From the Enlightenment to the Police State

From the Enlightenment to the Police State

The Public Life of JOHANN ANTON PERGEN

Paul P. Bernard

UNIVERSITY OF ILLINOIS PRESS
Urbana and Chicago

Library of Congress Cataloging-in-Publication Data

Bernard, Paul P.
   From the enlightenment to the police state : the public life of
Johann Anton Pergen / Paul P. Bernard.
      p. cm.
   Includes bibliographical references and index.
   ISBN 0-252-01745-5 (alk. paper)
   1. Pergen, Johann Anton, 1725–1814. 2. Police—Austria—
History—18th century—Biography. 3. Political crimes and
offences—Austria—Prevention—History—18th century. 4. Austria—
Politics and government—1740–1789. 5. Austria—Politics and
government—1789–1815. I. Title.
HV7911.P44B47 1991
363.2'83'092—dc20
[B]   90-38594
                                                         CIP

For I. J. W.

Contents

Preface

Joseph II's name will appear at, or close to, the top of any conceivable listing of the so-called enlightened despots. While historians are not always in agreement about precisely what meaning should be assigned to this term, there has never been, to my knowledge, any serious doubt expressed about his right to the designation. This is as it should be. The sweeping reforms that he introduced, sometimes from direst practical need, but in many cases doubtless from conviction, more than any other body of legislation brought about the Austrian *aggiornamento:* the monarchy was, in its internal workings, brought up to the standards of the West. While it is undeniable that his reforms owed much to the Theresian system that preceded them; and, equally, that the brief reign of his brother Leopold which followed his may have been marked by a greater generosity of spirit, to overlook Joseph's achievements would be to discard the body of the play in favor of the prologue and epilogue. In particular, Joseph's reforms of the Austrian legal system—although much opposed in some quarters, and, in the event, somewhat attenuated as a consequence of this opposition—went a long way toward establishing the rule of law in the monarchy. Of no lesser importance, they established once and for all that the judicial power rested in the state, which stood, symbolically, for all, and not in the estates, which represented the interests of the noble class alone. This was no mean achievement.

Yet when I first began applying myself seriously to a study of Joseph's reign some three decades ago, I quickly discovered that the picture of the revolutionary on the throne, so lovingly drawn by the nineteenth-century Austrian whigs and their latter-day followers, owed its sharpness and clarity largely to the systematic suppression of a part of the evidence. If one looks at Joseph not in the light in which he preferred himself to appear, as the detached statesman, concerned only with the greatest good accruing to the largest possible number of his subjects, translating social theory into practical reality, but rather examines his actions on the day-to-day level of mundane administration, the picture one arrives at is considerably different. Rather than a high-minded reforming spirit, as often as not one encounters pettiness, spite, arbitrariness, and excesses of zeal that would have done honor to almost any representative of the church, whose influence on the conduct of public affairs Joseph opposed so bitterly. It is only a partial exaggeration to say that Joseph had a penchant for attempting to implement an angelic program with measures that often verged on the satanic.

This contrast is particularly stark in the realm of the law, where, not to put too fine a point on it, Joseph, the great reformer of the judicial system, was also instrumental in establishing the secret police firmly upon Austrian soil. To be sure, the influence of that body was for the most part kept in check in his reign, and extra-legal proceedings were clearly the exception rather than the rule. Nevertheless, the basis for abusing the rule of law that would become so prominent a feature of the reign of Francis II had been firmly laid down. At the time, this struck me as a great paradox and I began a search for its resolution. Inevitably this search led me straight to Count Anton Pergen, the subject of this biography. It would be an understatement to say that Pergen, so far, has had bad press. For the most part, he has been dismissed in a few sentences as a peculiarly bloody-minded policeman, unable to think in terms more complex than brutal repression when confronted with any sort of opposition to public authority. The few analyses that tried to go beyond this primitive assessment of the man tended to portray him as the representative of reactionaries who, alarmed by the direction that a number of the Josephinian reforms were taking, attempted to stem the flood of change by convincing the emperor that he was playing into the hands of dangerous elements, who once they had prevailed, would not be satisfied to curtail the powers of the nobility but would want to abolish the powers of the crown as well.

As I began to study Pergen's career, it soon became apparent to me that none of these arguments corresponded to the facts of the case. Far from being a stupid and brutal policeman, Pergen was a man of considerable intelligence and sensitivity, who, moreover, was associated for a considerable part of his life with various reformist tendencies and who, in several responsible positions, took pains to defend positions diametrically opposed to those taken by the conservative opponents of Josephinian reform. Moreover, although he was a man who might be described as pathologically addicted to the keeping of records (over three hundred cartons of his papers survive in various Viennese archives, in spite of repeated cullings both by intention and by accidental loss), nothing in all his papers indicates that he entertained close contacts with these people. Rather, his intimates are to be found among those members of the Austrian nobility who had, for one reason or another, thrown in their lot with Joseph. Nevertheless, there can be no doubt whatever that Pergen was the principal architect of the Austrian secret police system in its original incarnation under Joseph, and again under Francis. This, too, is a paradox: a riddle wrapped in an enigma. The book which follows is an attempt, if not to resolve, at least to some degree to illumine this vexatious question.

It remains for me to carry out the most pleasant duty of expressing my profound gratitude to the many scholars and archivists who have helped me at one stage or another of my labors. Dr. Lorenz Mikoletky and his most efficient staff at Vienna's *Verwaltungsarchiv,* as well as Dr. Hedwig Benna and her most helpful assistants at the *Staatsarchiv* greatly facilitated my search through the vast collections over which they preside. Professors Adam Wandruszka and Erich Zöllner of the University of Vienna most generously listened to my ideas and gave me much good advice, as did Dr. T. W. C. Blanning of Sidney Sussex College, Cambridge. Professor Charlie Ingrao of Purdue University read the entire manuscript, pointed out various lacunae, and saved me from a number of factual errors. My research assistant at the University of Illinois, Charles Clark, went over the manuscript repeatedly, made a number of valuable suggestions, and introduced a measure of order into the rather chaotic rendition of proper names, which appear in contemporary sources in a variety of spellings. Dr. Ivan Jeanne Weiler of the University of Illinois not only read the whole of the book in several drafts, but also repeatedly pointed out to me where the argument needed to be tightened, ruthlessly excised errors of logic as well as those of diction, and more than once encouraged me to go on with the project when I was ready to abandon it. For the many errors and inadequacies that remain, the responsibility is mine alone.

1

The Education of a Diplomat

IT WOULD BE a slight exaggeration only to call the first half of the eighteenth century in Austria the age of the aristocracy. Those great noble families that had remained loyal to the Habsburg Monarchy were richly rewarded in the aftermath of the unsuccessful Bohemian revolt of 1618–19. The lands that a grateful crown lavished upon them enabled them, in an age of population growth and economic expansion, to amass really stupendous fortunes. Their great wealth, moreover, was buttressed by power. Under Leopold I and Charles VI representatives of prominent noble houses occupied the leading positions in the state. This, with some exceptions, continued to be the case under Maria Theresa.[1]

But wealth combined with power, if it does not always corrupt, invariably produces a certain lethargy. By the middle of the century the heads of the great houses, secure in their positions as the result of the *Fideikommisse,* the entails that the great families had secured from the crown, chose mostly to preside over the management of their estates, where the actual work could be left to overseers, rather than burden themselves with the rigors of state service. The younger sons, too, generally preferred to seek their fortunes in either the army or in the church, where the demands on one's time were less onerous and where the consequences of failure tended to be less drastic. This disobliging tendency on the part of the great nobles, in an age when the functions of the state were rapidly expanding, left the door wide open for others. The time had not yet arrived when members of a bourgeoisie, brought up to hard work by an ethic that equated individual effort with personal advancement, would be employed in leading capacities: the idea that it was the nobleman's place to lead was still too strongly entrenched, not least in the minds of the rulers themselves. Nevertheless, reasonably able people willing to work hard had to be found if the monarchy were to compete successfully with its rivals. What might well happen if this problem remained unresolved was demonstrated to everyone's satisfaction by the melancholy example of Poland, which already then had become a perpetual Question.

In the event, the gap was filled with members of lesser noble houses, mostly from the outlying provinces of the monarchy, generally in the west, where the position of the nobles was less secure and where they were more apt to have observed and, to some degree, been influenced by the bourgeois ethic. There were now great careers to be made for ambitious men with this background, and the potential rewards were considerable. Thus Johann Christoph Bartenstein, who entered state service under Charles VI practically penniless, retired in 1753 after the Kaunitzian reform of the government service, having amassed a fortune of 1,500,000 florins.[2] There were, however, difficulties. Maria Theresa, in particular, never liked to disappoint anyone who had ever rendered any service, no matter how minor or insignificant. The final result was that she would hardly ever dismiss a man from his post, no matter how badly he performed his duties. She preferred, instead, to create a new office to which the duties of the former would simply be shifted. This led, naturally, to a huge proliferation of officeholders and to a grossly inflated budget. This condition was anathema to Joseph II even before he became co-regent upon the death of his father, Francis Stephen, in 1765, and he concentrated his efforts on an attempt to rationalize the government service during the co-regency. The empress was able to shield the beneficiaries of her largesse so long as she lived, but upon her death, in 1780, heads began to roll. Thus, under the reign of Joseph it behooved every official anxious to remain on the payroll to demonstrate his worth and to produce results.

These then, in broad outline, were the factors that governed the career of the subject of this biography. Like many another scion of a noble but not particularly wealthy or well-connected family, he could look only to state service to make his mark in life. Being of frail health, and without an evident vocation for the religious life, this meant finding a niche in government. Like his contemporaries in similar situations, he was prepared for such a career by being given the best education available, an education in academies closely associated with the court. These schools were run by Jesuits, who were not of a mind to bestow upon their charges any notions capable of being thought modern, much less revolutionary. Yet the spirit of an age will out, so the majority of these young men, in the course of their educations, or perhaps quite outside of the classroom, came into contact with the basic ideas of the Enlightenment. As they went out into the world they, at the very least, were conversant with the idiom of that great intellectual movement; some of them doubtless subscribed to a number of its fundamental assumptions. This was the situation in which our hero, Pergen, found himself. Still, his mindset as well as that of the great majority of his contemporaries, did not go very deep, so that it would not have been a grievous loss if, under the pressure of events, it should turn out that it would have to be abandoned.

Johann Baptist Anton Pergen was born in Vienna on 15 February 1725, the son of Johann Ferdinand Wilhelm, Count Pergen, and Maria Elizabeth Pergen, born Baroness Olrich von Lazizka. The Pergens originally came from the Netherlands and could trace their nobility back to the sixteenth century. Johann Baptist's grandfather was made a *Reichsgraf* (Count of the Holy Roman Empire) by Joseph I on 28 July 1710.[3] His father served the monarchy in various administrative positions, achieving the rank of vice president of the Lower Austrian government in charge of the court system.

At the age of ten, Johann Baptist was made a page at the imperial court. There he received a good enough education and demonstrated sufficient ability so that, early in 1743, he was given a position in the Austrian diplomatic corps. His first job was that of junior secretary in the imperial legation at the court of the elector of Mainz. In 1748, when the Austrian minister at the Court of St. James, Baron Wasner, accompanied George II to Hanover to prepare for the peace negotiations ending the War of the Austrian Succession, Pergen was sent to London as the principal aide to the Austrian chargé d'affaires there, a most responsible assignment for so junior a diplomat. Although his stay in England was brief, Pergen conceived a lifelong attachment for that country and set out to master English, learning to write if not to speak it with tolerable fluency.

Upon Wasner's return to London, Pergen was reassigned to Mainz, upon the specific request of the minister there, Count Johann Karl Philipp Cobenzl, who had taken a liking to him.[4] In 1750, Pergen was attached to the staff of Baron Richecourt, who had been assigned to accompany the English king on an extended journey throughout Germany.[5] While so employed, Pergen kept in close touch with his old chief, Cobenzl, whom he evidently looked upon as his most likely patron and protector in government service. The two men exchanged frequent letters, which touched upon subjects that were to come up repeatedly in correspondence so long as he remained in the diplomatic service, and some of which, at least, were to constitute an underlying theme of Pergen's concerns throughout his life: prices in Germany are going up everywhere, they have risen by a third in the last two years;[6] could Cobenzl do him the favor of sending a few pounds of decent Spanish tobacco;[7] he is unable to make a go of it financially in spite of a salary augmentation of 200 florins monthly while on detached duty;[8] he wants to be remembered to the company of friends he left behind in Mainz;[9] he has encountered a lady of Cobenzl's acquaintance and hastens to assure him that (a) she is as beautiful as ever, and (b) Cobenzl is still very much in her thoughts.[10] Flattery and wheedling, arts for which Pergen seemed to have developed considerable talent at an early stage, were, it should be remembered, important constituents of every public servant's repertoire in the eighteenth century. The age of the baroque courtier was by no means over.

Upon his return to Vienna, where he was named chamberlain to the young Archdukes Karl and Leopold, he informed Cobenzl that he was worried about his career prospects, his present employment did not seem to lead anywhere; he had heard there was a possibility that he would be sent back to England, might not Cobenzl use his influence on his behalf? Cobenzl answered that he had put in a word for him with the chancellor, Count Ulfeld, and that if the English position should not materialize, Pergen would be returned to him in Mainz.[11] Pergen reported that he had called on Cobenzl's mother in Vienna, and that this lady was very angry with her son because of his numerous and well-publicized marital infidelities; would that this sort of opprobrium were leveled at him: his own affairs, due to his own indolence, were not worth mentioning.[12] He thanked Cobenzl for the efforts on his behalf and in return advised him that his own position was not as secure as it might be: he had a lot of enemies at court, although their mutual friends, the Harrachs, were doing all they could to protect him.[13] Within the year, however, Cobenzl was appointed minister extraordinary in charge of standardizing ceremonial within the *Reich*, and in 1753, Pergen, at the age of twenty-seven, replaced him as Austrian minister to the empire.[14]

The young man who now found himself presiding over the relations of the monarchy with a multitude of German princelings exhibited a curious and often seemingly contradictory set of behavioral patterns. By turns he could be a youthful *bon vivant,* a fawning and officious striver after promotion, a compulsive worker, a rather uncritical admirer of the French Enlightenment, and a pompous and sometimes shrill defender of authoritarian principles. In the position he now occupied he would have to cope with a bewildering variety of states, all of them nominally subject to Vienna. But in fact they looked upon themselves as sovereign members of a corporate body with well-established liberties anchored in ancient tradition, and they pursued convoluted and petty intrigues scarcely equaled in Europe outside the borders of the Ottoman Empire. Pergen's new job was hardly made to resolve the contradictions within a still partially unformed character; rather it seemed almost designed to encourage a man in the tendency to adjust his behavior to the situation of the moment.

Still, mid-eighteenth-century Germany afforded someone endowed with a normal quotient of intellectual curiosity, as Pergen undoubtedly was, a better opportunity to pursue his bent than Maria Theresa's Vienna, which had, so far, not emerged from the doldrums of the Counter Reformation. Mainz might be provincial and bigoted, but Frankfurt was not far away. And there Pergen would soon be availing himself of the many advantages of that city: booksellers with stocks of all the latest Enlightenment literature, charming and often accommodating ladies, expensive but marvellously stocked shops, a variety of theatrical productions, and a polyglot and cosmopolitan atmosphere. There were worse posts.[15]

Almost immediately after he had assumed his new duties, Pergen found out that being head of mission meant, in the first instance, doing favors for influential persons. Thus we find him writing to General Wirich Daun at the *Hofkriegsrat,* reporting that the elector's nephew wished to enter military service. Would Daun use his influence to gain admission for the young man to the Imperial Military Academy at Wiener Neustadt?[16] Another young gentleman of Mainz had just been appointed cornet in Archduke Leopold's guards regiment, but was unsure of what the lapel colors of the uniform of that regiment might be; Pergen duly wrote to Leopold's chamberlain, Count Hamilton, to elicit this information.[17] Shortly afterward, we find Pergen writing to Prince Salm-Salm, who was seeking the appointment of commanding general of the armies of the Catholic Electors, that he would of course use all his influence on his behalf.[18] Or, Field Marshall Batthany inquired whether his *Obristhofmeister,* von Beer, might not be appointed colonel in the Electoral Army.[19]

Not all favors asked of Pergen had to do with preferment. Thus a Baroness Benningsen wrote asking the minister's help in the matter of a Miss Starhemberg. This young lady's father had recently, it seemed, converted to Lutheranism, and her mother was afraid the girl would follow his example. Could Pergen not use his influence with the elector to have her placed in a convent? Pergen responded that he would do his best, but he doubted if it would be good enough: the elector not only tolerated Protestants in his territory, but recently he had given signs of being anxious to attract Protestant immigrants to Mainz. He would certainly not want to create a scandal.[20]

Doing favors for those in a position to repay them some day was by no means the only way for a young diplomat of no great personal fortune to improve his prospects. There was always outright fawning. Thus Pergen wrote Cobenzl that he had learned that Count Wenzel Anton von Kaunitz, who was to return shortly to take up his duties as ambassador to France, had, during a recent stay in Vienna, attained close to a complete ascendancy over Maria Theresa, and that his voice would henceforth be heard in all matters of importance. He had also heard that Kaunitz thought highly of Cobenzl, and it was by no means impossible that the latter would be appointed soon to "a more *convenable* place."[21]

Nor did Pergen blush to write to Bartenstein, whom, he insisted, he thought of as a second father, that his chief worry was that he had no assurance that Vienna considered his own place permanent. Could he not reassure him on this subject, or at least find out what the members of the ministerial conference thought of him?[22] Pergen also assured Cobenzl that, having called upon Kaunitz in Erfurt, he had spent the greater part of his interview with the ambassador singing Cobenzl's praises to him, and that Kaunitz had answered that he was very favorably disposed toward him.[23] In return, Cobenzl informed Pergen that Kaunitz, who he had just learned was about to be appointed state chancellor, thought equally highly of Pergen.[24]

It says something about Pergen that, in contrast to his penchant for flattering the great and near-great, he did not even bother to respond when his old teacher, Brognet, congratulated him on his being appointed minister, adding that he had always believed that his favorite pupil had a brilliant future before him.[25]

At least as important as flattery was the establishment of contacts that could produce valuable information. Heads of mission were frequently judged not just on how well they managed the assignments given them, but also on the degree to which their efforts fitted into the overall pattern of Austrian policy. Inasmuch as ministers in what Vienna regarded as minor posts were frequently informed late or not at all about important events, and not told about the consequences that great policy decisions would presumably have on their missions, it was up to these men to inform themselves as best they could. Knowing this, and wanting to be kept in the picture, Pergen almost at once initiated exchanges of letters with literally dozens of potential informants. Some were his ministerial colleagues, with whom he struck the simplest of bargains: they would agree to exchange whatever information they

[handwritten margin note: P – Learned early how to use informant]

possessed, allowing the other man to judge whether it were of any use to him. Others were diplomats below ministerial rank, whom he flattered assiduously, treating them as his equals, in return for being supplied with news, gossip, clippings from newspapers, posters, and proclamations.

Then there were various Jewish factors (privileged Jews who performed important, usually financial functions at the princely courts), from whom he elicited information in return for furthering their business, insofar as that lay within his powers. Finally, he did not hesitate, upon having identified a likely informant in some place where he had no other contacts, to pay for information. It did not seem to trouble him much that he was soon running an intelligence-gathering network that could easily compete with Vienna's official sources, nor that, consciously or not, he was the sole arbiter when it came to deciding how much of the information he gathered should be passed on to his superiors, and how much retained for future reference.

One of Pergen's major intelligence coups consisted of obtaining a detailed description of the person, habits, weaknesses, and strengths of Frederick II of Prussia. Whoever his informant was, he must have known his way around Potsdam very well indeed. While he evidently experienced some difficulty in distinguishing trivia from important matters, he nevertheless arrived at one extremely important political insight which, had Vienna chosen to take seriously, might well have resulted in considerable advantage: Pergen's informant insisted that whatever claims Frederick might make for himself, his genius was entirely limited to the field of battle; in all other matters he was a dilettante, and the mistakes he made in the determination of internal policy could easily be used against him.[26]

Among Pergen's most reliable informants was the Austrian resident in Cologne, Hofrat Roderigue. Pergen importuned him repeatedly for any information concerning not only local affairs but also for any news not available in Mainz. While he himself realized that information contained in the gazettes was often fragmentary and unreliable, he evidently felt that it was better than nothing at all, and was willing to repay Roderigue with detailed accounts of everything that went on at his post, as well as with elaborate accounts of what he heard from others.[27]

Assuming that Pergen would dictate an all-purpose informational bulletin to be sent to the majority of his correspondents, he would still have had to tailor this document to the various interests of his correspondents, which in itself must have been a hugely time-consuming process.

Even had he himself not been so eager to mind other people's business,

Pergen was being encouraged to do so by his patron, Cobenzl. For example, he was sent a thick bundle of correspondence from Regensburg, dealing with the cases before the *Reichskammergericht* there. Cobenzl accompanied this package with a letter indicating that he realized the material's dullness and unnecessary detail defied description, but that Pergen should read it anyway; he himself found it an indispensable source of information.[28]

Considerable attention, of course, had to be paid by every diplomat to questions of representation. In these matters, Pergen soon revealed himself to be a relative novice. In spite of being able to consult a protocol book that Cobenzl had left behind, he frequently found it necessary to inquire what to do in such important matters as what form of address to use when writing to various corporate entities of the empire.[29]

Vastly more important, in Pergen's eyes, than proper forms of address was making the right impression: after all, he represented the emperor. Upon his appointment, he had inherited Cobenzl's servants, house, carriages, horses, wine cellar, even his plate and silver. But he soon decided that these did not satisfy him. Before long, he was buying horses from the elector's stables,[30] linens and curtains from Lazarus Solomon,[31] and barrels of wine from a Frankfurt merchant, at prices ranging from 525 to 900 florins.[32] He also bought various small items of jewelry to be worked into reliquaries, meant as gifts for his pious friends,[33] as well as considerable quantities of silk stockings, both for himself and for several ladies of his acquaintance.[34]

And of course he bought books. Shortly after his arrival in Mainz, he opened an account with the Frankfurt bookseller J. G. Esslinger, with instructions that he was to be sent on approval all new publications in the fields of literature and statecraft.

Although he was undoubtedly a serious reader, Pergen by no means spent all of his leisure time with his books. Every fall there were numerous hunts, for boar as well as for lesser game, on the estates of the local nobility. On one occasion, he reported that his party had bagged two-hundred pheasants, fifty quail, and some two dozen rabbits, in less than two hours.[36]

And then there was always a profusion of little *affaires galantes,* although Pergen complained that in this respect Mainz hardly came up to his expectations.[37] Pergen thanked his friend Roderigue for having introduced him to a young lady who constituted the exception to the rule that the women of Mainz were unsightly and dull. As she was the illegitimate daughter of a great nobleman, he could not refrain from observing that this was yet another example of the dictum that the great of the world did all things well, not excepting even the production of bastards.[38]

Given his inclination to spend money freely, it is hardly surprising that Pergen, from the first, found himself running short. Not long after having assumed his duties, Pergen informed Cobenzl that the 7000 florins in salary that he received was simply insufficient; if he were to stay at his post for any length of time, he would have to receive a considerable increment, particularly as the elector had reneged on his promise to supply him with a coach and four. He would have to buy these himself, and the initial outlay, plus the upkeep, would by themselves amount to at least 1000 florins in the first year.[39] None of this did Pergen much good. He had to acquire his own coach and team, and he received no raise in salary. Cobenzl, while promising to bring the matter to Kaunitz's attention, advised Pergen that if he were really serious about having his salary increased, he would have to make official representations and make them often; this was the way things were done in Vienna. As we shall have ample opportunity to see, Pergen was to take this advice to heart. Throughout his long and varied career, he would launch concerted campaigns for increases in his pay, no matter how large it might be. Most of these would be crowned with success.[40]

Of course Pergen had not been posted to Mainz only for representational purposes. There was more than enough business to transact with various princely courts to which he was accredited. Given the circumstance that, theoretically, all of these princes were the emperor's subjects, Pergen's position was not quite the same as that of a diplomat accredited to a foreign court. For the most part, his duties consisted not of negotiating agreements—these were already in force as an integral part of the Reich Constitution—but rather of persuading the German princes to abide by the agreements that already existed. Also, he was forever arbitrating disputes between them.

In these circumstances, it is hardly surprising that the greater part of the day-to-day routine with which Pergen had to deal was repetitive, dull, and often trivial. The manner in which he dealt with this business, however, would become characteristic of his work habits for the rest of his career: no matter how insignificant the issue, he would expend inordinate amounts of energy upon it, and fill reams of paper reporting it to his superiors, which practice, as we have already noted, did not always please them.[41] While this tendency of his might have exemplified his zeal and devotion to duty, it also indicated a certain fundamental inability to distinguish between what was important and what was merely tangential.

In the first year at his post, Pergen mediated a dispute between Karl Friedrich of Baden-Durlach and the Franconian Circle, about the disposition of the fortress of Philippsburg, which the former claimed as an imperial fief, but which had been occupied by the *Kreis* for some time.[42] He assisted Cobenzl in rounding up sufficient supplies of wheat to feed the imperial garrison in Luxemburg.[43] He spent several hours a day making himself agreeable to the elector of Mainz's chancellor.[44] He made a number of unsuccessful attempts to have himself presented to the landgrave of Darmstadt.[45] He mediated another dispute between the elector of Mainz and the counts of Wurzburg and Fulda over a few miserable acres of ground.[46] And, by establishing a simple case of elopement, he interceded successfully on behalf of a young Austrian cavalry lieutenant who had been imprisoned in Mainz on the charge of having kidnapped the daughter of a leading merchant of that city.[47]

Then there were matters that, while relatively unimportant from the purview of Vienna, struck Pergen as being anything but minor. Such was what came to be called "L'affaire de la noblesse". It came to his attention that in Bamberg, an ecclesiastical principality, the bishop and chapter, for a fee, were registering various persons on the nobiliary rolls who would otherwise have had very great difficulty indeed in proving eight quarterings of nobility. As Pergen saw it, not only did this deplorable practice usurp the emperor's right to create nobles, but it amounted to a frontal attack on what he called "the nobility's most precious jewel, the purity of its blood." He protested in vigorous terms and, by threatening to take the bishop and chapter to court in Regensburg, succeeded in putting an end to these irregular ennoblements.[48]

Another incident to which Pergen attached considerable importance, although more because of its potentially damaging consequences for the imperial forces than out of any humane concern for those involved, was a case of desertion from the Bayreuth regiment. In June, while that unit had been drawn up for inspection in Lüneburg, sixteen troopers broke rank and fled. Thereupon, the officer in command detached a mounted company and gave pursuit. The deserters were soon caught up with and, when they ignored an order to halt, the cavalry opened fire. Three of them were hit, all fatally, but in the ensuing confusion the rest were able to escape across a nearby border. Now their commander indignantly demanded their return. Pergen, although by no means unaware of the difficulties this would create, promised his full cooperation: desertion could not be sanctioned, even in the ranks of another army, the example was too dangerous if it were to succeed.[49]

It is probably fair to say that in Pergen's own view, by far the most significant piece of official business he confronted in his first year was an incident involving Voltaire. As we have already seen, this gentleman's books were at the top of the list of Pergen's literary desiderata, although of course they figured prominently among the works whose importation into the Habsburg lands was strictly prohibited. Thus Voltaire was not just an abstract conceptualization of certain "enlightened" tendencies to Pergen, but someone whom, through his books, he had come to know well. Hence, we may imagine that it was not without a certain quickening of the pulse that Pergen learned, at the end of May 1753, that Voltaire was not only in Frankfurt but seemed to be involved in a convoluted affair that, if nothing else, constituted a direct challenge to Austrian sovereignty.[50]

The genial but equally mercurial Frenchman had arrived in Frankfurt on 29 May, having quarreled with his friend and protector Frederick II. The falling out had resulted largely from Voltaire's own hubris: he had not taken the trouble to conceal his own low opinion of Maupertuis, whom the king had recently installed as head of the Academy of Sciences in Berlin. In addition, Voltaire had made some impertinent remarks about the quality of Frederick's poetry, which of course had promptly been reported back to the king. In this situation, Voltaire, convinced that his position in Potsdam was hopelessly compromised, had asked leave to depart. In a gesture of self-effacement, he offered to give back the Golden Key that he had received upon his appointment as royal chamberlain, and the decoration that Frederick had bestowed upon him. The king, mollified by Voltaire's submissiveness, refused to accept these objects and told the philosopher that he was forgiven, thereby considering the incident closed. Voltaire, however, had had enough of Potsdam, and, deciding that this opportunity was as good as any, departed. The king was livid: he was in the habit of dismissing servants who did not give satisfaction; he did not take kindly to being left by them.

Believing that he had succeeded in escaping, Voltaire made no secret of his movements. At every stage of his journey away from Potsdam, he wrote numerous letters discussing his travel plans in great detail and mocking the king. Inevitably, some of these fell into the hands of the ubiquitous Prussian spy network, which routinely opened letters in all German places where a corruptible postmaster could be found. Frederick, already sufficiently incensed by Voltaire's departure, grew all the more furious when he learned from one of these intercepts that Voltaire had in his possession a book of royal poems that Frederick had had privately printed. Since these, in their published form, differed rather markedly from the drafts that the king had originally submitted to Voltaire for his opinion and correction, he had every reason to fear that Voltaire might amuse himself by publishing the original and amended texts in parallel columns, thus demonstrating, not unconvincingly, the degree to which the royal muse depended upon professional assistance. In one of his patented fits of rage, the king ordered his secretary, Fredendorf, to recover the booklet of poems and thereby demonstrate that he was not the incompetent he always held him for. For good measure, he was also to get back Voltaire's Golden Key and his decoration.

As it happens, Fredendorf took a back seat in his detestation of Voltaire to no man, with the possible exception of Maupertuis (who on one occasion had suggested to Frederick that Voltaire would make a splendid subject for one of his experiments in vivisection) and, encouraged in this manner, went a bit too far. He had learned that Voltaire and his secretary, Collini, had arrived in Frankfurt am Main and had taken rooms at the Golden Lion. At once he sent off a courier to the Prussian resident there, one Freytag, ordering him to arrest Voltaire and to keep him in confinement until all the required articles were back in the king's hands. The trouble with this procedure, of course, was that, Frankfurt being an imperial free city, no Prussian official there could exercise any police powers, certainly not over a subject of the king of France.

Nevertheless, Freytag, now that his sovereign had spoken, was resolved to act. In the company of one Schmidt, who, it later turned out, was a convicted felon, he appeared at Voltaire's inn and announced that he was putting him and Collini under arrest. A heated discussion followed, in the course of which Voltaire produced the key and the order, both of which, as he told Freytag, he had offered to surrender voluntarily before leaving Prussia, but regretted that he was unable to hand over the book of poems, as this had been included in the bags which he had sent ahead to Hamburg. In that case, Freytag told him, he would remain his prisoner. Voltaire begged the resident to dispatch an express letter to Hamburg, asking that Voltaire's luggage be sent back to Frankfurt, whereupon Freytag, protesting that his out-of-pocket expenses already exceeded three louis d'or, said that an ordinary letter would have to do.

Voltaire was now placed under house arrest. A day or so later, his niece, Madame Denis, arrived in Frankfurt, it having been agreed that she would accompany her uncle for the balance of the journey home. Learning what had happened, she confronted Freytag and raised a huge row, the consequence of which was that he had her put in custody as well. While being held in one of the rooms of the inn, she was, as she later alleged, sexually molested by Schmidt and one of the guards posted there by Freytag.

Pergen, who had been out of town, first heard of these events some ten days after Voltaire's arrest. His first reaction was rather cool and ironic. What these events showed, in his opinion, was the genuineness of the king of Prussia's admiration for the world of letters, and the ludicrous weakness and indecision of the imperial free cities, which could not even prevent a Prussian official on their territory from behaving as if he were on his home ground.[51] But as Voltaire's incarceration dragged on and the Frankfurt newspapers began to publish thinly veiled accounts of what had taken place, Pergen concluded that it behooved him, as representative of that power upon whose sovereignty Freytag had impinged, to take official notice. By the time he did, Freytag had consented to release his prisoners, but not before relieving Voltaire of a considerable quantity of precious objects and a large sum of money.

On 13 July, Voltaire addressed himself to Pergen, requesting an interview, and humbly asking that the imperial representative undertake whatever steps might be necessary to redress wrongs that had been done to him.[52] Pergen's position, to do him justice in the matter, was a complicated one. He was, after all, merely a diplomat accredited to the local government. He had no more executive powers in Frankfurt than Freytag had, but he did what he could. He advised Voltaire that the best course would be not to pursue his complaint through official channels, since, whatever the legalities of the matter, Freytag would not submit to any authority but that of Frederick, who was only too notorious for defining justice on his own terms. Nevertheless, he would write a strong letter of protest to the mayor of Frankfurt, in which he would remind this official of his duties and responsibilities, which included seeing to it that Voltaire was given back his property.[53] What he did not do was to lodge an official protest in Potsdam, which the circumstances would very well have warranted. It would seem that, notwithstanding his admiration for the great *philosophe's* ideas, the discomfiture of a mere scribbler did not strike him as sufficiently important to justify provoking a diplomatic incident. When Voltaire wrote from Strasbourg, asking for his help and support, he again answered that, while he would certainly use his influence to try to get the Prussians to return the valuables taken from him, he could not undertake any official steps.[54]

The Voltaire incident had clearly put Pergen's principles to a severe test. Much as he would have liked to offer additional help to a literary figure whose works he greatly admired, the diplomatic situation had been a delicate one. Whereas, of course, Frederick was heartily detested in Vienna and, in principle, any action resulting in the frustration of his will would be looked upon with favor there, it was always possible that in a matter of this kind he would have appealed to Maria Theresa for aid as monarch to monarch. In that case, Pergen, had he taken a more active role on behalf of Voltaire, might well have been caught between two great millstones—his career ground to pieces before it had properly begun. In these circumstances, he probably acquitted himself as honorably as the situation permitted.

In 1754, we observe Pergen settling down into a somewhat dull but by no means unpleasant routine of everyday diplomacy. And there were diversions to be looked forward to. If the carnival season in Mainz was boring beyond description, due to the elector's notorious parsimony, there were nevertheless numerous sledding parties, occasions on which it was quite proper to escort a lady married to someone else.[55] Also, whatever visiting dignitaries happened to be passing through had to be entertained, and this not only provided a good excuse for elaborate parties but, if one played one's cards right, resulted in the establishment of potentially useful social connections. Thus, when young Prince Philippe Lobkowitz arrived in Mainz armed with a letter of introduction from Cobenzl, Pergen not only squired him around the usual attractions and introduced him to a number of eligible young ladies, he also took the further trouble of arranging a joint visit to a bawdyhouse in Frankfurt. This last venture, it would seem, was not a total success, as Pergen later reported to Cobenzl that whereas the young man had been among the wedding guests in Galilee, there was no reason to assume that he had performed any great miracles.[56]

Frequently there were favors to be done for friends and friends of friends. Pergen seems to have put in a good deal of time buying and shipping hogsheads of the local wine, of which the Austrians could not get enough. On one occasion at least, he found himself picking out a fur cape in Frankfurt for a friend of Cobenzl's and then sending it on to Brussels to escape duty.[57] And, as always, Pergen devoted a considerable amount of his free time to his books. Among his purchases that year were a three-volume supplement to Bayle's *Dictionary, Manon Lescaut,* as well as a somewhat dubious item entitled *Délices du Sentiment.* He told Cobenzl, not without pride, that his library was about to pass the thousand-volume mark.[58]

Pergen also was a regular attender of Frankfurt theater performances, which led to a bizarre incident that he described in some detail to all of his regular correspondents. One evening, while he was sitting in his usual box, a part of the balcony directly over him collapsed, and he narrowly escaped being crushed to death by the fall of several Jewish spectators who had been sitting there. He himself lost only his hat and his wig, and none of them involved were seriously injured, but a scene of near-total chaos ensued. Pergen described this with some relish, particularly that part in which one of the Jews drew his sword (!) and demanded instant amends for his ruined clothing from the theater manager. In the old days, Pergen reflected, wagging tongues would have observed that it served the injured parties right, what were they doing attending a theater performance on the Sabbath? But now, *o tempora, o mores,* no one seemed to find fault with this.[59]

Pergen also was turning into something of an opera buff, attending whatever performances he found on his travels to the various German courts. His reputation as a music-lover came to the attention of the monarchy's leading opera patron, Prince von Thurn und Taxis, who approached him about joining a group of like-minded noblemen who intended to bring an opera season to Frankfurt.[60]

In his second year at Mainz, Pergen began to work on a project that at first seemed straightforward enough but would cause him more trouble and waste of time than any other during the whole of his diplomatic career. The *Hofkammer* in Vienna had decided that it would be useful to introduce a uniform coinage into all of the Upper Rhenish Circle. As there were so many evident advantages that this reform would bring— just to give an example, heretofore people traveling within the circle from one principality to the next often lost as much as a tenth of the value of their money each time they were forced to exchange it—Pergen foresaw no difficulties in its acceptance and rather high-handedly informed the various courts to which he was accredited that this step was being contemplated, and that they would be notified when to turn in their old coinage for the new. It soon turned out that Pergen's optimism had been incredibly naive. The German princes, as Pergen by then should already have known, were inflexibly determined to hold on to every last one of their privileges, no matter if it could be logically demonstrated that in doing so they were harming their own interests. A huge hue and cry arose in all quarters. Complaints about Pergen's arbitrary conduct were heaped upon not only the *Hofkammer* but also a half-dozen other Viennese ministries, and soon enough Pergen found that, if he were to retain any influence at all, the outraged parties would have to be placated with large doses of humility and flattery. Even then, it would take him the better part of a year to get this relatively simple reform accepted.[61]

A duty that Pergen undertook rather reluctantly was the introduction of the newly created imperial lottery into the *Reich*. This enterprise was being launched as a trial balloon (an economic theory, holding that lotteries were an ideal way of raising state revenue without increasing taxes, having recently reached Vienna) with its headquarters in the Austrian Netherlands. Consequently, it was now up to Cobenzl, who had just been posted to Brussels as chief administrative officer under the regents, to make as good a showing as possible. He hastened to write to his protégé describing the lottery and expressing the hope that Pergen would see to it that a large number of lots would be sold in Germany; after all, the individual ticket cost only 14 florins, and top prize would be 200,000 florins. Pergen answered that he would of course do his best for his friend, but that Cobenzl should not nourish any inflated hopes: he knew as well as he did that the Germans, when there was question of parting with hard money, were nowhere to be found.[62]

In Vienna's eyes, the matter of the imperial succession was by far the most important responsibility Pergen had so far been entrusted with. Recalling all the trouble and confusion that had preceded the election of Maria Theresa's consort, Francis Stephen, to the throne, the empress and Kaunitz were determined to avoid a repetition of these events. This time, the succession was to be settled well in advance of the demise of the emperor, by convincing the electors to elect the Archduke Joseph, then fourteen years of age, as king of the Romans in his father's lifetime. This procedure in the sixteenth century had become quasi-automatic, really only a formality; however, the electors had gotten wind into their sails as the result of the Charles VII episode, and could no longer be expected to rubber-stamp Vienna's proposals. Since in the existing political climate there was no chance whatever for the election of any but a Habsburg candidate—and the electors knew this to be the fact— they were in no hurry to act. The longer they held out, the greater the chances were of collecting additional bribes from a Vienna anxious to resolve the issue. Pergen, not any wiser for his experience with the currency reform, originally was sanguine about securing Joseph's election with a minimum of difficulty. He was soon informed of his mistake and was forced to report back that a good deal more effort would have to be expended, and money spent, to secure this goal. In particular, the king of England, in his capacity as elector of Hanover, decided to play a waiting game. In order to put pressure on Vienna, he, very much against his usual habit and inclination, announced that he would not be visiting his continental domains that year, so that no meeting of the college of electors could take place. And Pergen was forced to report that the issue would have to be dropped until at least the following year.[63]

Pergen also functioned as a sort of clearing-house for requests for special consideration, petitions, proposals for reform, and inventions that the residents of that part of Germany wished to have forwarded to Vienna. It would take him a while to develop sufficient judgment and self-confidence to consign most of this material unanswered to the wastebasket. So far, he continued to waste many hours of his own working time in corresponding with the authors of evidently quixotic if not demented proposals, and actually would forward this material to Vienna, where it caused a good deal of head-scratching.

To give an example, he corresponded over the period of six months with a certain Colonel von Pruseken, who claimed to have invented (a) a pistol that would shoot a ball at a distance of two-hundred paces with more impact velocity than current models, and that had a range of no more than thirty; (b) a musket that would guarantee accurate fire at one thousand paces, whereas existing models were reliable only up to three-hundred; (c) a means of doubling the range of field guns while using smaller quantities of powder; and (d) a mixture that, when lit, produced an inextinguishable fire that would burn on the surface of water and could thus be used to destroy enemy fleets without sustaining any damage to one's own.

Pergen immediately sent all of these materials, as he received them, on to Vienna. The commander in chief of the Austrian artillery, Prince Joseph Liechtenstein, not unnaturally replied that, before he was willing to invest any money in any of these schemes, he would have to see their efficacy demonstrated. Stung by the skeptical tone of this note, Pergen asked von Pruseken to come to Mainz to demonstrate his inventions. All he received in answer was a letter carefully explaining that, in order to do so, von Pruseken would need an advance of 6000 florins. He also sent a brace of pistols, which proved to be in no respect different from any other.[64]

Another of Pergen's duties was to arrange for the stays of a variety of people sent by Vienna to be trained in this or that technical discipline. Thus he found a place for a young man whom the chancellor, Count Ulfeld, wanted instructed in the newest Dutch methods of planting gardens, so that he could introduce these at Schönbrunn. Pergen did as he was asked, but not without complaining to Ulfeld that this was no easy assignment. The best gardening, by far, was being done at Kassel, but the landgrave there was no friend of Austria, and was, moreover, extremely particular about whom he permitted to work in his gardens. In addition, as the young fellow in question was tall and well put together, he would be an obvious target for the Prussian recruiters, who swarmed all over that region and were not particular about what method they used to enlist likely candidates in the army of their king. We may suppose that this catalogue of difficulties that Pergen put together was not entirely disinterested, as it was followed by a complaint that Kaunitz had lately turned down his urgent request for an increase in his wages. He complained bitterly that he was unable to live without using up his capital; he could go on doing so for at most two years, but after that he would have bankrupted himself and would have had no alternative but to resign his post. Could not Ulfeld find him a second job, not to put too fine a point on it, a sinecure that would pay him a salary without requiring his presence?[65]

Ulfeld did his best to return the favor, securing an increase of 600 florins yearly in Pergen's salary; but this, as Pergen was quick to complain, while a gracious token of Their Majesties' confidence in him, in no way addressed itself to the gravity of the situation.[66] Still, as Ulfeld had rendered him this service, Pergen did not hesitate to ask for another. He wrote to him, wanting to know in strictest confidence what Kaunitz really thought of his abilities, and what he might do to raise himself in his estimation.[67]

Pergen had good reason to be concerned about Kaunitz's opinion of him, as it had come to his attention that the arrogant manner he liked to effect had aroused the anger of the elector of Mainz. He had been warned that it was not the custom to appear for an audience with that prince while carrying a walking stick; but he had nevertheless refused to leave his at home, telling the elector's chancellor that His Majesty's ambassador went about his business dressed as he saw fit. The elector, thereupon, wrote him a letter of protest, and now Pergen had reason to fear that the episode had also been reported to Vienna.[68]

By the time Pergen settled into his third year in Mainz, he was complaining routinely to all of his correspondents about the onerous nature of his job. Onerous no doubt it was, but this was in large part because he insisted on concerning himself with any number of matters at best marginal to his formal responsibilities, and for good measure reported on these in detail to all of his regular correspondents, who now numbered not just in the dozens but in the hundreds. For instance, he conducted an exchange of letters with a Baron Buchenburg about the fate of some Protestants who had lately, at Maria Theresa's command, been expelled from her dominions.[69] Regrettable though this incident might have been, it was a matter of purely internal concern, and as Pergen knew nothing whatever about the background of the affair, beyond the official version being disseminated by Vienna, he could well have spared himself the embarrassment of defending a policy that he neither himself supported nor was responsible for defending. Pergen, it would seem, suffered from the constitutional inability to remain on the outside of any dispute that came to his attention.

Although continually complaining that he could barely keep up with the mass of information that crossed his desk, Pergen deliberately set about trying to add to it. In this vein, he asked Cobenzl whether he could be supplied with a regular correspondent who would report to him on the activities of the *Reichstag* in Regensburg. He would, he said, gladly pay up to 100 florins a year to such a person.[70] It should be pointed out that very little that went on in this body had any practical consequences; moreover by far the greater part of the questions debated there had no bearing whatsoever on the states to which Pergen was accredited.

Pergen involved himself quite gratuitously in a dispute over precedence between Mainz and Koblenz, and afterward could not understand why neither side had shown any gratitude for his intervention.[71] Shortly thereafter, he went about a routine task of diplomatic housekeeping, settling the gambling debts of young Austrian gentlemen who had fallen in with bad company in Mainz, as if he were suppressing a conspiracy of malefactors of major international significance.[72] He displayed such an utter lack of tact in resolving an argument arising out of the arrogant behavior of an Austrian officer on leave, that it took considerable restraint on the part of various Mainz officials to prevent the affair from escalating into a full-blown diplomatic incident. This officer, who, having been taken to task for galloping his horse through a planted field, proceeded to cane the objecting farmer, and was subsequently stabbed by his victim.[73]

Finally, Pergen's complaints about being constantly overworked should also be weighed in the light of the fact that he never hesitated a moment in taking upon himself the most wearisome of tasks when it was a question of doing a favor for a friend or an acquaintance. Thus, when the director of the newly founded Frankfurt Opera Company came to him with the tale of woe that one of his best tenors had left for Darmstadt, although there were still two months to go on his contract, Pergen immediately offered to arrange for the fellow's return, although it was by no means clear by what authority.[74]

Whether because he never tired of bombarding various ministries with complaints,[75] or because the sheer volume of paper he generated was beginning to make a cumulative impression in Vienna, the rewards Pergen constantly demanded were not withheld from him entirely. So, in June 1755, he was appointed imperial observer at the election of a burggrave of Friedberg. He complained that this was one of those situations best avoided, where no advantage was in sight: if the wrong candidate were to be elected he would harvest all of the blame, and if he succeeded in securing the choice of the Austrian candidate, no one would appreciate his efforts. But he was nevertheless happy enough to pocket the 1000 florins he was allowed for what turned out to be the work of less than a week.[76]

Pergen's first major coup came in 1755. It consisted of winning over landgrave William of Hesse-Darmstadt to the imperial cause. The genuine friendship that developed between these two men seems to have been based on nothing more elevated than their mutual interest in women. In their correspondence, Pergen described at some length the various balls and social functions which he attended, commenting on his chances of achieving this or that conquest. The landgrave urged him on and expressed the hope that he would soon prove the equal of his predecessor Cobenzl in bedding the belles of Frankfurt.[77] Before long, Pergen and the landgrave discovered that they had other interests in common. Both tended to prefer works of political theory for their leisure time reading, and they fell into the habit of exchanging lengthy, if not always very profound, analyses of what they had read.

Both men were also confirmed hypochondriacs and reported to one another in copious detail on their never-ending illnesses. In Pergen's case, he complained again and again about his unremitting headaches and his chronic insomnia. He had tried every known remedy, but none of these had provided him with any relief, until he had consulted a Jewish physician who had ordered him to take the waters at Schwalbach, which seemed to help him somewhat. This Jew, he told the landgrave, was a most astute fellow, and he had come to rely upon him for more than medical advice. In fact, it was fair to say that the man had come to represent a confidant and father-confessor to him.[78]

Throughout 1755, Pergen kept a watchful eye on the political developments in the world at large. As he saw matters, the resumed hostilities between France and England in the American colonies could not fail to lead to another European war. Being kept, as he was, on the fringe of diplomatic negotiations, more often than not finding out about great and consequential events from the gazettes to which he subscribed, as Kaunitz did not deem it necessary to inform him beforehand about even those policy decisions that directly affected the *Reich,* Pergen naturally assumed that if war were to come, Austria would once again be fighting its old enemy, France. As a confirmed Anglophile, he took great pleasure in every report of English victories in America. He expressed profound suspicion of the new French foreign minister, Vergennes, whose considerable abilities he was willing to concede but whom he regarded as the most devious man in France. He was outraged at the report that the French had promised to free the black slaves in the English colonies if they would revolt against their masters. He warned his friends in England not to expect the French to observe the traditional rules of diplomacy; they were undoubtedly capable of descending upon Hanover without benefit of a declaration of war.[79]

It was not until the very end of the year that Pergen began to suspect what Kaunitz was up to. Even then, this was not because the chancellor had given him any intimation about a possible change in course—a change that could not, after all, help but influence Pergen's mission in Germany in the most fundamental way—but rather because the great secrecy that descended upon various comings and goings of senior diplomats in Vienna seemed to him to signal some sort of important event.[80]

When Pergen finally found out about the reversal of alliances, which Kaunitz had fashioned, it came as a considerable shock to him. The policy that he had regarded as immutable, and with which he had most strongly identified, eternal friendship with England, had suddenly been abandoned. Whereas previously Pergen had exchanged analyses and comments on foreign affairs with dozens of his regular correspondents, he now became much more circumspect. Having found out to his horror that he had been drastically out of step with Vienna, he did not feel like taking any further chances. His sole comment, upon hearing of the signing of the Convention of Westminster between England and Prussia, was that such an extraordinary event was bound to have profound consequences.[81]

The new year promised to be a troubled one. Not only were there omnipresent rumors of war, but an unmistakeably apocalyptic feeling took hold of the populace in many parts of Europe. The terrible earthquake that destroyed Lisbon on All Saints' Day, 1755, in which entire congregations had been wiped out while attending Mass, captured the imagination of Catholic Europe. Throughout Germany itinerant preachers predicted the approaching end of the world, and in many a rural district the populace was transported into a state of near panic. Pergen, who saw this as a consequence of the "ravings of superstition-riddled lunatics," thought that his duty required him to exert a calming influence. He appealed to various local authorities to expel the doomsayers before they succeeded in stirring up dangerous rioting, but these appeals fell upon deaf ears.[82]

A source of considerable annoyance that, as Pergen soon enough realized, might have an extremely negative effect upon his career, was his falling-out with William VIII, landgrave of Hesse-Kassel. Pergen had alienated this gentleman a year earlier by reproaching him for corresponding directly with the imperial court on questions of *Reich* policy, rather than funneling his correspondence through him.[83] The prince now avenged himself by accusing Pergen of having fomented a conspiracy whose purpose was to alienate the heir to the throne from his father, to encourage him to flee the country, and, worst of all, to convert to Catholicism. Nothing would satisfy him, William now wrote to Vienna, short of Pergen's dismissal and condign punishment.[84] Although Prince William's version of these events was much exaggerated—all that Pergen seems to have done was to encourage the young man to make his own decisions—and although Pergen could feel reasonably secure in the belief that Maria Theresa would always look with favor on any action that led to the winning of a soul for the Universal Church, no matter how incompatible with the canons of diplomatic behavior it might be, Pergen nevertheless thought he had reason to fear that if not the empress, Kaunitz would take a dim view of his involvement in this affair. He decided that it would be necessary to make an appearance in Vienna in order to attend to the task of repairing whatever damage had been done.

There were other reasons as well, in Pergen's eyes, which made his presence in the capital desirable, in spite of the rapidly deteriorating political situation, which would have seemed to require his presence at his post. So far as his personal affairs were concerned, Pergen had become involved in a liaison that appeared to be more serious than his usual casual flirtations. His friends began to tease him. One of them compared the lady to "that good woman who had succeeded in turning a bad canon into a worthy husband," while Pergen himself after his departure, wrote one of his intimates who was to dine with the *inamorata* that he should be sure to find an occasion, while at table, to play footsie with his beloved Nannerl and, on his behalf, to implore her not to forget how one kicked out with both feet.[85]

For a brief moment also, Pergen had reason to think that his financial situation was about to improve dramatically. Soon after his arrival in Vienna, he received a breathless letter, informing him that he had won the first prize in a lottery held in Darmstadt, where, as a favor to his friend the prince, he had bought several tickets. But it turned out that the Darmstadt lottery was on a scale with the rest of the principality: Pergen collected all of 45 florins.[86]

When he found out that, contrary to his fears, the Hesse-Kassel affair had not made any serious trouble for him in Vienna, Pergen decided to take advantage of his presence in the capital to conduct in person his unremitting campaign to have his salary raised. The results he had achieved by correspondence had not been brilliant. The only concession which the chancellery had made was to procure him a further supplementary appointment, this time as imperial commissioner to observe the election of a new bishop in Ellwangen. This Pergen had dismissed as the merest drop in the bucket.[87] He was also very much concerned about a rumor then circulating that he was soon to be replaced in his post, so it is hardly astonishing that he haunted various government offices from the day of his arrival and attempted to mobilize whatever support he could among his friends.[88]

Note : imperial position
w HRE honed his skills of
collecting
information

At first the going was slow. In July, Pergen complained that he had been unable to get so much as a promise to have his salary situation studied.[89] The breakthrough came when he succeeded in securing a private interview with Kaunitz. As there are no references in the papers of either man to what might have been discussed at this meeting, it is of course impossible to do more than surmise what the substance of their conversation might have been. But it is not unreasonable to assume, given the fact that the chancellor, from that point on, began to take a systematic interest in Pergen's career, that in some way or other Pergen had been able to convince him not only of his useful qualities but also that he would be his man.[90] At any rate, by September Pergen had been given an increase of 1000 florins yearly, and a gift of another 1000 to settle his most pressing debts.[91]

Although 2000 florins hardly represented a fortune, the increment seems to have gone to Pergen's head. He decided at once that upon his return to Mainz he would need to occupy more spacious quarters. He was, at any rate, involved in a running dispute with his landlord, who had insisted, not unreasonably, that as Pergen was occupying only one floor of the house he was renting, he either pay him for the space he was not occupying or allow this to be rented out to a third party. Pergen had answered haughtily that, had he wished to take quarters in a public inn, he would have done so in the first place, but without his increase he would presumably have had no choice but to share the house with someone else. Now he wrote to his secretary, Nagel, that he would not dream of negotiating further with the scoundrel. Nagel was to find him other quarters, regardless of the expense. What Nagel came up with was a palatial villa belonging to a Baron Schmidberg, which rented for 500 florins yearly, an almost unheard-of sum for that city.[92]

While in Vienna, Pergen also pursued another of his favorite occupations, that of amassing potentially useful informants. He had met a Josef von Hockenthal, an aulic councilor of limited personal means, whom he now persuaded to report to him on all the goings-on at court that might conceivably be of interest to him, and assured Hockenthal that he would not only reimburse him for the cost of the correspondence but would also be happy to pay his expenses for any steps he might take on his behalf.[93]

On balance, whereas Pergen seems to have been persuaded that he had failed to accomplish the goals he had set himself before journeying to Vienna, he had in fact taken a decisive step forward. He had been granted a lengthy interview with Kaunitz and succeeded in impressing him as a young man of ability and sound views. And once the chancellor formed a favorable impression of someone, that man's future was assured:

Kaunitz never liked to admit that he had made a mistake in making a professional judgment.

NOTES

1. For the following, see H. G. Schenk, "Austria," in Albert Goodwin, ed., *The European Nobility in the Eighteenth Century* (New York & Evanston Ill., 1967), 102–17, and now the truly magisterial P. G. M. Dickson, *Finance and Government under Maria Theresia, 1740–1780* (2 vols., Oxford, 1987), particularly I, 78–114.

2. B. Schimetschek, *Der österreichische Beamte* (Vienna, 1984), 80. The Austrian gulden, or florin, was the principal unit of currency, although monetary amounts were often given in thaler. There were roughly two gulden in the thaler, although there was also a *Reichsthaler* in circulation that was worth only 1½ florins. The ducat, which also circulated, was the equivalent of about 4 florins. There were approximately 8½ gulden to the pound sterling. As for purchasing power, it was estimated that the minimum income on which a man could live nobly, if not always well, was 5,000 florins annually. Anything below that would condemn him to a genteel poverty at best.

3. Vienna, Verwaltungsarchiv (hereafter V.A.), Adelsinkolate.

4. Cobenzl assured Pergen's father, who regularly wrote to thank him for the patronage extended to Johann Baptist, that he was most favorably impressed with the young man's abilities and that he would without fail ask that he be returned to him in Mainz in case no permanent post should materialize, either in England or in Hanover. Cobenzl to Pergen senior, 24 June 1750, Vienna, Haus-, Hof- und Staatsarchiv (hereafter S.A.), Grosse Correspondenz (hereafter G.C.), 347.

5. The only, albeit fragmentary, account of Pergen's childhood and earliest beginnings in the diplomatic service is to be found in C. v. Wurzbach, *Biographisches Lexicon des Kaiserthums Österreich* (60 vols., Vienna, 1856–91), XXII, 1 ff. The account in *Beiträge zur Geschichte der Niederösterreichischen Stadthalterei* (Vienna, 1897), 336 ff., merely paraphrases Wurzbach. Wurzbach fails to cite his sources, and because the files holding Pergen's early correspondence were apparently dispersed in the last century, a degree of uncertainty about these events remains. For a detailed discussion of the possible fate of various collections of no longer extant Pergen materials see L. Bittner, *Gesammtinventar des Wiener Haus-, Hof- und Staatsarchivs*, 5 vols. (Vienna, 1936–40), II, 207. What follows in this chapter is mainly an attempt to reconstruct Pergen's early career on the basis of his extensive correspondence.

6. Pergen was accredited to the diet of the empire at Regensburg; to the electoral Rhenish, Swabian, Franconian, Upper Rhenish, and Westphalian Circles; and separately to all electors and princely courts with territories in these dominions. His position carried with it the honorary title of chamberlain to the emperor (*wirklicher Kämmerer*).

7. Pergen to Cobenzl, 8 May 1750, S.A., G.C. 348.

8. Pergen to Cobenzl, 26 June 1750, S.A., G.C. 348.

9. Pergen to Cobenzl, 29 June 1750, S.A., G.C. 348.

10. Pergen to Cobenzl, 9 August 1750, S.A., G.C. 348. This letter, as well as the immediately following ones, is written in English, the language that Pergen would use for the rest of his diplomatic career when touching upon highly personal or potentially compromising subjects. Since he was certainly aware that even correspondence at the ministerial level was subject to being opened by the censor, he must have felt that whoever was engaged in this capacity would be less likely to be able to read that language.

11. Pergen to Cobenzl, 30 August 1750, S.A., G.C. 348.

12. Cobenzl to Pergen, 6 September 1750, S.A., G.C. 348.

13. The various circles to which Pergen was accredited were in effect voluntary associations into which the imperial knights had entered with the blessings of the emperor in order to be better able to resist the continual encroachments of the princes into their miniscule domains. Cf. T. C. W. Blanning, *Reform and Revolution in Mainz 1743–1803* (Cambridge, 1979), 58–59, 65–67. For this reason the knights, who exerted considerable influence on the ecclesiastical electors, tended to be pro-Habsburg. As for the elector, who as *Reichserzkanzler* was ex officio a member of the imperial government, this was Johann Friedrich Karl von Ostein. Unlike a number of his predecessors, Ostein was thoroughly loyal to the empire (if not as loyal as Vienna would have liked), but also something of a champion of the Enlightenment. Pergen, who apparently could never forgive him his disinclination to sponsor, or even to allow, fancy dress balls in the preLenten season, consistently deprecated his abilities in his reports. Blanning, 65. F. G. Dreyfus, *Socités et mentalités a Mayence dans la seconde moitié du xviiième siècle* (Paris, 1968), 26–27, 46–47.

14. Pergen to Cobenzl, 30 October 1750, S.A., G.C. 348.

15. Pergen to Cobenzl, 29 November 1750, S.A., G.C. 348.

16. Pergen to Daun, 15 April 1753, S.A., Reichskanzlei, Ministerial Korrespondenz (hereafter M.K.), 27.

17. Pergen to Hamilton, 15 June 1753, S.A., M.K. 27.

18. Pergen to Prince Salm-Salm, 1 September 1753, S.A., M.K. 31.

19. Pergen to Batthàny, 13 April 1753; Batthàny to Pergen, 8 November 1753, S.A., M.K. 25. Pergen assiduously courted Batthàny, who was a great favorite of Maria Theresa. Thus in March he had sent to him four bottles of Italian perfume as a gift for his wife.

20. Mme. Benningsen to Pergen, 14 September 1753; Pergen to Mme. Benningsen, 30 September 1753, S.A., M.K. 25.

21. Pergen to Cobenzl, 9 October 1752, S.A., G.C. 379. The letter is entirely in Pergen's somewhat quaint English.

22. Pergen to Bartenstein, 23 May 1753, S.A., M.K. 25. This last inquiry was not only the result of free-floating anxiety on Pergen's part. He had just learned from Cobenzl that the reaction of the ministerial conference to the reports he had been sending in was mainly negative: they were considered to be too detailed, above all too diffuse, and weighted down to the point of caricature by

the endless *Beilagen* that he insisted on including. Cobenzl to Pergen, 29 April 1753, S.A., M.K. 25.

23. Pergen to Cobenzl, 8 April 1753, S.A., M.K. 25.

24. Cobenzl to Pergen, 26 May 1753, S.A., M.K. 25.

25. Brognet to Pergen, 30 June 1753, S.A., M.K. 25.

26. S.A., M.K. 33. Whoever compiled this document does experience a certain difficulty in distinguishing trivia from genuine political appeçus. Perhaps his most interesting observation is that Frederick's genius was strictly limited to the military sphere; in all other fields he was to be considered no more than a willful dilettante.

27. Roderigue to Pergen, 18 February 1753; Pergen to Roderigue, 21 February 1753, S.A., M.K. 30. Similarly, Pergen exchanged weekly letters with the Austrian resident at the court of the Prince-Bishop of Liège. Cf. Pergen to Hetzler, 11 February 1753, S.A., M.K. 27.

28. Cobenzl to Pergen, 25 February 1753, S.A., M.K. 26.

29. Pergen to Cobenzl, 11 March 1753, S.A., M.K. 26. The proper forms were, respectively, *schuldig ergebenster Diener* and *dienstbereitwilligster.*

30. Pergen to Brettendorff, 3 June 1753, S.A., M.K. 25.

31. Solomon to Pergen, 27 February 1753, S.A., M.K. 29.

32. Pergen to Lohy, 19 March 1753, S.A., M.K. 29.

33. S.A., M.K. 30.

34. Pergen to Balay, 4 December 1753, M.K. 25.

35. Esslinger to Pergen, 16 October 1753, S.A., M.K. 27. Among Pergen's first purchases was a volume of Voltaire's *Essays.* Pergen agreed to buy most of what Esslinger sent him, but urged the bookseller to keep his prices within reasonable limits. Pergen to Esslinger, 25 October 1753, S.A., M.K. 27. The prices Esslinger asked ranged between 50 kreuzer and 4.30 florins per item, which hardly seems excessive. Pergen particularly wanted a periodical called *Le Cosmopolite* and the collected works of St. Evremond.

36. Pergen to Breidbach, 20 October 1753, S.A., M.K. 25.

37. Pergen to Cobenzl, 5 December 1753, S.A., M.K. 26.

38. Pergen to Rodrigue, 29 November 1753, S.A., M.K. 30.

39. Pergen to Cobenzl, 14, 20, and 22 May 1753, S.A., M.K. 25. The sum of 7,000 florins yearly was by no means scant. For a discussion of diplomatic salaries of the period, see P. P. Bernard, "Kaunitz and the Cost of Diplomacy," *East European Quarterly,* XXVII/1 (March 1983), 1–14.

40. Cobenzl to Pergen, 9 June 1753, S.A., M.K. 26. Pergen was not to be dissuaded. In July, while Cobenzl was on home leave in Vienna, he wrote him another wheedling letter, asking him to use all his influence on his behalf because his chances of obtaining an increase would surely be nil once Cobenzl had left the court. Pergen to Cobenzl, 19 July 1753, S.A., M.K. 26.

41. Cobenzl to Pergen, 16 May 1753, S.A., M.K. 26, in which he repeats these strictures: *"je vous dirai que l'on souhaite, que vous sussiés moins diffus dans vos relations et sur tout, que vous ne les chargiés pas de Beylagen superflues."* Although Pergen was greatly alarmed upon hearing that he had not been giving

complete satisfaction, he never went so far as to remove the cause for this discontent. It seems rather that Kaunitz, at Cobenzl's urging, decided to take Pergen as he was and to put up with his verbosity. Cf. Cobenzl to Pergen, 23 April 1753, S.A., M.K. 26. Kaunitz had also objected that, not only was Pergen drowning him in a sea of superfluous detail, he was also running up huge bills for special couriers to bring these reports to Vienna. In one month alone in 1753 Pergen ran up 664 florins in courier charges. Cf. his account sheet, S.A., M.K. 52.

42. Karl Friedrich of Baden-Durlach to Pergen, 14 May 1753, S.A., M.K. 25. Phillipsburg was eventually restored to Karl Friedrich.

43. Cobenzl to Pergen, 21 February 1753, S.A., M.K. 26.

44. Pergen to Cobenzl, 1 April 1753, S.A., M.K. 26.

45. Pergen to Cobenzl, 28 July 1753, S.A., M.K. 26. This campaign would be spectacularly successful, as we shall presently see.

46. Pergen to Cobenzl, 17 September 1753, S.A., M.K. 26.

47. Pergen to Cobenzl, 10 November 1753, S.A., M.K. 26; Pergen to Harrach, 17 October 1753, S.A., M.K. 27.

48. Pergen to Cobenzl, 29 July 1753, S.A., M.K. 26; Mercy-Argenteau to Pergen, 20 October 1753; Pergen to Mercy-Argenteau, 25 October 1753, S.A., M.K. 25.

49. Rindsmaul to Pergen, 28 June 1753, S.A., M.K. 30.

50. The incident which follows is described in varying detail in the standard biographies of Voltaire. Cf. T. Besterman, *Voltaire* (New York, 1969), 328–333, and J. Orieux, *Voltaire* (New York, 1979), 270–80. Orieux, however, fixes Voltaire's arrival in Frankfurt on 1 May, which is clearly wrong. Cf. the *Journal de Francfort* (July 1753), which carries an extensive account of these events.

51. Pergen to Roderigue, 11 June and 8 July 1753, S.A., M.K. 30.

52. Pergen to Harrach, 13 July 1753, S.A., M.K. 27.

53. Pergen to Fickart, 20 July 1753, S.A., M.K. 27. Fickart tried to excuse his behavior on the grounds that, although Freytag had seemed to him to be proceeding along dubious lines, he and the city council had not received any instructions in the matter, and so had no reason to restrain him. Fickart to Pergen, 23 July 1753, S.A., M.K. 27.

54. Voltaire to Pergen, 10, 15, and 27 August 1753; Pergen to Voltaire, 27 August 1753, S.A., M.K. 32.

55. Pergen to Cobenzl, 11 January 1754; Cobenzl to Pergen, 23 January and 13 February 1754, S.A., M.K. 35. The lady in question was identified only as Mme de S . . . Pergen didn't lack a sense of humor about these gallantries, as the poem that he sent to his young friend Lobkowitz attests: *"Die Schlittenlust regieret, / Es stürmet, es schneiet und friert, / Klagt Pfad, Knecht und Diener, / Freut Euch, die Mediziener."* Pergen to Lobkowitz, 19 January 1755, S.A., M.K. 48.

56. Cobenzl to Pergen, 7 February 1754; Pergen to Cobenzl, 14 February 1754, S.A., M.K. 35. After young Lobkowitz's departure Pergen continued to court him assiduously. Thus he reported that the young Countess Hoheneck had only fond

memories of his visit and reassured Lobkowitz about the constancy of the lady's feelings by quoting him this little verse: *"L'absence est á l'amour / Ce qu'est au feu le vent. / Il éteint le petit / Et allume le grand."* Nor did Pergen neglect to ask Lobkowitz to mention his name occasionally at court so that it should not be completely forgotten in his long absence. Pergen to Lobkowitz, 1, 23 April and 11 June 1754, S.A., M.K. 37.

57. Champigny to Pergen, 26 October 1754, S.A., M.K. 35. It is not without interest that Pergen, after all a public official of high rank, seems to have had absolutely no scruples about abetting this bit of illegality. On another occasion Pergen asked Roderigue to see to it that a certain M. de Peigne, who was traveling with a considerable number of dutiable *objets d'art* in his luggage, be given free passage through customs on his arrival in the Austrian Netherlands. Pergen to Roderigue, 25 May 1755, S.A., M.K. 48.

58. Cobenzl to Pergen, 27 February 1754, S.A., M.K. 35; also Esslinger to Pergen, 19 February 1754, S.A., M.K. 38. Pergen in no manner hesitated to circumvent the already lax censorship obtaining in Mainz when he wanted to buy a work forbidden there. Thus he asked a London acquaintance to send him Lord Bolingbroke's *Memoirs,* which, as he himself admitted, were based on extremely dangerous principles. Pergen to Bährein, 14 February 1754, S.A., M.K. 42.

59. Pergen to Roderigue, 10 October 1754; Roderigue to Pergen, 8 October 1754, S.A., M.K. 42. For reasons best known to himself, Pergen penned a memoir describing this incident in great detail. N.d., S.A., M.K. 44.

60. Girolamo Bar to Pergen, 1 March 1755, S.A., M.K. 45.

61. Cobenzl to Pergen, 10 August 1754; Spangenberg to Cobenzl, 7 August 1754, S.A., M.K. 35. Pergen to Schaffgotsch, 12 August 1754, S.A., M.K. 39. It would seem that Pergen's high-handedness generated like behavior in Mainz. Thus when he questioned the prime minister, Vogel, about the reasons for the arrest of the Jew Riedel, he was told that, since Pergen had assured the elector that the monetary reform would go through without a hitch, it had been decided that the man, easily the most adroit speculator in the region, should be put behind bars. Otherwise he would unfailingly have made a financial killing in the circumstances. As it happened, Riedel was the guiding spirit behind Pergen's scheme for effecting a smooth transition in implementing the currency reform, so that the man's arbitrary arrest was a major embarassment to him. Nagel to Pergen, 20 August 1754, S.A., M.K. 43. This incident delayed the implementation of the currency reform, which was, as a result, put off until the next January. Cobenzl to Pergen, 11 January 1755, S.A., M.K. 46.

62. Cobenzl to Pergen, 14 September 1754; Pergen to Cobenzl, 21 September 1754, S.A., M.K. 35. Pergen would catch the lottery fever himself and become an enthusiastic supporter of such schemes.

63. Pergen to Prince Louis of Hesse-Darmstadt, 18 February 1754, S.A., M.K. 36.

64. Prüseken to Pergen, 30 August, 26 September, 12, 15 October, and 14 December 1754. Pergen to Prüseken, 3, 23 September, 14 October, and 22 December 1754. S.A., M.K. 38.

65. Pergen to Ulfeld, 25 March 1754, S.A., M.K. 39.

66. Pergen to Ulfeld, 4 May 1754, S.A., M.K. 39.

67. Pergen to Ulfeld, 18 June 1754, S.A., M.K. 39.

68. Von Vorster to Pergen, 5 July 1754, S.A., M.K. 41.

69. S.A., M.K. 45.

70. Pergen to Cobenzl, 4 January 1755, S.A., M.K. 46.

71. Pergen to Cobenzl, 23 January 1755, S.A., M.K. 46.

72. Pergen to Cobenzl, 15 June 1755, S.A., M.K. 46.

73. Pergen to Cobenzl, 1 July 1755, S.A., M.K. 46.

74. Pergen to Riedesel, 1 April 1755, S.A., M.K. 49.

75. Pergen to Harrach, 3 February 1755, S.A., M.K. 47.

76. Pergen to Cobenzl, 15 June 1755, S.A., M.K. 46. As matters turned out, the imperial candidate was elected with a plurality of eighty-five votes, forty-seven of which were cast by Protestants. Pergen was particularly proud of having brought these in. Pergen to Hetzen, 11 July 1755, S.A., M.K. 47.

77. Pergen to Landgrave William of Hesse-Darmstadt, 16 January 1755; Landgrave William to Pergen, 18 January 1755, S.A., M.K. 47. Pergen had first been noticed by the landgrave as the author of a tract, circulated in manuscript, defending the house of Hesse-Darmstadt against some territorial claims of Hesse-Homburg (a court on notoriously bad terms with Vienna). S.A., M.K. 50. Pergen revealed himself capable of a remarkably coarse tone in entertaining his friends. When Roderigue wrote him about the serious concern of the Dutch authorities regarding the spread of homosexuality in the province of Zeeland, he replied with the following anecdote: A novice in a monastery was discovered by the abbot *in flagrante delicto* with a Jewish lad. He calmly explained, *"Ce per rompere il culo à questo nemico del Cristo."* Pergen to Roderigue, 17 October 1755, S.A., M.K. 49. As for the landgrave, he seems to have been something of an eccentric. A passionate hunter like so many of his princely contemporaries, he had himself driven through the streets of Darmstadt with his mistress in a coach drawn by six tame stags. His endless hunts were the despair of his subjects, not a few of whom chose to emigrate to Prussia during his reign. At the same time he took an interest in philosophical discussions and devoted consider-able money and energy to the care of orphans in his lands. E. G. Franz et al., *Darmstadts Geschichte* (Darmstadt, 1980), 252–55.

76. Pergen to Landgrave William, 15 June 1755, S.A., M.K. 47. Nevertheless, Pergen made a great point of the fact that, despite his various debilitating ailments, he never missed a day of work. Pergen to his father, 16 November 1755, S.A., M.K. 48.

79. Pergen to Hetzler, 4, 15 February, 3, 14 April, 9 May, 20 August, 21 September, 5, 29 October, 15 November, and 2 December 1755, S.A., M.K. 47.

80. Pergen to Hetzler, 28 December 1755, S.A., M.K. 47.

81. Pergen to Hetzler, 9 February 1756, S.A., M.K. 54. Even so, Pergen underestimated the immediate effects of the Convention of Westminster. Admit-ting that it was, from his point of view, a piece of unequivocally bad news, he

nevertheless insisted that, as long as George II was on the throne, there would be no irrevocable consequences. The time to worry would be during the minority of his successor. Pergen to Roderigue, 17 January and 1 February 1756, S.A., M.K. 57. It took Pergen a good month of reflection to come around to the view that a terrible storm was now bound to break out over Europe. Pergen to Roderigue, 2, 5 February and 4 March 1756, S.A., M.K. 57.

82. Pergen to Roderigue, 4 January 1756; Pergen to Cobenzl, 4 January 1756, S.A., M.K. 57.

83. Pergen to Landgrave William of Hesse-Cassel, 10 March 1756, Hessisches Staatsarchiv, Marburg (hereafter H.S.A.M.), Politische Akten nach Philipp dem Grossen: Kaiser-, Reichs- und Kreisakten (hereafter P.A.).

84. Landgrave William of Hesse-Cassel to Emperor Francis Stephen, 16 March 1756, H.S.A.M., P.A.; for a fuller discussion of the Hesse-Kassel crisis see Charles W. Ingrao, *The Hessian Mercenary State* (Cambridge, 1987), pp. 17–19.

85. Bürisch to Pergen, 7 January 1756, S.A., M.K. 52. Pergen to Adelmann, 2 May 1756, S.A., M.K. 53.

86. Colonel Hoffmann to Pergen, 29 January 1756, S.A., M.K. 55.

87. Pergen to Cobenzl, 24 February and 24 March 1756, S.A., M.K. 53.

88. Pergen to Ulfeld, 24 January 1756, S.A., M.K. 58. Cobenzl wrote that he had learned that Pergen was to be relieved of his post in order to make way for a young protégé of Maria Theresa, Count Neiperg, and that Pergen would do well to mobilize all his friends at court in order to block this maneuver. Cobenzl to Pergen, 30 March 1756, S.A., M.K. 52. Pergen had also heard that he was about to be replaced by General Bretlach. Pergen to Roderigue, 1 April 1756, S.A., M.K. 57.

89. Pergen to Cobenzl, 22 July 1756, S.A., M.K. 53.

90. Pergen to Cobenzl, 23 August 1756, S.A., M.K. 53.

91. Pergen to Cobenzl, 23 September 1756, S.A., M.K. 53.

92. Nagel to Pergen, 6 August 1756; Pergen to Nagel, 14 August 1756, S.A., M.K. 56.

93. Pergen to Hockenthal, 25 September 1756, S.A., M.K. 58.

CHAPTER

2

Dead End in the *Reich*

ALMOST IMMEDIATELY AFTER his return to Mainz, Pergen had to
deal with a thorny and potentially explosive issue. The duke of
Pfalz-Zweibrücken, who, as a major German prince, was regularly courted
by both Vienna and Versailles—he was in fact little better than a French
client—had negotiated an exchange of territory with the prince of
Nassau. No sooner had Zweibrücken taken possession of the villages for
which he had traded than he issued orders to chase out the priests and
to turn over the churches to the Protestant clergy. To be sure, this was
his right under the provisions of the Religious Peace of Augsburg,
as reaffirmed in the treaties of Westphalia, but the ousted Catholics
now addressed themselves to their imperial protector, demanding
redress. Pergen realized that he would have to tread extremely carefully
here.

If the dispute were to be referred to Vienna, Maria Theresa, who saw
herself as the protector and patron of Catholics everywhere, would
undoubtedly order him to undertake all measures necessary to restore
the dispossessed priests to their positions. While threats alone could
conceivably achieve this end—Zweibrücken could hardly afford an
open breach with the empire—the duke would assuredly complain
loud and long to Versailles, all of which might well lead to a bitter
quarrel between the new allies. Pergen decided to appeal to the duke's
vested interest in the constitution of the empire. He had done some
research of his own and now came up with the following argument:
whereas it was certainly true that the clause *Cuius regio, eius religio*
gave Zweibrücken the right to impose his religion on his new subjects, this had been abrogated and superseded by the article of the
Peace of Ryswick, which guaranteed the inhabitants of Nassau the
right to exercise free religious choice. Surely, Pergen asked, the duke

would not wish to seem to be breaking solemn treaties in these perilous times?[1]

The times indeed were perilous. Within a week of Pergen's return to Mainz, the war that he had so long been predicting broke out. And with its onset, the whole nature of Pergen's responsibilities underwent a drastic change. Now, instead of arbitrating endless petty disputes and presiding over the mostly ineffectual attempts to introduce some degree of cohesion into the *Reich,* Pergen was to engage full time in mustering what support he could for the imperial cause. Given the unremitting material and manpower needs of the Habsburg monarchy in the war, this circumstance was sufficient to elevate Pergen from the position of a distinctly minor envoy to that of a key figure.

Pergen soon enough found that it would be anything but easy to meet Vienna's expectations of him. As had been the case in the previous war, a good many of the German princes, whatever they might say in public, were determined to commit themselves as little as possible to either side, until it became clearer from whence the wind blew. The first casualty of this attitude of caution on their part was Maria Theresa's plan to have the Archduke Joseph elected as king of the Romans. This scheme, whose success Pergen had confidently predicted some months previously, now had to be dropped entirely.[2] Pergen found that he had to adjust his expectations considerably downward. It took him days of wheedling to persuade the elector of Mainz to permit a brochure to circulate in his dominions explaining the justice of Austria's position in the war.[3]

Nor did Pergen have much better luck in Frankfurt. Two weeks after the outbreak of war, the mayor and council of what was, after all, an imperial free city, bound to support the emperor in all matters of foreign policy, protested to Vienna that Pergen had dared to demand that they put an end to the activities of Prussian military recruiters on their territory and that Prussian propaganda leaflets be removed from the municipal bulletin boards. The imperial vice chancellor, Count Colloredo, was forced to remind them that they governed not some neutral state but an integral part of the empire.[4]

But these, as Pergen was soon to find out, were mere pin pricks. Far more difficult, as it turned out, would be what was to constitute his principal task over the next years: gathering together materiel required by the allied armies. In July of 1757, the imperial commander, the duke of Hildburghausen, declared that before he could move his force toward the enemy he would require several hundred barges to be used as pontoons in the numerous river crossings he would have to undertake. The problem was that although there was no shortage of barges on the Main and Rhine, their owners, seeing them in such great demand, were asking exorbitant prices. Pergen was finally reduced to applying to Vienna for permission to requisition the barges if it turned out that he could not buy them.[5]

While many of the German princes were reluctant to take sides too blatantly in a war whose outcome was unclear and in which it was by no means manifest where their true interest lay, Pergen's problems in getting them to cooperate with him were caused in great part also by Vienna's heavy-handedness. Thus, he was informed from one day to the next that a force of sixteen thousand foot and eighteen hundred horse would be passing through the Upper Rhenish Circle within a fortnight. He was instructed to make the appropriate arrangements for the supplies and quarters that this army would require, but was not assigned so much as a single additional commissary agent to assist him in the huge amount of additional work this would involve. In desperation, he begged Cobenzl to send him some people from his staff in Brussels, or else utter chaos would inevitably result.[6]

Equally infuriating to Pergen must have been a communication from the vice-chancellor in answer to a report of his in which he had chronicled his continuing efforts to persuade his friend, the landgrave of Hesse-Darmstadt, to support the imperial cause in spite of the circumstance that his own ministers were undeniably pro-Prussian. Colloredo thereupon instructed Pergen to pay two hundred florins to a Hofrat Langstorff at that court, one of the few known Austrian supporters there. Pergen was to continue to bribe that official, although, as Colloredo now informed him, and as Pergen had been unaware during the entire period he courted the landgrave, Langstorff was a double agent who passed on all the information that came his way to the Prussians. Not only was Pergen informed, at this late date, of this circumstance that conceivably could and did have a negative effect upon his negotiations in Darmstadt, but he was instructed to continue cultivating Langstorff; at least the man was a known quantity, and perhaps he might at some time in the future betray his Prussian paymasters, just as he had betrayed the Austrians.[7]

If Pergen had frequent reason to complain that the state chancellery showed an almost total disregard for the nature of his problems, he could console himself with the reflection that as the nature of his duties had acquired a much greater importance in Vienna's eyes, his own stock had risen correspondingly. He was no longer regarded as a troublesome eccentric with a tendency to drown each minor concern in an ocean of words. Colloredo personally took the trouble to inform him that not only he, but the sacred person of the emperor as well, was extremely pleased with Pergen's work in Darmstadt. They realized that, had it not been for his unrelenting efforts, the landgrave's prime minister, aptly named Teufel (devil), would long ago have profited from his master's lethargy and overall disinterest in public affairs to take Hesse-Darmstadt into the Prussian camp.[8] And soon enough there was a reward forthcoming for Pergen. He was given yet another special appointment, that of representing the empire at the election of a new bishop of Fulda; the result was a foregone conclusion, so that Pergen had to invest hardly any time, but was given a very generous 1000 ducats for his services.[9]

As the war grew more and more to monopolize his attention, Pergen found that most of his troubles were neither the result of machinations of the enemy nor even of the lukewarm cooperation he received from the rulers of various German states. Rather his troubles were caused by the deep set antipathy for Austria's French allies, which was an ineradicable element of popular sentiment in that portion of Germany. Pergen fumed and fretted, maintaining that if he himself, who had been until very recently in the habit of denouncing Versailles as the ultimate seat of perfidy, was flexible enough to adapt to the new circumstances, so should others; but this did him no good.[10] Many German princes saw in the French armies, which were crossing and re-crossing the territories of the various German states, a much worse danger than in the Prussian enemy.

Thus, Prince Charles of Waldeck reminded Pergen that he had been the only prince of the empire who had not, at one time or another, gone over to the Bavarian Charles VII in the bad old days of the Silesian wars. Now this loyalty was being rewarded by forcing him to allow the French to take up quarters in his lands. The commanders of these forces never tired of making demands, which either simply could not be met at all, or which would lead to his bankrupting himself in fulfilling them. If Pergen did not soon find a way of moderating the appetite of the French, he would be forced, most reluctantly, to rethink his position.[11] Soon afterward, Waldeck was complaining that the French had requisitioned some five hundred horses in his domains, and all the wagons that would roll, and had not paid a *sou* for any of this.[12] Pergen did his best to calm the prince, but in substance all he could come up with was a rather lame expression of confidence in his great nobility of character, which surely would not allow him to make good his threats.[13]

Especially alarming, from Austria's point of view, was the increasingly equivocal attitude displayed by the good burghers of Frankfurt. When the French commander informed the mayor of that city that he intended to quarter several regiments there, that dignitary distributed arms to the citizenry and had cannons drawn up on the ramparts, just as if the town were about to be invested by the enemy. For good measure, the town council voted to recall its contingent serving with the imperial army, and Pergen himself was threatened with physical violence if he should venture to support the French demands. As a result, he spent weeks in locating appropriate quarters for the French outside the walls of the city.[14] The independence of spirit displayed by the Frankfurters did not stop there. Soon Pergen saw himself forced to ask that Vienna put a halt to their large-scale sales of wheat and other foodstuffs to the enemy, as none of his representations in the matter had had the least effect.[15]

The French did nothing to facilitate Pergen's task. There were continual incidents in which they behaved with an arbitrariness that seemed to suggest they were campaigning somewhere deep in enemy territory. In one such incident, a French colonel, upon learning that an imperial fusilier had debauched a young trooper in his force, had the man arrested and proposed, after a drumhead court-martial, to shoot the fellow on the spot. Pergen, learning of these events in the nick of time, was forced to point out to the French commander, the duc de Broglie, that relations between the French military and the German population were bad enough as it was. Exacerbating them with such a provocative step was indefensible. Unless the man was turned over to his own unit for punishment, he could not guarantee the reaction of the German populace.[16]

If the French were making themselves enormously unpopular in Germany, they too had more than enough reason to be displeased with their allies. Under the terms of the alliance, they were not only entitled to receive material assistance equal to the cost of maintaining an army on German soil, but they had also been promised that this force would be augmented by various regiments in the German free cities and principalities. Yet, as of mid-May 1757, this force remained almost entirely on paper. The French ambassador to Austria complained bitterly that no contingents at all had so far been raised in Mainz, Cologne, Trier, the Palatinate, the Franconian Circle, Swabia, or in the Rhenish Circles, and that it appeared to him that it was Austria's intention to slough off the responsibility for waging the war in Germany entirely upon France.[17] To add insult to injury, the Austrians were now caught red-handed spying upon their allies. A certain Captain Ongania was stopped while carrying away secret documents from the headquarters of the French commander in chief, Marshal d'Estreé. Pergen, to whom the furious French commander addressed his protest, was faced with the unpleasant and difficult task of having, at one and the same time, to try to save the unfortunate man's life—as d'Estreé was all for shooting him—while also denying any Austrian responsibility for him.[18]

Pergen could not come up with much beyond evasiveness in a case such as that of Captain Ongania, and no one really expected him to, but the French complaints about the continuing absence of an effective force in the *Reich* were more difficult for him to explain away. And to make matters worse, these complaints could fairly be placed at his door, as he had been specifically instructed to see to it such a force was raised. If so far he had not succeeded in the attempt, it was not for lack of trying. As a result of his efforts, practically all the princes and free cities in the region had agreed to the free passage of Austrian troops through their territories, and promised to raise contingents for incorporation into the imperial army.[19] Sadly, it soon turned out that promises were one thing and actions another. Pergen kept assuring Vienna that he was working day and night to light a fire under the Germans; he could not be blamed if they chose to move so slowly.[20] Not until June was he able to report that a few regiments had actually been raised and were marching to join the main body of the Austrian forces in Franconia. There were 2600 men from Mainz, 1200 from Trier, 1000 from Cologne, and even the Palatinate, where reluctance to support the imperial cause was greatest, was sending 1200 men and 460 horses.[21] Pergen failed utterly, however, in getting any action out of Frankfurt. The authorities there had indeed raised a force of some 4000, but proffered the flimsy excuse that their weapons all needed to be overhauled; the city council refused to allow them to leave the city.[22]

The Rhenish and Swabian Circles also were still dragging their feet, a circumstance that Pergen attributed to the fact that most of the territories in these entities were Protestant, and thus sympathized with Prussia. In all probability, he reported, it would be unwise to persist in getting the promised contingents from them, as even if they were ultimately raised, they would doubtless prove totally unreliable. He had recently heard that in Darmstadt, where the landgrave had insisted on raising the force he had promised over the objections of his ministers, the soldiers had refused to affix the green cockade of the allied armies to their hats. Even worse news arrived from Württemberg, where a regiment that had been given its marching orders mutinied, killed its officers, and deserted.[23]

Pergen's doubts about the fighting spirit of the *Reich's* auxiliaries were only too well founded and, as it turned out, the Catholic troops were hardly any more reliable than the Protestant. As he ruefully noted, at the first encounter with Prussian detachments the auxiliaries had fled, practically without having taken any casualties, and what remained of them could only be described as rabble.[24] Still, to a remarkable degree Pergen had done the job that he had been assigned, and it was hardly his fault that the troops he squeezed out of the German states did not, for the most part, choose to fight. On this occasion his efforts did not go unrecognized. When in the spring of 1757 Frederick, hard pressed on all fronts, was unable to detach sufficient forces to defend the Prussian territories in Northern Germany and in the Rhineland, and these were occupied by the imperial army, Pergen was appointed to the post of president of the administration of the conquered territories, a position that brought an addition of 4000 florins to his salary.[25]

In his new post, Pergen could function in a manner very different from the one that he had been accustomed to. Rather than having always to fall back on his powers of persuasion,—the princes, imperial knights and city governments with which he had to deal invariably insisted on exercising their independent judgments on all questions, no matter how absolute their dependence on Vienna might be—he could now administer and give orders. Although he was responsible to the central government for his decisions, and would have to answer to it if these proved unsuccessful, at least he did not have to spend the greater part of his time defending them. Given the fact that his country was at war and that the territories in question had, after all, been conquered from the enemy, Pergen could certainly have behaved in an arbitrary, perhaps even in a tyrannical, fashion without incurring much danger of serious reprimand. Vienna was chiefly interested in results. In fact, Pergen performed his new duties, which were not always straightforward or uncomplicated, with a good deal of fairness and circumspection. In the instructions sent to him at the time of his appointment, he was told that the occupied territories must under no circumstances produce less revenue under his administration than they had brought into the coffers of the Prussian government. Clearly this was a mandate to squeeze the territories as hard as he could, since the disruptions of the war had hurt the German North Sea ports particularly hard, and their income had correspondingly diminished, all of which had an inevitably negative effect on their hinterlands as well. Pergen did not hesitate to point this out to Vienna. He reported *inter alia* that Cleves, in the previous year, had paid the equivalent of almost 280,000 florins into the Prussian exchequer. It was extremely unrealistic to expect a like contribution, or indeed much of anything, out of the district at this time. In addition to the already-mentioned economic miseries that plagued the inhabitants, they also were having to meet the huge financial demands that the French were making on them to reimburse the cost of keeping a part of their army stationed there.[26]

Pergen also took it upon himself to argue that, as a matter of plain humanity, it would prove necessary to assume the payment of Prussian invalids' pensions in the conquered territories. He was only too painfully aware, he wrote, that this would constitute a heavy additional load for the already overburdened imperial treasury; he was not unfamiliar with the arguments that this was no responsibility of Austria, and that it would be preferable somehow to squeeze the money out of the territories themselves and, when peace returned, to present Prussia with the bill; but he felt very strongly that it was more important to demonstrate Austria's generosity toward a conquered enemy.[27]

Not long after this exchange, Pergen was intervening on behalf of the Jew Philip Israel of Cleves, who had become involved in a dispute with a merchant of Münster. This man, claiming that Israel owed him a sum of money, and having failed to get the town council to collect it on his behalf, went instead to the commander of the Austrian garrison, whom he persuaded to put a squad of soldiers at his disposal. With the assistance of these men, he then broke into the home of Israel's son, from whom—at the point of the bayonet—he took the money he claimed he was owed. When Pergen learned what had happened, he delivered a severe dressing-down to the officer responsible for this action, ordered the return of the money, and let it be known that under his administration all persons, regardless of their religion, were to feel safe in the possession of their property.[28]

Pergen's relations with Jews, uncharacteristically cordial for an Austrian nobleman of his time, transcended mere self-interest. Anyone in his position would have been well advised to maintain friendly relations with the more prominent Jewish factors. Their help was essential, and had been for almost a century, in supplying the army commissariat with the materiel and foodstuffs it needed. But in the case of the factor, Nathan Aaron Wetzlar, Pergen went well beyond this. Much as in the case of his Jewish doctor friend in Frankfurt, he treated Wetzlar as a confidant and, the occasion arising, was not too proud to ask him to put in a good word on his behalf at the court in electoral Hesse.[29]

Pergen did his best to ease the situation of the merchants in the conquered territories, who not only had lost the greater part of their markets due to the war but who were now suffering under a myriad of new export regulations imposed by Vienna. In this manner, the port of Emden was all but closed down because, as Pergen ruefully explained to a committee of local shippers, every single man aboard one of their vessels bound for sea would now need to have in his possession a passport signed by the sovereign himself.[30] And, as he further explained, although he forwarded all passport requests as soon as he received them, accompanied by cover letters explaining the urgency of the matter, it took a minimum of six weeks for a passport to be made out and returned to him. The inevitable consequence was that the trade of Emden was being slowly strangled, as most shipowners refused to dock there and subject themselves to this kind of delay.

Pergen repeatedly protested to Vienna that this sort of bureaucratic vexation, coupled with the exhorbitant demands and exactions of the commanders of the French troops stationed in the territories, would lead to total financial collapse.[31] He endorsed the plea of Baron Seckendorf, chief minister of Clèves, who pointed out the impossibility of coming up with the sums demanded of him, and assured Seckendorf that he was using whatever influence he had on his behalf. At the same time, however, he told Seckendorf that he could be of no help at all in the matter of the French, over whom he had not the slightest influence.[32]

Notwithstanding his scrupulous regard for the rights of the inhabitants of the conquered territories and his sympathy with their financial plight, Pergen managed to make an excellent financial showing. In January of 1758, he was able to report to Vienna that in the previous half-year the amount of money raised there by his tax-collectors had come to just under 5 million louis d'or, whereas the expenses of the Austrian administration had amounted to $3\frac{1}{2}$ million, thus leaving a surplus of $1\frac{1}{2}$ million.[33] No province of the monarchy, at any time during the war, was able to show so positive a balance.

But if Pergen exhibited a genuine concern for the well-being of the people under his administration, he very badly wanted this fact to be generally known. He reacted with a considerable show of hurt feelings to an article attacking him as a tyrant that appeared in a gazette published in The Hague. Complaining that the writer of this piece had very evidently not taken the trouble to inform himself about the true nature of conditions in Cleves, he pointed out that the town council there had unanimously passed a resolution of thanks to him, in which it was explicitly noted that the most salient quality of his administration was his extreme regard for everyone's rights. As he himself saw it, he could be reproached only for being a realist: he had never hesitated to inform one and all that they would have to make the best of prevailing circumstances; after all, Austria was at war, its government needed money desperately, and the inhabitants of an occupied enemy territory could not expect to escape all taxation merely because they had had the misfortune of being on the losing side.[34]

Pergen's new responsibilities brought other annoyances with them. Kaunitz now took it upon himself to demand daily reports from him. If necessary, these were to be sent not by the regular post but by special courier.[35] As Pergen would have had to bear the considerable costs from his own budget, he decided instead to apply to the chancellery for permission to open a post office at Wesel, which would accommodate this increase in postal traffic. When the permission was duly granted, Pergen appointed a certain Heger as postmaster and thought that this problem, at least, had been solved.[36] Instead, he soon received a furious protest from Prince von Thurn und Taxis, the *Reichsgeneralerbpostmeister,* who insisted that the privilege of running post offices in Germany belonged to him alone. Feeling secure in his position, Pergen responded with irony and *hauteur:* the post office at Wesel had been established at His Majesty's direct order; if the prince had objections to make, he should address these to the state chancellor.[37] Unfortunately, it soon turned out that von Thurn's connections at court were substantially better than Pergen's, who now had to inform Heger that, as His Majesty had no intention of sustaining his claims against von Thurn, he would have to close up shop. The fact that Pergen tried to shift the responsibility for this fiasco onto Heger, whom he blamed for having begun operations before having received official permission from Vienna, does not exactly speak well for his magnanimity.[38]

No less of an embarrassment was the affair of young Count Bergen. This gentleman had been put under arrest by an Austrian officer in the conquered territories upon presentation of a document bearing the signature of Charles Frederick of Hohenzollern, burggrave of Nuremberg. This warrant, which seems to have been the German equivalent of the notorious *lettre de cachet,* alleged that Bergen was governed by passions so tumultuous that, for his own good and that of society, it was necessary to place him under permanent restraint. Acting without Pergen's knowledge, one of his deputies, a certain Van de Velden, had thereupon arranged for Bergen's transport to the Austrian Netherlands, where he was imprisoned in the fortress at Antwerp. The unfortunate young man's wife, however, soon discovered his whereabouts and undertook to secure his release. Bergen was a citizen of the United Provinces, and the countess prevailed upon the Dutch government to protest his arbitrary arrest to Vienna, which in due time demanded an explanation from Pergen.

Things did not look too good for him as he, or rather his deputy, for whose behavior he was responsible, had acted in a clearly illegal manner. But Pergen found a way out of the dilemma by stressing a side of the affair he knew would have a powerful effect on Maria Theresa: he insisted that the young count's transgressions were unimaginably horrible; he was a habitual seducer of women. And, indeed, Pergen's tactics were rewarded when the empress ordered Bergen locked up in a monastery prison without trial or investigation.[39] In spite of this, Pergen did not escape unscathed. The incident led to a break between him and his old friend and benefactor Cobenzl, who was a close friend of the Bergen family.[40]

An incident which demonstrated that, in spite of his quick temper, Pergen was learning the ways of diplomacy, took place about this time. He received a letter from a Countess Linange, informing him that she desired to become a Catholic and asking for his help. Although himself anything but a religious zealot, he would normally, calculating that such an action would surely benefit him, in view of Maria Theresa's deep religious convictions, have assisted the countess in realizing her intention without giving the matter a second thought. He had acted in just this manner a few months before, in the case of a young Lutheran minister wanting to leave his church for that of Rome, sending the fellow to Vienna with a personal recommendation that made it plain that he himself had been instrumental in making this conversion possible.[41]

The Linanges, though, one of the most prominent families in the *Reich,* were another matter entirely. Upon making some discreet inquiries, Pergen discovered that the lady's husband, a pious Lutheran, had no inkling whatever of her intentions and that helping her to convert was tantamount to breaking up the marriage. Such a scandal might well have serious consequences among leading German Protestants. Deciding that discretion was indicated, Pergen temporized, and in the meantime wrote to Maria Theresa's trusted personal secretary, Baron Koch, asking him to find out in a circumspect manner what the empress wanted to be done.[42]

As Pergen had probably surmised, the empress, although she clearly saw the undesirability involved in an affair of this sort, was also unwilling to allow an immortal soul to escape. She finally resolved her dilemma by instructing Pergen to stay well in the background, but also to see to it that the countess was put in touch with a suitable priest to instruct and help her.[43] As Pergen apparently could not or would not come up with an appropriate candidate, the empress finally took matters into her own hands and dispatched the emperor's own confessor, the Jesuit Bittermann, to Germany. This cleric, unwilling to make an enemy of the minister, trod extremely lightly upon his arrival there, and finally gave up the whole enterprise as probably ill-advised.[44]

On one of his inspection trips through the occupied territories, Pergen traveled in the company of a young visitor from Vienna with whom he would become fast friends. This was Gottfried van Swieten, the son of Maria Theresa's personal physician and close adviser, Gerhard van Swieten. Upon the completion of Pergen's official duties, the two gentlemen went off on a week's visit to the United Provinces, where they seem to have had a very jolly time indeed.[45] In the aftermath, the two began a correspondence that lasted over many years, and in which, in spite of the considerable difference in their ages, Pergen not only treated the younger van Swieten as an intellectual equal but also divulged to him many of his innermost concerns. As van Swieten, like his father, tended toward Jansenism in theological questions, and, in contrast to the former, was something of a liberal in political ones, Pergen's friendship with him may be taken as providing some insight into what his own positions at that stage of his life were. Perhaps the speculation may be permitted that the strongly reactionary opinions, which Pergen occasionally voiced in official communications at this time, were inserted more for show than out of conviction. At the very least, what emerges from this correspondence is that Pergen had not just bought the principal works of the philosophes; he had read them with some care.

By the beginning of 1758, Pergen's job was rapidly becoming impossible for one man, and not merely, as had been the case frequently in the past, because he insisted on minding everyone else's business as well as his own. As the quick victory the allies had confidently expected at the outset of the war failed to materialize, the German forces that Pergen had helped to raise were near dissolution. He was under constant pressure, both from Vienna and from Versailles, to come up with replacements.

The problem of course was that it was well-nigh impossible to convince the German princes and free cities to put themselves out any further in supporting what was beginning to look suspiciously like a losing cause. Still, Pergen tried manfully. While admitting that the war news was bad—he could scarcely have done otherwise—he asked the Germans to trust Kaunitz's genius for finding unexpected solutions, to rely on the bravery of the Austrian commanders, and, over the long run, to be confident that the strength of numbers would always be on the side of the allies.[46] He argued that, especially in these dangerous times, the duty of all princes and corporations was clear; they would have to acquiesce in the incorporation of their territorial militias into the imperial army; it would of course be best if they did so without insisting on any payment in return, but if they objected to this, money could be found for them. What he needed was men.[47]

While putting up a brave front for the benefit of the Germans, Pergen did not bother to disguise his doubts and fears when writing to various French commanders. Thus, he admitted to General Dupuy that the military situation looked desperate. The previous campaign had shown that Frederick was capable of mobilizing his army for use on any given front within forty-eight hours. As it routinely took the Austrians at least two weeks to reach their assembly points, the Prussian king could, if he chose, strike a decisive blow at any time.[48]

Pergen's complaints about the slowness of the Austrian reactions were true, *a fortiori,* of the Germans, who if they agreed to participate in a campaign at all, unfailingly marched with such agonizing slowness that generally their forces managed to arrive too late to participate in the critical phases of most operations. But of course Pergen was not responsible for the fighting qualities of the German troops; it was all he could do to see to it that at least some reinforcements reached the imperial army from this quarter. And even so, he was frequently forced to admit total failure, as with the elector of Trier, who baldly answered a request for the dispatch of the troops he had previously committed to the imperial cause, by saying that the *Renitenz* (obstinacy) of his subjects prevented him from sending any help at all.[49]

Nor did Pergen's difficulties with the French abate. Soon he was interceding on behalf of the citizenry of Hanover, which had complained to him that the tax burden imposed by the French command was so crushing that all economic life in the city had come to a standstill.[50] Later in the year, the German nobles, through their representatives at the Regensburg *Reichstag,* protested directly to Vienna about the unceasing French demands for supplies and quarters, having gotten nowhere with Pergen. Now, as he pointed out to the French intendant in Mannheim, the fat was in the fire. An official complaint from a corporate constituency in the *Reich* would certainly not be ignored there, and there was sure to be trouble between the allies at the highest level.[51] Much worse would come. The French commander, the Prince de Soubise, decided that he needed a secure base of operations for himself and that Frankfurt was the logical place to satisfy this purpose. He addressed himself to the mayor of that city, asking for permission to quarter his troops there. The request was promptly turned down, whereupon Soubise asked if he might march two battalions through the city on their way to the front; this would save them a good part of the distance they had to cover. As French troops had previously passed through Frankfurt without incident, this request was granted. No sooner were Soubise's battalions inside the city walls than they proceeded to disarm the local militia, and to open the gates to the whole French army, which marched in and without further ceremony took quarters wherever they found them. Like it or not, the Frankfurters found themselves submitting to foreign occupation. That Pergen, as chief Austrian representative in the district, had been unable to prevent Austria's allies from perpetrating this outrage, and that he on instructions from his government—which did not want any trouble with France at this point—did not make so much as a formal protest to Soubise, hardly endeared him to the citizenry.[52]

Still another element exacerbated Pergen's already difficult situation. As he complained bitterly and repeatedly, he was being hampered in the performance of his duties because, to his certain knowledge, the Elector Palatine had a highly placed informant at the Court of Vienna. This person supplied him with the details of the most secret discussions in various governmental councils. Being so well informed, the elector was always able to parry Pergen's arguments, in their many differences of opinion, as soon as these were advanced. As matters stood, Pergen saw no way to exert pressure on the elector to support Austrian policies. Either the information leak would have to be plugged, or the Palatinate must be written off.[53] It had been one of Pergen's fondest hopes, at the outbreak of the war, that the enormous amount of random information and intelligence that could be extracted from the vast network of correspondence he had built up, in various parts of Germany and the Netherlands, would serve the allies well. And throughout the early phases of the war, he bombarded both his own government and that of France with the information he had been able to gather.

He was deeply disappointed when this information was ignored—if not treated with actual disdain—in both places. To be sure, his tips, based for the most part on second- and third-hand information, often bore no particular resemblance to actual conditions. He certainly overreached himself when he passed on various dubious rumors, already discounted in other places, that a plot to assassinate the leading German princes supporting Austria had been hatched in Potsdam. On that occasion, he was curtly told not to traffic in such gossip.[54]

When Pergen decided to turn strategist, and sent a warning to the Prince de Soubise that a Prussian corps moving rapidly through Saxony would soon present a threat to his flank, this warning did not elicit so much as an acknowledgment from the marshal.[55]

Pergen was not much more successful as a transmitter of scientific information, an area in which he took a particular interest. This fact had become known sometime before, and the scientific innovators, the inventors, and the charlatans in all of northern Germany submitted him to a regular bombardment of proposals ranging from quack cures for various epidemic diseases to helpful advice on how the monarchy might reform its public health policies. After a time, Pergen learned to weed out the most insubstantial of these, but he remained an easy mark for any halfway plausible scheme suggested by someone with bona fide scientific credentials.

In June 1758, a Dr. Strock, known to Pergen as a reputable physician practicing in Mainz, wrote him that he had discovered a cure for that terrible scourge of armies, dysentery. The specific which he had discovered was a readily available substance that, if administered at the right moment, would unfailingly do its job. No reputable physician, once the method was explained to him, could fail to recognize its efficacy. Strock further informed Pergen that he had already received overtures from the English. If he would reveal his cure to the medical authorities there, he was promised an appointment to the Royal Academy. Like all other men, he was not insensitive to honors and awards. Still, as a loyal subject of the empire, he would prefer to turn his discovery over to the friends rather than to the enemies of his country. Could Pergen smooth the way for him in Vienna?[56]

Pergen at once answered that he himself entertained no doubts about the efficacy of Strock's newly discovered cure; his standing in the medical profession alone guaranteed this respect. He added that he was deeply affected by his evident loyalty to Austria; this did him great honor; and he begged to be sent a description of the miracle cure by return mail, so that it could still be put to use during the present campaign, in which hundreds of men were dying of dysentery. He proposed to call upon Strock that very evening personally to pick up his manuscript and to send this to the dean of Austrian medicine, Gerhard van Swieten, who would undoubtedly see that the information was passed on to all of the monarchy's physicians serving the army.[57]

The matter, however, was proceeding much too rapidly for Strock's taste. What guarantees, he asked, did he have that van Swieten would not simply steal his discovery? In that case, he would never collect any reward at all. A whole month of undignified haggling followed before Strock finally agreed to send van Swieten a description of his method, but only on condition that the latter be sworn to absolute secrecy, and that not a single detail of his cure be divulged to anyone but him, before Strock collected his reward.[58]

In the meantime, Pergen had, however, sent off a breathless note to van Swieten announcing the impending arrival of Strock's great discovery. The old doctor's reaction was considerably less enthusiastic than Pergen might have hoped. First of all, the great man pontificated, dysentery was not nearly as terrible a disease as was commonly thought; all soldiers got it, most survived. Second, van Swieten informed Pergen, in a tone that left no doubt that in his opinion he felt Pergen should have been aware of it, that he himself had just published a little monograph outlining a cure for that disease. His own method had already been tested in the field and an epidemic that had broken out in a Hungarian regiment had been completely suppressed.

Nor could van Swieten refrain from adding that, in his view, a physician conscious of his duty at all times is primarily concerned about benefitting his fellow human beings. Thus, when some years ago he had developed a successful treatment for the Venetian sickness (gonorrhea), a treatment that had been adopted with great success in the British army, it had not entered his head to ask the king of England for a reward. Furthermore, it struck him as highly unlikely that the English would be willing to reward Strock without having first tried the method. To his certain knowledge, they had recently paid out 5,000 pounds to a Mrs. Stevens for a remedy against kidney stones that had subsequently turned out to be worthless, and they would not so soon have forgotten that lesson.

Still, van Swieten did not wish to be unfair to Strock. It was barely possible that the man had discovered something of value. If Strock were really unwilling to publicize his cure and look to heaven for his reward, van Swieten would read the manuscript and reveal its contents to no one. If it turned out that Strock had come up with something really useful, he would see to it that Strock would get his reward. If not, van Swieten would point out his errors. In the meantime, van Swieten proposed to go on in his humble way, curing dysentery as he had been doing for some months.[59] There the matter had to rest, because Strock had evidently changed his mind and never sent van Swieten anything.

If a number of Pergen's pet projects miscarried in the course of 1758, there was a decided upturn in his private life. He began to see the young Baroness Großschlag on a regular basis, and wrote her numerous letters from his inspection trips to the occupied territories.[60] His health, however, left something to be desired. Whether because of overwork, or because of some chronic disorder, or simply as a result of pure hypochondria, he complained of suffering from continual headaches and eye strain. His doctor bled him regularly, but without achieving any improvement. He himself attributed his symptoms to "a weakness of the nerves in the head," and lived in continual terror of suffering a stroke. As he repeatedly assured Vienna, he needed nothing so much as a prolonged respite from work, but in the existing circumstances would not even consider applying for one; he would prefer to die rather than neglect his duty.[61] It did turn out, though, that there were limits to his devotion. By the summer of 1759, he had become sufficiently alarmed about his general health that, in spite of the continuing pressure of affairs, he applied for and was given permission to take the waters at Spa.[62]

Pergen's cure seemed to have done some good, as he was able to resume work by autumn. His romance with Mlle. Großschlag had now progressed to the point at which marriage was being seriously discussed, which, in the eighteenth century, meant in the first instance talking about money. As both families were only moderately well off, and since running a regular household would be notoriously costlier than keeping up bachelor's quarters, Pergen now launched into yet another major campaign to extract additional funds from Vienna. Since he was already drawing two salaries, he could not expect his pay to be raised; so instead he concentrated his efforts on having himself appointed *wirklicher geheimer Hofrat* (secret court counsellor), a position with no duties but with a regular emolument. He also did not hesitate to write his acquaintance Koch, Maria Theresa's principal secretary, that a generous wedding gift from the empress would be most appreciated.[63]

Pergen's appointment came through in the New Year's Honors List of 1761,[64] but the wedding itself was several times postponed and did not take place until August 1762.[65] Maria Theresa's wedding present, because the war was still in progress and money was as short as ever, did not consist of a cash grant, as Pergen had hoped, but rather took the form of a pearl brooch for his bride.[66]

So far as his duties went, these had by now settled into a predictable routine. Pergen regularly reported on the movement of the French armies stationed in Germany, information that was ardently desired by Vienna as the French, for the most part, never troubled to inform their allies of their intentions.[67] He continued to represent the monarchy's interests in various episcopal elections in Germany, such as that of the new archbishop-elector of Cologne, when much to Vienna's satisfaction he persuaded the chapter to select a pro-Habsburg candidate.[68] Having succeeded there, he next exerted himself on behalf of another imperial client, Prince Clement of Saxony, as archbishop of Münster.[69] He continued to try his hand at the difficult task of recruiting in Germany for the Habsburg forces, although he had already become disillusioned about the usefulness of dissipating his energies in this manner; and he did not hesitate to inform Vienna that the money spent on recruitment far outstripped the value received.[70]

Nor did Pergen neglect the interests of his own family. Repeatedly he attempted to intercede on behalf of his brother, a Dominican canon who aspired to become the vicar general of his order, although well below the canonical age. Pergen wrote to Koch, asking him to test the wind: if Maria Theresa could be persuaded to put a word in the right place on behalf of the canon, this would be excellent, but Koch should ask her to do so only if he were convinced that the request would not turn the empress against Pergen himself.[71] On personal instructions from Maria Theresa, Pergen looked into the plight of a Baroness Buccon, who had been recommended to her as a young woman of upright morals and great personal piety, but who unfortunately had recently fallen upon hard times. When he reported back that the lady was indeed worthy of being helped, the empress, in spite of the circumstance that the monarchy was then in the fifth year of an ever more ruinous war, and was being kept financially afloat only by secret French subsidies, instructed Pergen to pay out an annual pension of 400 florins to the Baroness.[72]

In 1762, we discover Pergen newly married, and having moved into a larger house, desperately trying to squirm out of having to put up the young Count Starhemberg. This young gentleman had been sent to him by Maria Theresa herself for the purpose of being schooled in the rudiments of diplomacy. Hence there was no possibility of refusing him his appointment, but providing him with bed and board was another matter. As Pergen plaintively noted, his house was already stuffed like an egg with domestic servants; there was simply no room for anyone else. Still, as he wrote Koch, if Starhemberg were to live somewhere else, he would undoubtedly fall into the clutches of some local seductress, and while he himself did not begrudge him the pleasure, Maria Theresa would be extremely angry if she found out that this had happened. He simply could not extricate himself from this situation without damage to his reputation.[73]

If Pergen's relations with the various German states with which he had to deal had been difficult from the outset of the war, they were now rapidly becoming impossible. The death of Empress Elizabeth of Russia, followed by the accession of Peter III, whose Prussophile tendencies were well known, gave rise to the wildest rumors, some of which at least would prove only too accurate. In particular, the French high command openly declared that, as the war would now undoubtedly have to be ended, there was no point in undertaking further military operations.[74] When the new Russian tsar issued a manifesto in which he characterized himself as the last-minute savior of the German princes, who would have been reduced to mere Austrian lackeys were it not for his decision to come to terms with Prussia, he found many attentive listeners.[75] In these circumstances, Pergen reported, it was really hopeless to expect any further war contributions in Germany.

The Russian defection led both the Austrian and the French governments to the inescapable conclusion that the war could no longer be won, and so early in 1763 peace was concluded. In Europe, the powers agreed on a status quo ante arrangement. This, for Pergen, had catastrophic results, as the conquered territories that he had been administering were now returned to Prussia and Hanover, so that his second income disappeared overnight. Complaining bitterly about this to Koch, he let a rather large cat out of the bag: not only was he facing the loss of a substantial part of his salary, but over and beyond that this would mean a loss of more than 12,000 florins yearly. As his salary as governor of the conquered territories had been only 7,000 florins, this meant that the position had, in one way or another, put an additional 5,000 florins into his pocket every year. The charitable assumption would be that most of this had been derived from various fees for the performance of certain duties that it was customary, if not always legal, to collect.[76] He went on to lament that, faced with this loss of income, there was simply no way for him to keep up a decent standard of living; he would have to go into debt; surely he would be ruined in short order.

Pergen's incessant complaints about his salary must be viewed in the light of the fact that a gentleman could live decently, if in somewhat retired circumstances, on 3,000 florins a year. Even if part of Pergen's very large salary was meant to defray the expenses of office, that he was continuously complaining about so large an income would indicate he was determined to make a large splash in the fashionable world.

For the moment, Pergen's only financial salvation consisted in obtaining as many special commissions as possible. As the election of a new archbishop of Liège would show, such occasions presented opportunities for recouping one's losses well beyond the already generous allowance granted the imperial representatives for their services. As the *Gazette de Liège* now alleged, Pergen, in return for material considerations, had supported not one but two candidates for the vacancy. Normally this would not have had any lasting consequences as those aspiring to high ecclesiastical office were accustomed to being outbid by wealthier rivals; but in this case, the chapter, not wishing to offend the imperial representative, chose the path of discretion and elected both men. Pergen tried with all available means to prevent the publication of this number of the *Gazette,* but without success, and soon complaints about his conduct were being sent both to Rome and to Vienna, complaints that did not hesitate to characterize his conduct as flatly villainous.[77] Fortunately for Pergen the confused threads of this affair apparently were not unraveled by the responsible agency in Vienna, or there might well have been serious consequences for him. What it does reveal is a certain venality in his character that would continue to crop up in the future on occasions when he thought he was unobserved.

But even squeezing the last kreuzer out of every commission, by means both fair and foul, would not have kept Pergen financially afloat had not a unique opportunity for making a large profit just then presented itself to him. Once the war was over, Maria Theresa decided that her idea of having Joseph elected as king of the Romans, which some years before, on Pergen's advice, had been dropped as premature, should now be revived. Pergen was informed that henceforth this matter would constitute his major responsibility. Although the empress wrote that she had not yet decided what official new appointment to bestow upon him in conjunction with this project, Pergen should be secure in the belief that he would not be forgotten.[78]

As it soon turned out, he himself had in mind to be named special imperial ambassador, a dignity that by tradition was coupled with a very high emolument. Pergen realized that his expenses for representation and entertainment in such a capacity would be considerable, but with a little management, he was confident that a substantial portion of this salary could be put aside. Unfortunately, there were others who aspired to the position. At one time, the princes Liechtenstein and von Thurn und Taxis had expressed an interest, and when for one reason or another both of them withdrew, Prince Esterhàzy announced his candidacy. The claims of so distinguished a magnate could not very well be ignored, and so Pergen, who would as matter of course be saddled with all the work, had to be content with being named second ambassador at a much reduced salary.[79]

Even now in peacetime, Pergen's task turned out to be anything but an easy one. Although Frederick II, as part of the peace settlement, had promised not to oppose Joseph's election so that there was no real chance of another candidate's receiving effective support, the ecclesiastical electors would have to be brought around, and this, as usual, turned out to be a question of bribes and favors. At one point the vote of the elector of Mainz was all but lost when he took umbrage because it had been decided that the election would not, as originally planned, take place in his city, but in Frankfurt. It was only when he was assured that a sum equal to that being put aside for the ceremonies in Frankfurt would be accorded to him, that he pledged his vote.[80]

Once Pergen felt that he had managed to assure the success of the project, he began to campaign in earnest for every advantage he thought might be extracted for his own person. As second ambassador, he wrote, he would of course be expected to bring his wife to Frankfurt. The difficulty there was that she owned very little in the way of diamonds. To make a decent impression at the galas and festivities they would be attending, she would need, as a bare minimum, a brooch, a necklace, and a plume. Could Maria Theresa lend her the appropriate pieces for the occasion?[81] The empress—would it be too cynical to speculate that Pergen had had precisely this in mind all along?—did better than that. She presented the pieces to the countess as a gift.[82]

However, Pergen's main concern, the size of his honorarium for

B - devotes lengthy space to Pergen imperial diplomat. This is good

DEAD END IN THE *REICH*   51

serving as second ambassador, proved to be more troublesome. He had not blushed to ask for 20,000 florins, the sum which Esterhàzy had been allotted. He was now informed that, in the natural course of things, differences were made between a first ambassador and a second. Esterhàzy, who was a very rich man, would undoubtedly pay for the greater part of the entertainment that would be a part of their joint mission out of his own pocket; and there was thus no justification for such a large sum to be paid to him. It was decided that as an extraordinary favor Pergen would be granted 8,000 florins, but only on condition that he tell no one of this. Finally, the court informed him that it would be a good idea for him to outline his needs to Kaunitz, who would, if his argument was convincing enough, presumably come up with a contribution of his own.[83] While this was far from everything Pergen might have hoped for, it was nevertheless enough to tide him over rather nicely for at least a year.[84] Nor was the extra salary all that the court proposed to do for Pergen. Maria Theresa now bestowed upon him the Commander's Cross of the Order of St. Stephen, a decoration ranked just below the coveted Golden Fleece and which normally went only to members of the imperial family and to a few of the most important ministers.[85]

By this time Pergen's stock had risen sufficiently so that he was often in the position to negotiate special favors for those who applied to him, and so to build up a clientele of his own. Thus when he recommended a young acquaintance of his, serving as second lieutenant in an imperial regiment, for a captaincy, Maria Theresa addressed herself to the case. She objected that the moment was hardly opportune, since the general demobilization at the end of the war had created some eight hundred unemployed officers for whom she now would have to provide, but, she said, since it was Pergen who asked, she would consent to promote his friend to first lieutenant.[86]

A further mark of high favor was shown Pergen when he informed the court that his wife was pregnant with their first child. Maria Theresa at once replied that she had prevailed upon her husband, the emperor Francis Stephen, to act as godfather to the infant. If it were to turn out to be a boy, it should be named Francis Joseph, if a girl, Maria Anna Josefa.[87] Although the empress did not say so, it was of course understood that the emperor would in the normal course of events bestow more than one rich gift upon his godchild.

In spite of the marks of high favor, Pergen was becoming increasingly discouraged with his post. As he now regularly complained in his reports to Vienna, the difficulties facing him had, if anything, increased with the end of the war. To prevent actual harm being done to the imperial interest was the best he could accomplish. Doing any real good was out of the question. The minor successes he did achieve were, he reported, due solely to the personal attachments he had been able to form to several ruling princes. But such successes were rare.

He was frequently on the road, forced to negotiate every trifling issue with each of the governments to which he was accredited, so that more often than not, by the time he had reached the end of his rounds, those to whom he had spoken first had once more changed their minds. He had to do all his negotiating face to face, not daring to commit any really important points to paper. This was not so much because he feared that his letters would be opened, although this did happen from time to time, but rather because the instructions he received from Vienna were more often than not so vague that he lived in constant fear of committing himself irrevocably to a position that, it would later turn out, did not accord with official policy. Moreover, he had no way of finding out what, in the broader sense, this was, since Vienna never bothered to inform him about what was taking place in other parts of the world. He added that he would not presume to complain so much were it not for the fact that he knew Kaunitz to be a man who valued frankness in his subordinates above all.[88]

As none of these complaints referred to conditions that had undergone any substantial change since Pergen had first assumed his post, and since he had been aware of the inherent difficulties of his job for a good many years, it is fair to surmise that he was now in fact mounting a campaign for another and better position. As soon as he heard that the entire court would travel to Innsbruck to be present at Archduke Leopold's wedding, Pergen let it be known that he, too, wished to attend.

There can be little doubt that he intended to argue his case directly before Their Majesties. He was, however, told that in order to do so he would first have to get permission from Kaunitz.[89] As the prince was notoriously reluctant to allow his diplomats the privilege of reporting to anyone but himself, Pergen thought it prudent to write again. He begged Pichler, who had replaced Koch as Maria Theresa's chief secretary, to point out to Their Majesties that the situation in Germany could not be weaker so far as Habsburg interests were concerned, and that it was absolutely necessary for him to report on it directly to them; whereupon he was granted permission to come to Innsbruck.[90]

While it is by no means clear that Pergen's audience with Maria Theresa and Francis Stephen resulted in the improvement of the monarchy's position in the *Reich,* there can be no doubt that he succeeded in bringing about a substantial improvement in his own. Maria Theresa promised to nominate him and his brother-in-law Großschlag for the Grand Cordon of the Order of St. Stephen, a distinction that was accompanied by a substantial yearly emolument; and she listened sympathetically to his recital of his financial woes. He told her flatly that he could no longer live on his salary (by now 15,000 florins annually); this had been possible only so long as he had earned a second salary as governor of the conquered territories. During the past year he had been forced to use the entire sum that he had been granted— theoretically to repay him for his representational duties at Joseph's election and coronation—to meet his expenses. The last nail in his coffin was the exchange rate. Every time he changed the Austrian currency into German money, he lost at least 10 percent.

Although Pergen had revealed a fairly serious impropriety by admitting that he had diverted the sums allowed him for his entertainment to other purposes, Maria Theresa received his expositions in a benevolent mood. The expedition to Innsbruck had turned into a delightful vacation for the whole court; the emperor's attentions to her, which had lately been flagging, were considerably restored, and she was feeling expansive. She promised Pergen a salary increase of 4,000 florins.

Almost immediately after this audience, the emperor died of an apoplectic stroke while leaving a theater performance in Innsbruck. Maria Theresa, who had never hesitated to criticize and even to rebuke him while he lived, now responded to his death with an unprecedented display of bereavement. She went into what appeared to be a protracted state of shock, all but withdrew from the conduct of affairs, and spoke openly of wishing to abdicate. These circumstances, however, in no fashion prevented Pergen from writing Pichler that while this might not be the ideal moment for bringing up the point, he wished him to remind the empress of the commitment she had made to him.[91]

By January 1766, Pergen had convinced Maria Theresa and Kaunitz that his usefulness in Germany was over. It was decided that he should be recalled to Vienna to assist in the formulation of new policies for the *Reich*.[92] During the period following Francis Stephen's death, Joseph's influence had been considerable, as Maria Theresa was for long stretches incommunicada, and various ministers reported to him. This state of affairs had not lasted long, because the empress, as soon as she recovered from the first shock, quickly took the reins back in her hands. But in the meantime, Joseph had gotten a taste of power and, rather than resign himself to a renewed political impotence, was now looking for specific projects where he could exert his influence.

As Maria Theresa guarded her prerogatives most jealously in the realm of *internalia*, Joseph's best chances to carve out a sphere of influence for himself were clearly in foreign affairs. He now proposed that Pergen assist him in working out what would become a pet project of his, to be returned to on several occasions: to acquire all or at least part of Bavaria.[93] Pergen was not the man to miss perceiving what the benefits to him of such a special relationship with the emperor would be. As he saw it, his diplomatic career was at a dead end. He had failed to win the confidence of Vice-Chancellor Colloredo, with whom he had had continual differences over policy matters, and who, for that reason, had tended to bypass him whenever possible. Pergen's family relationship with Baron Großschlag, who in the meantime had become chief minister to the elector of Mainz, had turned out to be a hindrance rather than an advantage, because everyone in Germany now automatically assumed that Pergen and Großschlag would always be of the same mind, and therefore made a common front against them.

By now Pergen was past forty, and if ever there were to be a leap forward in his career, now would be the time. In spite of these considerations, Pergen, having been in much closer touch with German reality than Joseph, who then as later formulated his ideas for pursuing foreign policy exclusively on theoretical grounds, was appalled at what Joseph proposed. He had excellent reason to know that the emperor's conceit would raise a storm of protest throughout the *Reich*. Thus he found himself facing a major dilemma: how to dissuade Joseph from pursuing a plan that he knew was bound to fail, and that would inevitably reflect discredit on those who had been instrumental in working it out, first of all on himself; and yet how to avoid giving the impression that he was anything but totally enthusiastic about the prospect of serving Joseph in a special capacity. Under the circumstances, he did the best he could, arguing that it would be a great pity if Joseph were to begin his reign as emperor by giving his German subjects the impression (mistaken, of course) that he intended to alter the basic constitution of the *Reich*. He ended by assuring Joseph that whatever special knowledge he had gained in his long stint in Germany would be laid at His Majesty's feet, for whatever use he cared to make of it.[94]

As Kaunitz had independently poured cold water on Joseph's ardor for Bavarian acquisitions, Pergen's lack of enthusiasm for the project does not seem to have harmed him in the emperor's eyes, or it may also be that Pergen's objections had been couched in such opaque language that they escaped Joseph's attention altogether. At any rate, by March 1766, Joseph and Kaunitz were agreed that Pergen should return to Vienna for a higher appointment, without necessarily having settled what this would be. Pichler informed Pergen that Joseph, who regularly attended the meetings of the *Staatsrat*, leaned toward placing him in that body to be assured of having someone at his side there whose career he had personally furthered, and upon whom he could thus count for support. But as Pichler thought it necessary to warn Pergen, money was short and he was not to expect a salary anything like what he was drawing in his present post. Nor would he need nearly as much money, as he would not be expected to do much in the way of official entertaining. This warning, viewed with great alarm by Pergen, who was always extremely sensitive when it came to the question of his salary, was to some extent mitigated by the communication that Maria Theresa had graciously agreed that Joseph should be godfather to Pergen's second child, which would mean a substantial gift of money.[95]

The reason for Pergen's elevation to the *Staatsrat* from what had been, after all, a series of relatively minor posts, is no great mystery. Joseph II, ever since his father's death, had taken a very lively interest in the affairs of the *Reich*. Here, at least, was an area in which he was not likely to encounter any direct interference from Maria Theresa with his policies and decisions. Soon after his accession, Joseph drew up a list of twenty-three questions pertaining to imperial affairs, which he submitted to Kaunitz, Colloredo, and Pergen. The latter's answer, as it happens, came closest to corresponding to Joseph's own notions that, without striving to achieve any fundamental changes in the constitution of the *Reich,* he owed it to his dignity as emperor to restore, at the very least, the situation that had obtained before 1740. Then the Bavarian Charles VII had bartered away the greater part of the remaining imperial powers in exchange for the support of various powerful princes and corporations.[96]

While the other two ministers had urged great restraint from Joseph, emphasizing the difficulties involved in accomplishing even the least of projects within the *Reich,* Pergen's recommendation, while not precisely sanguine, had at least encouraged Joseph in the belief that the old position might yet be restored. Thus, Pergen had managed to focus Joseph's attention on himself at a moment in which the emperor was determined to make a sally in imperial affairs. Hence Pergen's promotion, which doubtless also owed something to the circumstance that Kaunitz was anything but loath to install one of his protégés—on whose support he would presumably be able to rely—in the *Staatsrat.*

Given Pichler's repeated warnings that Pergen should not expect to receive anything near his diplomatic salary in his new post, it is hardly surprising that the latter now bombarded Vienna with a veritable volley of appeals. He protested that even on his present larger salary, he had been obliged repeatedly to spend his own money; how could he possibly survive on less? All this got him nowhere, as the inevitable rejoinder was that he could not expect a similar rank and seniority; this would create jealousies, which would inevitably be detrimental to the service. Pergen, however, had learned long ago that the way to get what one wanted out of Vienna was to repeat and intensify one's demands.

This stratagem stood him in good stead once more. When his appointment was finally confirmed in May, he was informed that the empress had graciously decided to award him an annual pension of 6,000 florins, in addition to his salary.[97]

Most men in Pergen's position would have declared themselves satisfied at that point, but this news merely served to spur him on to greater efforts. Accepting his appointment in the most obsequious terms, he now begged Pichler to inform Her Imperial Majesty that it would be necessary to make an exception for him in the matter of salary, otherwise he would inevitably be bankrupt within the year.[98] Upon hearing this, Joseph, who perhaps was unaware that his mother had already granted Pergen the aforementioned pension, and having made up his mind that Pergen should be returned to Vienna as quickly as possible, allotted him, as special sign of his favor, an additional 10,000 florins a year for life.

Now, at last, Pergen had what he wanted: a combined pension large enough to support himself in style, so that whatever salary he received could be spent for the more expensive appurtenances of noble life: land and houses. He tried to justify his painfully obvious greed by maintaining that he would be no better off than before; in 1761, after all, he had drawn a salary of 15,000 florins, with an added 12,000 florins that had come to him as governor of the conquered territories.[99] There was, however, no disguising the fact that he had succeeded in scoring a major financial coup; it would have been difficult, if not impossible, to name another member of the middle nobility who had been treated with equal generosity by the court.[100]

As if all this would not have sufficed, Pergen now also put through a request for free quarters in the Hofburg. He was told, however, that nothing was available at the moment; the best that could be done would be to put him on a waiting list. In the meantime, Pichler informed him, a small house that had belonged to the late Baron Dorn was for rent. If he did not mind being somewhat cramped, he might consider this for his temporary residence, until something more suitable could be found.[101] Pergen's answer to this offer, which he made after his financial situation had been settled, was that the Dorn house, which, as he had heard, was up for sale for a mere 18,000 florins, and which struck him as being a good investment, would indeed suit him if Joseph would be so good as at least to assign him apartments in the Hofburg where his servants could be housed. Also, he reminded Pichler that it was customary for the court to grant an allowance to a minister returning from a foreign assignment, for the purpose of moving his effects. As he had accumulated a rather considerable amount of furniture, porcelain, glassware, books, and the like, he could only put his trust in His Majesty's generosity.[102]

When every conceivable advantage had been accorded to Pergen, and every special privilege applied for, it only remained for him actually to move to Vienna. This was by no means as straightforward a proposition as one might suppose, because in Maria Theresa's Austria the customs and censorship regulations were extremely strict, and, as Pergen was now to find out, they were strictly applied without any exceptions for even the most prominent persons. As soon as he learned of his posting to Vienna, Pergen inquired whether there would be any problems about bringing his household possessions back into the country. He was told that there would probably be no great difficulties in this, so long as the articles concerned were not new.[103] But what about his wines, and his books? He had put down a goodly number of barrels of German wine, which in Germany would be resellable only at a great loss, and his library, too, was vast.

The wines proved to be the lesser problem. He was informed that upon submission of a complete list of what he proposed to import, along with a written guarantee that they were for his use only, customs would be instructed to let them through. As for the books, however, while a returning minister was not customarily subjected to the same stringent censorship applied to the general public, nevertheless, he would be forbidden to bring into the country any work hostile either to religion or to morals. Pichler informed him that Maria Theresa was inflexible on this point, and so it would be best if Pergen were to submit a complete catalog of his library before packing it into crates. This he now declared himself utterly unable to do: there were many thousands of volumes, and he just did not have the time. He would, however, be happy to assure the empress that he owned not a single book that could be said to fall into either of these categories; practically all of his books dealt either with political theory or with literature. Of course the former, particularly, did of necessity include works by Protestants. Pichler hastened to inform him that it would be hopeless to try to import these, and Pergen saw himself, in spite of his previous protestations, forced to draw up a catalog and to dispose of such titles as might meet with the empress's disapproval.[104]

Before leaving Mainz for good, Pergen summed up his thirteen years' mission in the empire in a letter to an old and trusted friend. In contrast to the opinions he had expressed in his answer to Joseph's questionnaire, the verdict that he arrived at was deeply negative. He was seized with fear and trembling, he wrote, whenever he considered the future of the *Reich*.

In spite of his best efforts, and those of his ministerial colleagues, the political situation in Germany was, if anything, less satisfactory from the Austrian point of view than it had been when he first was appointed to his ministerial post there. Vienna could count on no reliable friends. Even the three ecclesiastical electors, all men carefully handpicked for their positions by Austria, were unreliable. They were so consistently at one another's throats that it was hopeless to expect all of them to support a single line of policy. As for the secular princes, their respective political principles bore about the same relationship to one another as did those of the elector of Mainz to the emperor of China. In Franconia and Baden, prominent people did not hesitate to talk openly of sedition, and he had absolutely no doubts that one soon would be facing armed revolt in those provinces.[105]

While of course Pergen gave no inkling of this pessimistic appraisal in his official dispatches, a course of action that would have inevitably raised the question of whether the manner in which he had performed his duties had led to this deplorable situation, it was clear that he left Germany with a sense of discouragement and of failure. He may have, in his most private thoughts, in part at least blamed himself. What is certain is that he felt that he had been insufficiently supported at court. He was determined that, in his new responsibilities, all this would have to change.

NOTES

1. Pergen to the duke of Pfalz-Zweibrücken, 14 April 1757, S.A., M.K. 68.
2. Cobenzl to Pergen, 18 February 1756, S.A., M.K. 53.
3. October 7, 1756, S.A., G.C. 412.
4. Mayor and council of Frankfurt to Colloredo, 18 October 1756; Colloredo to Pergen, 17 October 1756, S.A., G.C. 412.
5. Pergen to Stadion, 1 July 1757, S.A., M.K. 71.
6. Pergen to Cobenzl, 21 October 1756, S.A., M.K. 52.
7. Colloredo to Pergen, 20 January 1757, S.A., G.C. 413.
8. Colloredo to Pergen, 8 March 1757, S.A., G.C. 413.
9. Pergen to Colloredo, 20 February 1757, S.A., G.C. 414. Baron Großschlag—who would become the leading political figure in Mainz under Ostein's successor, Emmerich Joseph von Breidenbach—congratulated Pergen on the success of his mission and on his generous reward, adding that this would doubtless someday make a nice addition to his future bride's dowry. Großschlag to Pergen, 24 January 1757, S.A., M.K. 63. Since Pergen would marry Großschlag's sister five years later, it is tempting to speculate that such a marriage was already under discussion, although Pergen answered with the remark that, despite his varied exploits, to date he had not found a girl willing to marry him. Pergen to

Großschlag, 25 January 1757, S.A., M.K. 63. Shortly afterward he told Lobkowitz that his courting of Countess Hatzfeld was progressing no better than had Lobkowitz's dalliance in Darmstadt, but he may, in this case, have had something besides marriage in mind. Pergen to Lobkowitz, 13 February 1757, S.A., M.K. 66.

10. Pergen to Zuckmantel, 16 January 1757, S.A., M.K. 75. Pergen wrote that "the whole of human ingenuity had not come up with a torment terrible enough to serve as punishment for so sacrilegious a deed," which would seem to suggest that similar pronouncements of his as minister of police in later years were by no means only attempts to ingratiate himself with the various rulers he served in that capacity.

11. Waldeck to Pergen, 14 June 1757, S.A., M.K. 73.

12. Waldeck to Pergen, 7 July 1757, S.A., M.K. 73.

13. Pergen to Waldeck, 14 July 1757, S.A., M.K. 73.

14. Pergen to the landgrave of Hesse-Darmstadt, 26 June 1757, S.A., M.K. 61. Pergen to Koch, 2 July 1757, S.A., M.K. 66. It availed Pergen nothing to object that the actions of the Frankfurt City Council were *"contre l'ordre, contre les loix, et contre la bienséance. . . . "*

15. Pergen to Stadion, 24 June 1757, S.A., M.K. 71.

16. Pergen to the duke of Broglie, 10 May 1758, S.A., M.K. 79.

17. 16 May 1757, S.A., G.C. 415.

18. Pergen to Georg Starhemberg, 11 and 20 June 1757, S.A., M.K. 72. Pergen ventured, privately, to express a criticism of Kaunitz for having insisted on placing a spy in the French headquarters, and put the blame for Ongania's discomfiture on the man's own monumental incompetence: no self-respecting spy should ever allow himself to be captured with compromising documents on his person.

19. Pergen to Zuckmantel, 20 December 1756, S.A., M.K. 59. The one major exception was the elector of Palatine.

20. Pergen to Cobenzl, 10 March and 4 June 1757, S.A., M.K. 61.

21. Pergen to Cobenzl, 17 June 1757, S.A., M.K. 61. Pergen considered that his success in persuading the government of the Upper Rhenish Circle to commit auxiliary troops to the imperial cause had constituted the turning point, since the Swabians chose to follow this example. Pergen to Zuckmantel, 20 June 1757, S.A., M.K. 75.

22. Pergen to Zuckmantel, 1 July 1757, S.A., M.K. 75. This constituted a serious setback, as the Frankfurt contingent would have made up fully a third of the auxilliary army.

23. Pergen to Cobenzl, 24 June and 19 July 1757, S.A., M.K. 61. The Hessian landgrave was in fact completely isolated in Darmstadt. His own son had fled to join the Prussian army, and he was proposing to disinherit the boy, going so far as to ask that Pergen persuade Maria Theresa to strip the ingrate of his imperial fief of Botenhausen and to bestow it upon him. Pergen thought this would be an exemplary step and hastened to recommend it. Pergen to Koch, 2 July 1757, S.A., M.K. 66.

24. Pergen to Cobenzl, 20 November 1757, S.A., M.K. 61. This admission apart, Pergen deprecated the importance of Frederick's victory: the honor of the Austrian army was now at stake, surely it would react with great vigor. Moreover, it was inconceivable that the French would be content to end so promising a campaign with an ignominious retreat. He was of course merely whistling in the dark. Pergen to the landgrave of Hesse-Darmstadt, 16 November 1757, S.A., M.K. 62.

25. Pergen to Cobenzl, 9 and 16 May 1757, S.A., M.K. 61. As Pergen saw matters, his new duties would not remove him from his post for more than two weeks at a time, three or four times a year. Pergen to the landgrave of Hesse-Darmstadt, 12 May 1757, S.A., M.K. 62; cf. also Pergen to Nagel, 11 July 1757, S.A., M.K. 67. The conquered territories consisted of East Frisia, Emden, Minden, Ravensburg, and Clèves.

26. Pergen to Koch, 13 August 1757, S.A., M.K. 66.

27. Pergen to Nagel, 6 July 1757, S.A., M.K. 67.

28. Maale to Pergen, 8 August 1757, S.A., M.K. 67; Pergen to Nagel, 22 September 1757, S.A., M.K. 67.

29. Wetzlar to Pergen, 10 and 18 June 1757; Pergen to Wetzlar, 16 November 1757, S.A., M.K. 68. *"Den guten Freund ersuche viel schönes von mir zu melden...."*

30. Pergen to de Pottere, 22 September and 13 November 1757, S.A., M.K. 62.

31. Pergen to General Piza, 5 November and 26 December 1757, S.A., M.K. 68. Pergen did not content himself with placing the blame for the financial distress of the territories on the French, which would have absolved him of the responsibility. In fact, he went directly to the French commander in chief, the duc de Richelieu, to argue his case. Pergen to duc de Richelieu, 17 August 1757, S.A., M.K. 69.

32. Pergen to Seckendorf, 12 July 1757, S.A., M.K. 69.

33. Pergen's report of January 1758 in S.A., M.K. 81.

34. Pergen to Reichasch, 22 June 1757, S.A., M.K. 69.

35. Vogel to Pergen, 8 June 1757, S.A., M.K. 67.

36. Pergen to Weger, 22 August 1757, S.A., M.K. 64.

37. Pergen to Prince von Thurn und Taxis, 27 October 1757, S.A., M.K. 72. *"Also war meine gehorsamste Meynung, da Eure Excellenz diesen Anstands selber sich ohnmittelbar an den Herrn Hof- und Staatskanzler Grafen von Kaunitz zu wenden geruhen wollen."*

38. Pergen to Heger, 4 December 1767, S.A., M.K. 64.

39. Van den Velden to Pergen, 10 October 1757; Pergen to Van den Velden, 23 July and 22 October 1757, S.A., M.K. 72. It is entirely possible that this Count Bergen was a relative of Pergen's, whose family spelled its name in this manner before coming to Vienna.

40. Pergen and Cobenzl had had a falling out over another matter as well. Cobenzl had sent a young man to Mainz armed with a letter asking Pergen to find him a place on his staff. But since the fellow had no experience of any sort, Pergen told him that he was running a diplomatic mission, not a training

school for raw beginners, and sent him packing. This had greatly offended Cobenzl, who felt, not without reason, that Pergen owed him more than one such favor. Pergen to Nagel, 19 June 1757, S.A., M.K. 67. Although the two men were eventually to be reconciled, their breach was never entirely healed. Thus when Cobenzl's wife gave birth to a boy, Pergen learned this only from reading the gazettes. Pergen to Cobenzl, 5 November 1758, S.A., M.K. 79.

41. Pergen to Koch, 24 March 1757, S.A., M.K. 66.

42. Pergen to Koch, 5 November 1757, S.A., M.K. 66.

43. Pergen to Koch, 13 December 1757, S.A., M.K. 66. This proved to be more difficult than anticipated. Almost a month later the countess again wrote Pergen, complaining that nothing whatever had been done for her. Countess Linange to Pergen, 8 January 1758, S.A., M.K. 84.

44. Koch to Pergen, 28 January 1758; Pergen to Koch, 21 February 1758, S.A., M.K. 83; bittermann to Pergen, 25 February 1758, S.A., M.K. 87. As Pergen had been strongly urged by Colloredo to stay out of the whole business, he must have been in a quandary about how best to compose an acceptable reply. In the end it would seem that he opted for discretion and sent none.

45. Van Swieten to Pergen, 6 September 1757; Pergen to van Swieten, 22 September 1757, S.A., M.K. 72.

46. Pergen to the landgrave of Hesse-Darmstadt, 6 January 1758, S.A., M.K. 80.

47. Pergen to the landgrave of Hesse-Darmstadt, 21 January 1758, S.A., M.K. 80.

48. Pergen to Dupuy, 11 January 1758, S.A., M.K. 81.

49. Pergen to Cobenzl, 19 February 1758, S.A., M.K. 79.

50. Pergen to de Lorges, 5 July 1758, S.A., M.K. 84.

51. Pergen to Foulon, 30 November 1758, S.A., M.K. 80.

52. B. Strauss, *La culture française à Francfort au xviiième siècle* (Paris, 1964), 49–70.

53. Pergen to Koch, 16 September 1758, S.A., M.K. 83.

54. Pichler to Pergen, 23 September 1758, S.A., M.K. 87.

55. Pergen to Prince de Soubise, 3 July 1758, M.K. 89.

56. Strock to Pergen, 4 June 1758, S.A., M.K. 89.

57. Pergen to Strock, 10 June 1758, S.A., M.K. 89.

58. Strock to Pergen, 12 July 1758, S.A., M.K. 89.

59. Gerhard van Swieten to Pergen, 22 June 1758, S.A., M.K. 90.

60. Molitor to Pergen, 1 December 1758, S.A., M.K. 85.

61. Pergen to Koch, 23 February 1761, S.A., G.C. 242.

62. S.A., M.K. 90.

63. Koch to Pergen, 10 July 1760, S.A. G.C. 242.

64. Koch to Pergen, 6 January 1761, S.A., G.C. 242.

65. Koch to Pergen, 11 August 1762, S.A., G.C. 242.

66. Koch to Pergen, 17 November 1762; Pergen to Koch, 5 November 1762, S.A., G.C. 242.

67. Pergen to Koch, 30 March 1761, S.A., G.C. 242.

68. Koch to Pergen, 9 May 1761, S.A., G.C. 242.

69. Koch to Pergen, 15 May 1761, S.A., G.C. 242.

70. Pergen to Koch, 20 May 1761, S.A., G.C. 242.

71. Pergen to Koch, 30 March and 9 May 1761, S.A., G.C. 242.

72. Koch to Pergen, 9 and 15 May 1761, S.A., G.C. 242; see also P.P. Bernard, "Kaunitz and the Cost of Diplomacy," *East European Quarterly* XVII, no. 1 (March, 1983), 1–14, for a full discussion of Maria Theresa's financial competence.

73. Koch to Pergen, 26 January 1762; Pergen to Koch, 20 April 1762, S.A., G.C. 242.

74. Pergen to Koch, 15 March 1762, S.A., G.C. 242.

75. Pergen to Koch, 6 May 1762, S.A., G.C. 242.

76. Pergen to Koch, 25 February 1763, S.A., G.C. 242. Actually, the treasury turned over 2,000 florins monthly to Pergen, but part of this went for the salaries of various assistants in the territories. Maria Theresa gave instructions to stop these payments on 3 January 1763. Cf. Posch to Colloredo, 3 January 1763, S.A., Staats Kanzlei: Interiora, Personalia 9.

77. Pergen to Pichler, 22 April 1763, S.A., G.C. 242.

78. Pichler to Pergen, 30 March 1763, S.A., G.C. 242.

79. Pichler to Pergen, 6 May and 17 August 1763, S.A., G.C. 242.

80. Pichler to Pergen, 27 October 1763, S.A., G.C. 242. Pergen worried that the Prussians would go back on their word, but Pichler was able to reassure him on this point: Frederick had let it be known that he would cast his vote as elector of Brandenburg for Joseph. Pichler to Pergen, 13 January 1764, S.A., G.C. 242.

81. Pergen to Pichler, 15 December 1763, S.A., G.C. 242.

82. Pergen to Pichler, 6 January 1764, S.A., G.C. 242.

83. Pichler to Pergen, 24 January 1764, S.A., G.C. 242.

84. In the event, Pergen received not 8,000 but 11,000 florins, and a purse of 1,000 gold ducats as a personal gift from Joseph. Pergen to Pichler, 8 October 1765, S.A., G.C. 242.

85. A. von Helfert, *Das System der österreichischen Volksschule* (Prague, 1861), 191.

86. Pichler to Pergen, 7 November 1763, S.A., G.C. 242.

87. Pichler to Pergen, 13 December 1764, S.A., G.C. 242. A girl was born to the Pergens in January 1765.

88. Pergen to Pichler, 4 January 1765, S.A., G.C. 242.

89. Pichler to Pergen, 15 May 1765, S.A., G.C. 242.

90. Pergen to Pichler, 29 January 1765, S.A., G.C. 242.

91. Pergen to Pichler, 6 August and 8 October 1765, S.A., G.C. 242. Pergen's importunings did not speed matters up substantially and his raise went through only at the start of the next year. At that point, however, it was made retroactive to 1 August 1765. Pichler to Pergen, 13 February 1766, S.A., G.C. 242.

92. Pichler to Pergen, 7 January 1766, S.A., G.C. 242.

93. P. P. Bernard, *Joseph II and Bavaria* (The Hague, 1965), 5–11.

94. Pergen to Pichler, 4 February 1765, S.A., G.C. 242.

95. Pichler to Pergen, 4 March 1766, S.A., G.C. 242.

96. H. Voltelini, "Eine Denkschrift des Grafen Johann Anton Pergen über die Bedeutung der römischen Kaiserkrone für das Haus Österreich," *Gesamtdeutsche Vergangenheit* (Munich, 1938), 153–68. Voltelini was able to demonstrate that this document, previously attributed to Kaunitz, came from Pergen's hand.

97. Pichler to Pergen, 8 April, 9, 20 May 1766, S.A., G.C. 242.

98. Pergen to Pichler and Pichler to Pergen, 10 May 1766, S.A., G.C. 242.

99. Pergen to Pichler, 28 May 1766, S.A., G.C. 242.

100. A few years before, when Kaunitz was made state chancellor, his salary had been fixed at 30,000 florins. Haugwitz, as president of the *Directorium in publicis et cameralibus,* received 24,000 florins. Harrach, in his capacity of president of the *Hofkriegsrat,* was paid 12,000 florins. H. Ehalt, *Ausdrucksformen absolutistischer Herrschaft* (Munich, 1980), 61–62. To be sure, Kaunitz's income, counting all his benefits and pensions, was probably nearer 80,000 florins. Still, for Pergen to receive so large a salary in a relatively obscure position is an indication that he was being extraordinarily well treated, probably as a result of Kaunitz's patronage.

101. Pichler to Pergen, 6 June 1766, S.A., G.C. 242.

102. Pergen to Pichler, 28 May 1766, S.A., G.C. 242.

103. Pichler to Pergen, 6 June 1766, S.A., G.C. 242.

104. Pichler to Pergen, 1, 17, 24 July and 12 August 1766; Pergen to Pichler, 18 June, 10 July, and 21 August 1766, S.A., G.C. 242.

105. Pergen to Spangenberg, 23 June 1766, S.A., G.C. 242.

3

Staatsrat and Educational Reform

THE STAATSRAT, IN whose deliberations Pergen would now take part, was founded in 1760 to effect a more unified control of policy matters after the Haugwitzian system had failed to produce sufficiently positive results during the Seven Years' War. This body concerned itself with the various affairs of the separate ministries and, after due consideration, made recommendations directly to the sovereign. So that no member should be tempted to argue on behalf of the direct interests of his department over that of the others, membership in the *Staatsrat* was not to be combined with any ministry or other leading executive post. The issues would be debated on their merits alone. The single exception to this rule was the state chancellor, Prince Kaunitz, who continued to occupy his various offices while presiding over the *Staatsrat*. In practice this meant that Kaunitz's prestige, power, and influence so overshadowed that of the other members that the council became, in essence, a means for him to extend his influence over the internal as well as the external affairs of the monarchy; and that no one could stay on that body for very long, once he had directly opposed the chancellor's policies.[1] Those who made the attempt, like Haugwitz, who was a member of the *Staatsrat* until his death in 1765, or Count Blümegen, soon found themselves politically isolated.

Kaunitz had played with the notion of bringing several of his protégés, notably Cobenzl, Adam Starhemberg, and Pergen, into the *Staatsrat* from its inception; but had eventually concluded that, for the time being at least, they were more useful to him in their respective diplomatic posts. The situation had, however, changed drastically by 1765. Even before Joseph's elevation to the co-regency in August, Kaunitz had convinced himself that his advice in various questions had been insufficiently followed, and offered his resignation on the ground that his health no longer permitted him to carry out his duties. Maria Theresa, who not only was genuinely convinced that the prince was a supernal genius, but who above all disliked new faces, refused to accept the resignation and assured Kaunitz that she would never dismiss his advice without the most thorough consideration, and that in order to lighten his burden, his favorite pupils, Starhemberg and Pergen, would be brought back to Vienna to work at his side.[2]

After an initial show of reluctance, Kaunitz agreed to stay, but, he insisted, only for the time it would take him to initiate his new assistants, at most for two years. He informed the empress that it was his wish that Pergen be given the title of minister of state (what we would today call a minister without portfolio), and should, along with his membership in the *Staatsrat*, be given the title of vice-chancellor of the *Staatskanzlei*, so that he would be available for any special missions with which Kaunitz might wish to entrust him.[3] Starhemberg would be groomed as Kaunitz's successor. At this point, however, Starhemberg raised some objections. While disclaiming any ambition to succeed Kaunitz, except perhaps in the very remote future, he nevertheless complained that were it to come to that, he would not want to have his freedom of action very considerably reduced by the creation of what he chose to call "an independent satrapy" for Pergen.

As a result, Maria Theresa in the end decided that Pergen was not to receive the titles that Kaunitz had requested for him, but would be employed in whatever capacity the chancellor might find useful.[4] At first Kaunitz seemed willing to make use of Pergen as an all-around troubleshooter.[5] Soon enough, however, it became evident that Pergen needed an institutional base to negotiate as an equal with the other ministers, and in spite of Starhemberg's objections he was given the title of minister of state and made a voting member of the *Staatsrat*.[6] This appointment seemed also to have been the result of Kaunitz's rapidly growing distrust of Starhemberg, whom the chancellor, within a couple of months, came to look upon not only as a rival to his power but also in some degree as a successor appointed during his lifetime and, worst of all, as the mouthpiece of Joseph, who since his father's death in August and his appointment as co-regent, had begun to interfere much more directly in Kaunitz's bailiwick than Maria Theresa had ever done. To some degree, Pergen in his new position was to be a counterbalance to Starhemberg.[7]

Pergen, who did not take long to perceive the direction of the prevailing winds, was not the man to make a stand against Kaunitz, even though he was no longer as dependent on the prince's patronage as he had been while serving in the diplomatic corps. And he soon found that it would be anything but difficult for him to support the chancellor's positions, as these in the main tended to accord with his own. It was normal procedure in the *Staatsrat* to refer questions submitted to it by the court to one of its members within whose approximate area of competence these seemed to fall. The referee would then prepare a detailed report that would be debated by the full membership. This procedure had turned out to be rather more cumbersome than the empress had originally expected, as the referees were very much aware that their reports, no matter how these fared in the discussions, would, before they arrived at their final destination, have to undergo a detailed critique by Kaunitz, who never left an *i* undotted; and, as often as not, also by Joseph, whose analyses were not nearly as thorough as the chancellor's, but who could be scathingly critical when something displeased him.

Thus the *Staatsrat* members tried to cover their flanks in every conceivable manner, and their reports took correspondingly long to prepare. To balance this evident disadvantage, the reports were not only exceedingly thorough, but were frequently based on a profound knowledge of the subject, even if their author had had to acquire this as he went along.

So far as Pergen was concerned, there was no question at all as to which area of expertise would be assigned to him. Even while still posted in Germany, he had been a kind of consultant to the *Staatsrat* in questions dealing with taxation of the clergy. In March 1762, in the sixth year of the war with Prussia, with money running desperately short in Vienna, he had been instructed to search the *Reich* archives for any documents whatsoever supporting the rights of the crown to tax the clergy. Eventually he reported back his discovery that in the years 1404–43 very different norms had prevailed than was now the case. Not only had the clergy been taxed on a regular basis, but frequent extraordinary exactions had been imposed upon it during that period, without it having in the least occurred to anyone at all that papal permission for such a step would have to be sought.[8] When a similar question was put to Pergen some years later, he reported that he had consulted the leading German canonists in Mainz, who were of the opinion that, although the monarch should not levy taxes without first having secured the agreement of the church as a matter of policy, in practice it was evident that since the monarch, in any given case, had a much more precise knowledge of the financial situation of his realm than did the pope, it was therefore all but unthinkable for the Holy See to refuse such a request. Nevertheless, Pergen was of the opinion that even so slight a qualification of royal rights was inadmissible—in cases of dire need, natural law gave the sovereign the right to undertake whatever measures seemed to him necessary for the preservation of the state; and that the church possessed no special immunities whatsoever vis-à-vis this right.[9]

As this opinion fitted in very closely with the views held by Kaunitz on the subject, it was only natural that Pergen, shortly after his appointment to the *Staatsrat*, was put to work examining various proposals for changing church-state relationships to the advantage of the latter. During this period, either because his health was actually impaired, or because he had come to entertain serious doubts about the efficacy of the *Staatsrat* for implementing his views on policy, Kaunitz frequently absented himself from the meetings of that body. More often than not, Starhemberg would be in the chair. It did not take long for Pergen to discover that in the absence of the chancellor, his outspokenly anticlerical pronouncements were not heard with pleasure by most of the other members. In less than a year, he saw himself as hopelessly isolated. When his good friend Count Stadion asked him to use his influence on his behalf, he replied that while he would be happy to make the attempt, Stadion should not be overly optimistic; whatever influence he still retained was minimal.[10]

To add to his discontent, Pergen, in the absence of the chancellor's day-to-day support, soon found himself sidetracked. Instead of concerning himself with questions that genuinely interested him and that were close to his and Kaunitz's hearts, he spent most of his time reporting on matters of administrative detail, which were as tedious as they were far removed from his area of competence. Thus he spent months trying to sort out the confusion resulting from an ill-conceived and badly implemented scheme to resettle a group of Swabian peasants in Hungary, only to learn that the whole affair had been rendered moot by the actions of the imperial representative in Regensburg, who, lacking explicit instructions from Vienna, had refused the would-be settlers any kind of assistance, whereupon the Swabians had been snapped up by a Russian mission looking for settlers in that country.[11]

Occasionally Pergen would be consulted about some question pertaining to Austrian policy toward the *Reich*, but the principal result of these exchanges seems to have been that the emperor became convinced, even more than he had been before, that Germany was, at least for the foreseeable future, totally barren ground for any substantive intervention, and he therefore lost all interest in its affairs.[12] Pergen's closest approach to dealing with the area for which Kaunitz had intended him came when he was asked to adjudicate a dispute about censorship in Milan. The papal nuncio, Cardinal Visconti, had protested against Kaunitz's suppression of a papal letter addressed to the clergy of that province (the Milanese was ruled directly by the *Staatskanzlei*) and Pergen was instructed to prepare a report on the matter for Maria Theresa. But as he was reluctant to grasp this particular nettle—to do so would have forced him, in all probability, to take sides in a dispute between the emperor and the chancellor—he merely referred the whole question back to Kaunitz.[13]

In his years in the *Staatsrat*, Pergen might very well have transferred his allegiance to another powerful patron, given the circumstance that Kaunitz was taking less of an interest in the affairs of that body. He did not do so, possibly because no likely substitute appeared, or perhaps out of loyalty to the chancellor. Instead, he emerged not just as an always-to-be-counted-upon member of the prince's faction at court, but as his virtual factotum. Whenever the chancellor was away at his Bohemian estate near Austerlitz (and these absences came to extend for as much as four months every summer), Pergen would see to it that all documents addressed to the *Staatskanzlei* be sent on to him—if they were of sufficient importance. If not, he himself fashioned abstracts of them for Kaunitz's information. For his part, Kaunitz was delighted to have found a man whose attention to detail and whose capacity for sustained work came close to matching his own. Repeatedly he expressed his complete satisfaction with the manner in which Pergen was running things in his absence, and assured him that the chancery personnel, whom, as Pergen was aware, he regarded almost as his own children, were in good hands.[14] Pergen, in return, lost no opportunity to assure the prince of his zeal and total devotion. On one occasion, he apologized profusely for having missed work for part of one morning: the birth of his daughter and her baptism had prevented him from going to the chancery as early as he would have liked.[15]

By 1769, Pergen had advanced from one of Kaunitz's protégés to the chancellor's intimate friend. Countess Pergen and her children spent a part of the summer at the Kaunitz estate. On that occasion, the prince wrote Pergen that he had no intention of allowing such charming company to leave after a stay of only a few weeks. If necessary, he added, he would detain them by refusing them horses for their coach, even if this were to lead to an affair of honor between him and Pergen; anyway, he was of the opinion that Pergen had grown far too thin: continued forced sexual abstinence would fatten him up for another year of hard work to begin in the autumn.[16]

Pergen was now spending practically all his working hours as Kaunitz's right-hand man at the *Staatskanzlei.* Although he still attended the meetings of the *Staatsrat,* he no longer played any significant role there, and was not given any important issues to referee.[17] This state of affairs soon brought about a renewal of Pergen's dissatisfaction. Reflecting that, although he was doing the work of a vice-chancellor, he enjoyed neither the title nor the emoluments of that office, he told everyone that his career was at a dead end.

Finally, he unburdened himself in a long letter of complaint to Kaunitz. First, he wrote, his income was insufficient to maintain his household in Vienna. (At this time Pergen was drawing a greater sum from the public treasury than any other public servant except Kaunitz himself and a few ambassadors in major posts; but to be fair, it should be pointed out that many of the people with whom he was trying to keep up socially enjoyed vast private incomes.) Second, he lamented that none of the professional hopes he had cherished upon coming to Vienna had been realized. He himself could see no progress in his career, and it was by no means clear to him what the intentions of the sovereigns were toward him. Third, and from his point of view most hurtful, during the whole of his service on the *Staatsrat* he had received not a single mark of esteem from the court.

Therefore, he begged the chancellor to intercede on his behalf, should he consider these complaints to be well founded. He wished to underline that he could no longer pretend to himself that his continued presence on the *Staatsrat* was of any real importance, and although he was delighted to have been of help to Kaunitz at the *Staatskanzlei,* this was not a real job.

Recently, he confided to Kaunitz, he had learned in strictest confidence that the position of chief counsellor to the administrator of the Austrian Netherlands would soon be open. He realized that, looked at from the point of view of someone desiring a more active participation in the affairs of state, such a change of employment would be counterproductive. Politically the Netherlands were a backwater, and he would never make a real impact on policy formation from there. To balance this, however, the post was so handsomely rewarded that, by accepting it, he would be guaranteed a decent income for life. Only by this or a similar stratagem could he escape the necessity of selling off his possessions one by one, or of going hopelessly into debt. During the last year, he had been forced to run up a deficit of several thousand florins, a practice he could not afford to continue for long. He wished to assure Kaunitz that he was not an ingrate, and that he gladly put his trust in the assurance that had been made to him by the chancellor, namely that an appropriate post would eventually be found for him. If the chancellor should decide to go, as he frequently threatened to do, his own position would become hopeless; he had gone out on too many limbs on Kaunitz's behalf. Without the prince's powerful protection, he would be entirely at the mercy of the many enemies he had made in doing so.

After all this, Pergen finally came down to cases. If he were to turn down the offer of the Brussels post should it be made, and he had good reason to think it would, he would have to be given what he had been far too long denied: the Grand Cross of the Order of Maria Theresa, with the considerable emolument that went with it, and the title of vice-chancellor, which was nothing more than his due, as he had for some time actually been performing the duties of the position. If it were true, as he had also heard, that Kaunitz was serious in his intention to retire, and would be succeeded by Starhemberg, he wished to point out that he was prepared to work just as loyally under that gentleman as he had under Kaunitz.[18]

Things turned out differently than Pergen had thought. Kaunitz changed his mind about stepping down, and the continued presence of Starhemberg in Vienna would have constituted a considerable embarrassment for him. Thus it was Starhemberg, rather than Pergen, who was shunted off to Brussels.[19] Pergen, having long since despaired of being given an important assignment in a *Staatsrat* that looked upon him with suspicion as Kaunitz's protégé, almost by accident stumbled upon what he had been looking for. It all began in 1769 when a chance audit revealed that the Oriental Academy—a body created at Kaunitz's suggestion sixteen years earlier to train officials in the skills needed to represent Austria's interests in the Ottoman Empire—was hopelessly in debt, largely because of the financial mismanagement of its director, the Jesuit P. Franz. Although the school was fulfilling its academic functions admirably, Franz had turned out to be so unworldly an administrator that his creditors were now threatening to foreclose, an unheard-of turn of events. When Maria Theresa's attention was drawn to these circumstances, she agreed to settle the academy's debts, but only on condition that henceforth it be placed under the direct supervision of an official of the crown. A successor to the disgraced Franz was found in the person of Johann Nekrey, another distinguished orientalist, over whom Pergen was now installed as titular head.[20]

Pergen, of course, was not the man to preside passively over an enterprise. Only too anxious to demonstrate his zeal, he now proceeded to produce a long and detailed analysis of the course offerings at the academy, and concluded with the observation that apart from the way it had been administered—that of course was beneath all criticism—it was truly exemplary and could well serve as a model for all the instructional institutions in the monarchy.[21] Well it might: the aspiring diplomats were taught Arabic, Turkish, Persian, modern Greek, Italian, and Spanish, as well as receiving instruction in such mundane subjects as history and geography. Thus the academy was of necessity an elite institution, as by no means every young man, no matter how clever and ambitious, could withstand the onslaughts of such a curriculum. Those who survived commanded an enormous fund of knowledge, which far exceeded the relatively narrow purposes for which the academy had been founded. As Pergen saw it, every institution of higher learning in the monarchy should be brought up to this standard. While this was too evidently a counsel of perfection to be taken seriously, the proposal nevertheless had the important subsidiary effect of convincing Maria Theresa that here was a man with a sharp eye for educational questions.

Still, it is scarcely clear that Pergen was ever instructed to submit a plan for the reform of the whole of the Austrian educational establishment. He may very well have decided to do so entirely on his own. At any rate, on 16 August 1770, he submitted such a proposal directly to Maria Theresa with the urgent request that she not discuss it with anyone before submitting it to the *Staatsrat.*[22]

Pergen's submission, which filled a thick folio volume, was marked by the prolixity that had by then become his trademark. In ponderous sentence after ponderous sentence he described the existing school system down to the last detail, giving loving attention not just to its actual shortcomings, which were numerous enough, but to a large number of merely potential ones. With some effort it is possible to extract the following major points from this document: First, and of central importance to Pergen's argument, is the proposition that it would be worse than useless to attempt piecemeal changes. The entire educational apparatus would have to be submitted to systematic reform if it were, over the long run, to achieve its chief purpose, the production of learned but also docile Christian subjects.

Second, Pergen insisted, the state would itself have to supervise and direct the entire educational system in order to accomplish this end. Everything that was to be taught at even the lowest level must be known to the monarch, who must not merely have the theoretical power to revise the curriculum as he saw fit, but would have to exercise that power. A system of regular and frequent visitations would have to be instituted in order to assure the uniformity of teaching throughout the whole of the realm. State-directed teacher-training institutes would be created to ensure that all teachers met the minimum level of competence that the state should expect of them. The abler teachers were to be rewarded with both money and special honors; the disloyal and the incompetent were to be dismissed.

Third, and Pergen did not conceal that, in his eyes, this was the most crucial point in the whole proposal, instruction on all levels would be taken out of the hands of the monastic clergy at once. Hereafter all teachers were to be laymen, or, at worst, and for only so long as absolutely necessary, worldly priests. He saw such a step as inevitable because not only had the monks failed miserably at their task, falling short in every conceivable way of meeting the expectations that a modern society had a right to have of its teachers, but the whole character of the monastic life all but guaranteed that they would never be able to change sufficiently to do so.[23]

It is no great feat of detection to establish that this document's inspiration came almost wholly from the observations Pergen had made during his stint in Germany. In fact it can be traced back directly to some researches into the Prussian school system which he had commissioned while stationed in Mainz, when he was consistently making everyone's business his own. The conclusion that Pergen had come to as a result of studying this report had been that everything about education in the Protestant North was better: the curriculum, the teachers, the entire organization of the school system.[24] That he should have reached such a conclusion is not entirely surprising. The man who had undertaken this study for Pergen, Johan Melchior Birkenstock, had expressed his admiration for everything he had observed during his journey through Prussia in such glowing terms that Pergen was essentially left with no choice but either to endorse its conclusions or to discard the entire report. Since what Birkenstock had to say corresponded in large measure to Pergen's own prejudices in the matter, and since the report in its zealous endorsement of the North German model reinforced his inherent tendency to see things in black and white, Pergen proceeded to make Birkenstock's ideas his own. Inasmuch as, having done so, he persisted in clinging to them long after it should have been clear to the most sanguine of reformers that they had given rise to inflexible opposition in high places, we will do well to take a closer look at the document that inspired so much enthusiasm and loyalty in him.

Birkenstock had launched into his subject with a violent denunciation of what, even to the most pious of men, must be recognized as the ludicrously excessive wealth of the Catholic Church.[25] He quoted from a report recently published in Venice, according to which the church there disposed over an accumulation of over 130 million ducats, a sum equal to the whole of the Habsburg Monarchy's budget over a period of three fiscal years. In the monarchy itself, he added, the yearly income of the church amounted to 30 million ducats, which represented somewhat over two-thirds that of the state. Being able to dispense such vast sums enabled the church to pursue quasi-independent policies that by no means were always in accord with the interests of the state. In addition, the church's own interest clearly demanded that it reveal as little as possible about its affairs to the state, which otherwise would be in a position to interfere. The monastic orders in particular, given their direct subordination to the papacy, should be regarded as unblushing agents of Rome. In this capacity they were busily engaged in stripping the country's wealth, and forever invoking the arguments of religion as a defense against all attempts to gain any insight into the disposition of these gigantic sums. Manifestly, the orders had a vested interest in maintaining in the populace a spirit of superstitious acceptance of their authority, of moronic reverence for their holiness, and of fanatical generosity when it came to giving them money. The very least one might expect from the monks in return for all this was a scrupulous performance of their duties, which included providing a useful education for the people. Since this last, however, would unfailingly lead the beneficiaries to question the principles cited above, it would obviously be counter-productive for the orders to engage in anything of the sort.

In view of all this, the only practical way out of the dilemma, which was more than any other factor responsible for the fatal backwardness of the monarchy, was to staff the schools as soon as possible with right-thinking lay teachers. If the ruler's plans for the reform of the fundamental institutions of his realm were to have any chance of success, popular mentality would have to undergo a basic change, lest these always founder in a sea of passive resistance. It hardly needed elaboration that the church would refuse to preside over a program so injurious to its interests. Critical as the situation was, it was bound to worsen as others (the North German Protestant states, foremost among them Prussia, are clearly meant here), having found the right way, would leave the monarchy further behind with the passing of every year.

A further, and equally fatal, flaw of the prevailing system was that, as things stood, the most intelligent and ambitious products of the schools were systematically recruited by the church, which was in a position to influence them at an impressionable age, so that, excepting of course the aristocracy, only the mediocre and uninspired were left to serve the state. In sum, Birkenstock concluded, the decay was so far advanced that only heroic measures promised any help. Since it would be foolish to pretend that, at any time in the near future, the monarchy's schools could be staffed with qualified native Austrians—such people were simply not available in sufficient numbers—considerable numbers of foreigners would have to be recruited. But such men, hard enough to locate and attract under the most favorable of circumstances, would certainly refuse to come if they had every reason to assume ahead of time that, once in Austria, they would be continually subjected to specious controls and gratuitous humiliations. To create the sort of climate in which genuinely able and enlightened teachers would feel at home, it would first be necessary to liberalize the monarchy's institutions. Censorship would have to be, if not entirely abolished, at the very least significantly relaxed. As it functioned at present, it defended neither genuine morality nor even the real interests of the state, but the narrowest of theological *Vorurteile* (prejudices). Where error was defended with cannons, truth would never flourish.

Even to someone as innocent in questions of theological—as distinct from ecclesiastical—controversy as Pergen apparently was, the last arguments must surely have given the game away. Birkenstock's plea, although eloquent, was drenched in uncompromising Jansenism, there was just no overlooking the fact. And Pergen, who made it his business to know these things, could scarcely have been unaware that such views, while common enough among enlightened thinkers in Vienna, had of late come very close to representing something like anathema to Maria Theresa. Perhaps Pergen entertained some sympathies himself for the opinions of the Dutch bishop, or at least for those of his Austrian disciple, Febronius. We know so little of his religious beliefs that it would be foolhardy to exclude such a possibility on principle. Or it could well be that Pergen was so indifferent to religious zealotry of all descriptions that he was willing to adopt an argument that seemed to suit his purposes, whatever its provenance. At any rate, having decided to appropriate Birkenstock's proposals, he was careful to suppress the inflamatory rhetoric before submitting them as his own.

Even stripped of its Jansenist oratory, so radical a plan for the transformation of perhaps the most fundamental of institutions in the state (not for nothing had Maria Theresa observed that *Das Schulwesen ist und bleibt allzeit ein Politikum*) could hardly expect smooth sailing once it was opened up to the scrutiny of the various interested parties. The wonder of it was that, upon a first reading in the *Staatsrat,* the document on the whole was received with approval, the consensus being that it should be forwarded to the empress with an expression of thanks for the acuity and industry demonstrated by its author. To be sure, almost all the members of that body picked out of Pergen's proposal those elements that most closely corresponded to their own respective prejudices.

Thus Hofrat Gebler, a long-time patron of German as a vehicle of serious literary expression, waxed enthusiastic about Pergen's insistence that German replace Latin as the language of instruction at all levels; Binder, who had for years implemented Kaunitz's efforts to extend the controlling influence of the *Staatskanzlei* to various branches of the internal administration of the realm, could not agree warmly enough with Pergen's argument that education must be the prime concern of the state, and thus subject to its control; while Kaunitz himself in his *Gutachten* praised Pergen's achievement in terms that stopped just short of saying openly that the man had learned everything he knew at his feet.[26]

But when it came to Pergen's central recommendation, to take education entirely out of the hands of the monastic clergy, all the members were agreed that, however desirable such a step might be in theory, in practice it simply could not be carried out. Most of them were of the opinion that a series of small steps would have to be made before larger ones could be attempted. Perhaps a pilot program might be initiated, in which those lay teachers who could be found within the borders of the monarchy could demonstrate their abilities. The most conservative member of the *Staatsrat,* Count Blümegen, stated flatly that at present it was out of the question to dispense with the services of the monks entirely; it was no secret that what constituted a living wage for a lay teacher was at least triple the amount needed to keep a monk, and even if, contrary to the general expectation, enough of the former could be employed, the state would bankrupt itself in so doing.[27] In sum, the *Staatsräte* concluded that, while Pergen's proposals deserved much praise, he should now simplify them so that they might be implemented in practice.

Considering the importance that Maria Theresa attached to the subject of educational reform, one can only marvel at the glacial pace with which Pergen's proposal made its way over the various administrative hurdles that needed to be surmounted before it could be enacted into law. It would seem evident that, in large part, this was the consequence of a certain reluctance on the part of the empress herself to come to grips with its implications. Before she had so much as submitted it to the *Staatsrat* for consideration she had allowed six months to go by. When she finally did so, in January 1771, that body reported favorably on the substance of the plan, if not on the methods Pergen proposed to employ to achieve his aims. She had the proposal back in her hands in the first week of February, and allowed a further two months to elapse without taking any action. Finally, in April, she submitted the document to Joseph for his advice in the matter. Uncharacteristically, the emperor replied that he had neither the time nor the expert knowledge to comment upon it in any detail. In general, he said, he was inclined to agree with the suggestion that Pergen's ideas be given a trial on a limited scale; perhaps an academy specializing in the education of young nobles of limited means might be the appropriate place for such an experiment.[28]

At last, on 16 April, Maria Theresa communicated her decision to Pergen. Thanking him, in terms that came close to being fulsome, for his so evidently very considerable labors, she nevertheless informed him that his ideas would first have to be tried out on a small scale. Would he consider presiding over the experiment himself, in his own Oriental Academy? Further, there could be no question of eliminating the monastic clergy entirely from the ranks of schoolmasters.[29]

A prudent man would doubtless have accepted defeat at this point; after all, it was not just a matter of facing down the opposition of the entrenched conservatives in the *Staatsrat.* Maria Theresa had declared herself in sympathy with Blümegen and his supporters, and there was clearly no help to be expected from Joseph, who was taking no interest in the question. Normally Pergen too would not have gone on fighting against such odds. That he stubbornly stuck to his guns, and in so doing risked alienating the empress, was due to several factors. As he had demonstrated on various occasions before this, he had a tendency frequently found in men of superior intelligence but limited imagination: having come down on one side or the other of an argument, he identified with his newly acquired opinion to such an extent that it became next to impossible for him to admit that any right thinking individual could see the matter in another light. Clearly, he had been infuriated by the pettiness of his critics' objections. Thus Blümegen had employed as a clinching argument against Pergen's desire to make use of lay teachers the observation that, in practice, the system would prove unworkable because it was incapable of providing for the eventuality of a teacher's being ill; in a monastery there were always two or three possible replacements at hand, but who would take the place of a sick layman? And Baron Stupan had complained that, inasmuch as lay teachers would in the normal course of events marry, in the case of their deaths while still in service, the state would have to provide for their widows and orphans, which would constitute an intolerable burden on the exchequer.[30] As Pergen undoubtedly saw the matter, it would be intolerable for his so carefully worked-out proposal to go down under the impact of such trivial, not to say frivolous, arguments. Finally, the circumstance that his patron and protector, the powerful—if not all-powerful—state chancellor had consistently backed him during the debates in the *Staatsrat* must have convinced Pergen that all was not yet lost.

At any rate, instead of confining himself to working out a modest pilot program, as he had been instructed, Pergen, after three months of intensive labors, came up with a somewhat revised version of his original proposal, headed by a reasoned rebuttal of his critics' arguments.[31] His proposal began by addressing itself to the questions of where the financial resources to implement his plan could be found; where a sufficient number of lay teachers might be located; and what means could be employed to implement these changes with only minimal disruption in the task of educating the young? The answer to the first question, he insisted, was much more obvious than his critics would admit: the sovereign had the implicit right to appropriate whatever sums were necessary for the smooth governance of the state; specifically included in this were all sums of money derived from gifts formerly made to the church for educational purposes. Still, he did not propose to finance his plan completely with funds taken away from the church. Once again citing the North German example, he saw no reason why the schools should not be paid for, at least in part, by collecting tuition from the students; these students, after all, would be receiving something of great value in return. Also, there were no compelling reasons to pay schoolteachers on the same lavish scale that was used in determining the salaries of university professors in the monarchy. In Germany teachers got much smaller salaries than their colleagues in the universities and were glad to teach as many as six classes a day. He saw, of course, that charging tuition would create a social problem, but there was no reason why the children of the poor should not have their school fees paid out of various charitable funds under the control of the church (the so-called *Armenkassen*).

Should this plan not suffice, Pergen went on, there were still other means, successfully employed elsewhere, that could be resorted to: a tax levied on childless married couples; a differential tax rate, with the rich paying more and in return being assured that their children would be assigned better quarters in boarding schools; a campaign to raise voluntary contributions, with generous donors being accorded official praise in the gazettes; a special tax on artisans, who, after all, would be profiting from these improvements in the educational system by having access to better educated and therefore more useful apprentices; and finally—and he failed to see how Rome could object—the liquidation of all those benefices that no longer played a useful social role in favor of a general educational fund.

As for lay teachers, Pergen went on, regrettably there was no hiding the fact that, at first, there would not be nearly enough of them in the monarchy. But, as he was quick to point out, this deplorable circumstance was merely another argument in favor of accepting his proposals in toto: the prevailing system branded itself as a hopeless failure if, by admission of its most zealous defenders, it was unable to produce a sufficient number of teachers to meet the overall needs of society. It was necessary to ask oneself if, to cite just one example, there would be a sufficient number of qualified apothecaries in the monarchy, were the clergy to be made responsible for their training? A start would simply have to be made, a number of teacher-training institutions would have to be founded which, in a sort of crash program, would, before the passage of too many years, turn out the required number of teachers. And, if there should be a lack of trained personnel to staff these, foreigners would have to be brought in to get the job done.

Turning to the practical steps necessary to implement his proposals, Pergen argued that the most essential measure would be the founding of a *Schul- und Studiendirektorium* (central state agency) to supervise education on all levels. Here too, qualified individuals would doubtless have to be imported from such places as Prussia, Württemberg and Hamburg. By far the most important task of this body would be to institute a system of school visitation with the purpose of making sure that there were no deviations from the centrally mandated norm.

Once the teacher-training institutes were in operation and the directory was at work, the time would have come to relieve the monks of all their teaching duties. It was more than probable that, on mature reflection, they would themselves be more than grateful to have this burden lifted from their shoulders. In case this argument were to strike Maria Theresa as too transparently self-serving, Pergen added another to which, he must have thought, she could hardly be indifferent: central control of the schools as a political necessity. In the present, neglected state of the school system there was a grave danger that its graduates would emerge not merely ignorant, but tainted with deistic or, even worse, atheistic ideas. A uniform curriculum and a standardized method of instruction would have to be instituted in order to turn out graduates uniformly loyal to the state and secure in their religious faith.[32]

Pergen's critics, with Blümegen once more in the lead, now resumed their attack. Their task was by no means an easy one, as they themselves were convinced that the existing educational system was hopelessly inadequate. Thus, throughout their arguments they were forced to admit that something indeed needed to be done, but not that which Pergen had proposed. They did receive valuable help from the archbishop of Vienna, Cardinal Migazzi, who observed, horror-stricken, that the educational experts whom Pergen intended to import from North Germany might turn out to be—he was convinced that the count had simply failed to take the possibility into consideration—Protestants. Migazzi did not hesitate to remind Maria Theresa that her illustrious ancestors had gone to great lengths to oust the Protestant heretics, and particularly their teachers, from the monarchy. A monarch who so far forgot her responsibilities as to allow the Protestants back would surely have to answer before God at the Last Judgment for so horrendous a transgression.[33]

Pergen, however, was not lacking supporters, even in the inner circle of Maria Theresa's advisers. Unsure of her ground, confronted by radically diverging advice from the experts, the empress submitted the proposal to the man whose judgment she valued most highly, perhaps even more so than Kaunitz's, Gerhard van Swieten. She had often turned to him in trying to make up her mind on critical questions that surpassed her understanding; let him now decide this one. The grizzled old Dutch physician was no great friend of the ecclesiastical establishment. He saw a good deal of merit in Pergen's proposal, he told Maria Theresa. He was particularly incensed by the arguments being used by the defenders of the teaching orders, the Piarists and the Jesuits. These people were trying to absolve the orders from responsibility for the shortcomings of the present system by arguing that whatever faults it might have were nothing more than the result of the individual failings of some of the teachers, a condition that could not be expected to change if one were to go over to a lay teaching force. He wished to dispute this apologia most vehemently. He had seen with his own eyes, not once but repeatedly, how the Jesuits at the university had systematically ignored and even undermined Her Majesty's most explicit instructions in order to promote the interests of the society. He was convinced that so long as they retained control of education, the state would always find itself short-changed. In conclusion he declared that, in his opinion, Pergen's plan was solid, consistent, and clear, and furthermore, if it were to be put into practice, the most marvelous improvements would inevitably make themselves felt in a very short time.[34]

Perhaps what Maria Theresa had failed to take into account on this occasion was that van Swieten was a Jansenist to whom the very term Jesuit represented an abomination. Even so, while van Swieten's advice might not have corresponded to her deepest inclinations, she gritted her teeth and determined to act upon it insofar as her conscience would allow. Without wasting any further time, she informed Pergen by personal letter on 6 September that she had decided to institute a general reform of the educational system based upon his suggestions. She would begin by convoking a central school board as he had advised her to do. She would leave it up to this body to decide what substantive changes were to be made. Pergen should recommend the names of persons he thought suitable as members, and suggest a body of rules under which the directory should be governed.[35]

Ostensibly Pergen had carried the day. However, he knew better. There had been no mention of lay teachers in Maria Theresa's instructions, and for him this had become the crux of the matter. In his answer he quoted at length from his previous communications on the subject.[36] In particular, he reminded the empress that if "the whole of the school and educational system were from this point on to become truly a state concern, and the foremost pursuit of those in charge of regulating public affairs, it would be first of all absolutely necessary to lift up the schools out of the present state of confusion and disarray, which could be achieved only by replacing the present complement of teachers with laymen and/or secular priests." He emphasized that if this were not to be done, he failed to see any conceivable way of implementing this so necessary and salutory reform. As for the directory, he could assure those who entertained such fears that it was farthest from his mind to staff this body entirely with foreigners. On the contrary, every effort had to be made to attract whatever local talent could be found to this great task. Nevertheless, it was useless to attempt to conceal the sad truth: in educational questions, Germany was simply miles ahead of Austria. Not only was this a matter of possessing many more outstanding teachers, but in addition a whole specialized literature on education had come into being there, something which was quite unknown in the monarchy. There was no avoiding it, some of these German experts would have to be invited.

Coming down to particulars, Pergen named the men who, in his view, should be recruited for the central school directory. The Austrians he believed to be qualified were Gerhard van Swieten; Ignaz Müller, a Viennese priest of well-known liberal—not to mention Jansenist— sentiments; and Karl Anton von Martini, the one genuinely talented educational reformer in Vienna. With respect to Germany, Pergen continued, the best schools were to be found in electoral Saxony, Brunswick, and Brandenburg, with the gymnasia and academies of Berlin taking pride of place. As for individuals, the names of Ramler, Weisse, Büsching, and Sulzer came to mind. All possessed considerable experience in directing educational establishments in large cities, and thus were well prepared to cope with the problems that would confront them in Vienna. But, he concluded, he did not wish to hide the fact that none of these men were known to him personally. It might well be that there were others equally or even more suited, of whom he had never heard. Therefore, he suggested that Birkenstock, a man who had previously performed valuable services for him, and who was in Germany at the moment, be instructed to interview the candidates named above, as well as any others who might come to his attention.

Thereupon Maria Theresa once again sent Pergen's proposals to the *Staatsrat* for consideration. They were discussed there extensively in the second half of October. Their reception was in the main friendly. The consensus was that, as Pergen had taken such infinite pains with his various proposals, and acquired such a detailed knowledge of the subject, he himself was the only logical candidate to become chairman of the educational directory.[37] There were, however, some differences of opinion about Pergen's suggestions with respect to the personnel. Van Swieten had begged off, even before Pergen's report had gone to Maria Theresa, arguing that although he was very honored by the invitation, he felt himself to be just too old to take on so taxing a responsibility in addition to his other duties: he already was presiding over the censorship commission, over the faculty of medicine at the university, and over a special commission charged with reforming university education. On top of all this, his every spare moment was taken up with yet another task, with which Maria Theresa had entrusted him: drawing up a compendium of all the medical substances that the physicians in the monarchy were to be allowed to prescribe.[38]

Staatsrat Gebler took the occasion of van Swieten's withdrawal to point out that Weisse was even older, and would hardly consider making a move at his age. Why not instead bring in Riedel, from Erfurt? He was young, able, and, to Gebler's certain knowledge, inclined to accept a position in Vienna. Also, Abbot Felbiger of Sagan was a great authority on educational questions, and it would be a particularly brilliant coup to gain his collaboration.[39]

The conservatives, Blümegen once again in the lead, objected in principle to the employment of Protestants. Kaunitz, on the other hand, maintained that Protestants would have to be used, with good or bad grace, because there were simply not enough qualified Catholics.[40]

Maria Theresa, who had favored educational reform from the outset, but without a real sense of urgency, became convinced that drastic measures were necessary after reading a report describing what was actually passing for education in most of the schools. This document had been drawn up independently of Pergen's reform plan, so that his opponents were unable to dismiss it as something he had inspired in order to exaggerate the dimensions of the problem. The study in question noted that in Vienna and the surrounding countryside, out of

133,419 children of school age, no more than 23,292 were actually enrolled in school. Leaving aside the relatively small numbers of children of the aristocracy or of the wealthier bourgeoisie who were being privately tutored, what these figures meant in effect was that five out of six children were getting no instruction at all. And, as the empress was quick to note with horror, this meant not only that the majority of the inhabitants of one of her most economically developed provinces were growing up without even the rudiments of a formal education, necessary for them to be really useful subjects, but worse, that they were in all likelihood not even getting any religious instruction. Such conditions could not, she insisted, be allowed to continue. Turning to the source of the evil, she noted with sadness that it was undeniable that, at least in the rural areas, the church was fully to blame for these deplorable conditions. While theoretically there were enough monks within the borders of the monarchy to teach all school-age children, in practice the monks held school only in the larger villages, where there was a parish priest to organize the school. And, as the average parish in Lower Austria encompassed six or seven villages, the children living in the outlying settlements by and large never attended. Nor could they be reasonably expected to if they would have to walk an hour or more each way in order to do so.[41]

In spite of the empress's urgings that a solution to this problem would have to be found quickly, the *Staatsrat* found itself deadlocked between Pergen's supporters, who insisted that his plan, in order to be given a reasonable chance to work, would have to be adopted in its entirety, and the conservatives, who argued that reforms have always benefitted from being tried out piecemeal, a procedure that, in addition, would have the inestimable advantage of identifying problems and correcting insufficiencies before they could have a disastrous effect.[42]

As for Pergen, he refused to give as much as an inch. He told Maria Theresa, he had so far not heard a single cogent argument to make him doubt the practicality of his proposal. Of course there would be a teacher shortage at the beginning, any fool knew that much, but he was prepared to guarantee that it would be possible to bring in enough trained personnel from other countries to bridge the gap. And to buttress his claim that it was absolutely necessary to get rid of the teaching orders, he now resorted to a new argument: one of the most important concerns of the state was to educate the nobility. Until recent times, as Her Majesty was well aware, that class had on more than one occasion lacked a total commitment of loyalty to the august Arch-House. One had to be aware of the ever present danger that they might at any moment revert to their unfortunate autochthonous tendencies. The monastic clergy, whose economic interests were equally anti-monarchical, could only reinforce these. Only lay teachers, educated, paid, and supervised by the state, could ensure that the nobiliary class would be brought up to look upon state service as the chief social good, and so give an example to the rest of Her Majesty's subjects.

Finally, Pergen once more underlined his conviction that the exclusive use of laymen was the key to his entire program. Without it there would be no effective directory, as the monks would not bother themselves in the least about its pronouncements; no teacher-training institutes, since no one would chose to enter a profession still dominated by the same old clerical establishment; and, most harmful, no real possibility for the state to extend its influence over the curriculum and over the spirit in which it was taught.[43]

At last, given the apparent impossibility of getting a consensus in the *Staatsrat*, Maria Theresa was left facing a dilemma. She was, as always, except when it came down to a direct challenge of her powers, loath to offend the church, particularly her beloved Jesuits. She also did not wish to give Kaunitz the impression that she was ignoring his advice, and the chancellor had come down squarely on Pergen's side. Quick action was evidently essential, yet whatever course she chose would inevitably lead to trouble. As often before, when confronted by similar difficulties, she opted, for better or worse, to cut the Gordian knot by large-scale shifts in personnel: the obstreperous elements were to be removed by being kicked upstairs. On 15 December the Court Bulletin contained an announcement to the effect that Count Karl Hatzfeld was being named minister of state for internal affairs and would be replaced by Blümegen as president of the combined Bohemian-Austrian chancery. Pergen, as a reward for his services, was appointed *Landesverweser* (adjunct governor) of Lower Austria, under the *Landmarschall*, Prince Trautson. Binder was named first councillor in the state chancery, where he would function as principal assistant to Kaunitz. Barons Kressel, Qualtenberg, and Löhr were appointed to replace them on the *Staatsrat*.[44]

The intention behind these various shifts quickly became apparent. The three most inflexible disputants, Blümegen, Pergen, and Binder, were all given honorable promotions; the nature of their duties, however, necessitated their removal from the *Staatsrat*. Thereby the door was opened to a compromise settlement. Kressel, who commanded a considerable degree of expertise in educational questions, was now entrusted with the task of seeing it through. Unlike Pergen, he was willing to begin by making changes on a modest scale, expressing the pious hope that, should these prove useful—he did not doubt for a moment that this would prove to be the case—the monastic schools would not fail to note their success and hasten to imitate them. Also, as he let it be known, although he did not on principle object to bringing in foreigners, he rather thought that it would prove possible to locate sufficient domestic talent to make such a step unnecessary.[45]

Pergen was barely able to contain his rage when he learned of these arrangements. He now accused his opponents of having deliberately undermined his position by circulating false reports that he was intending to bring in not experts on education but rather a variety of people who had achieved a certain notoriety in Germany, namely Wieland, Riedel, Meusel, and the two Bahrdts. Nothing could be further from the truth. Not one of these names had ever figured in his recommendations to the empress. Wieland, while it could not be denied that he had published several works of genuine quality, had also written others which could legitimately be regarded as threats to the True Religion and to the purity of morals. This alone needfully disqualified him—in Pergen's eyes— from contributing to the only goals he had in mind in suggesting his reform plan, the propagation of the True Faith and the improvement of the standards of conduct among Her Majesty's subjects.

As for the other three, although they could not justifiably be criticized on these grounds, they all had a tendency to involve themselves in bitter polemics, a circumstance that would prevent them from being readily integrated into the Austrian school system. (Surely not?) Riedel, as a matter of fact, had not been proposed by him, but rather by Gebler, acting on a suggestion by Kaunitz. He wished to reiterate that Birkenstock, who had traveled up and down Germany on his orders looking for likely candidates, had been given strict instructions to avoid approaching those with a reputation either for freethinking or for mysticism. In his opinion both tendencies would disqualify anyone from implementing his plans in accordance with his true intentions.

Apparently neither Pergen's disclaimers nor his somewhat belated discovery of his own strict orthodoxy entirely convinced Maria Theresa, who appended a marginalium to his explanation that read, "I will never permit these four men to come here."[46] This proved to be rather an embarrassment to Pergen because, in spite of all his denials, his man Birkenstock had already gone so far as to make a firm offer to Riedel, who had thereupon resigned his post as school director in Erfurt, and who now appeared in Vienna expecting to be installed in his new position. While Pergen was still trying to decide how best to cope with the situation, an Augustinian monk of that city who happened to be in the Austrian capital at the time, learning of Riedel's presence there, promptly denounced him to the local religious authorities as a well-known freethinker and an immoralist to boot. This characterization was followed almost at once by another denunciation, in the form of a letter from a man who turned out to be an unsuccessful competitor for the post that had been offered to Riedel, calling him a free spirit and an epicurean. At that point Maria Theresa had heard enough and categorically refused to employ him, even if, as Pergen had been hinting, there was a definite possibility the man would convert to Catholicism. The best Kaunitz, to whom Pergen turned for help, was able to accomplish was to secure an indemnification of a thousand ducats for Riedel, along with Her Majesty's gracious permission that, if he wished, he might stay on in Vienna as a private tutor.[47]

As for Kressl's proposal, the empress happily endorsed it. On 15 December she resolved that Pergen submit a final revision of his plan, from which the insistence on getting rid of the monks and the Jesuits was to be stricken. An experiment would be tried at once insofar as a lay director of the Theresianum, the academy for educating the children of poor but deserving nobles that she had herself founded, would be appointed. Also, three laymen or, failing that, at least secular priests were to be added to the faculties of all the secondary schools of Vienna, as well as to all of the primary schools of Prague. However, all parents were to be offered the choice of having their children instructed by these men or by their old teachers. Finally, Sonnenfels would be instructed to hold a course of lectures at the University of Vienna prepare young men for a teaching career.[48]

In Pergen's eyes this constituted a total emasculation of his proposals. He now requested an audience with the empress, in the course of which he made one more impassioned plea on behalf of his plan as it stood. However, Maria Theresa would agree only that, as soon as the directory and the teacher-training institutes were functioning, she would turn over to the former all responsibility for instituting further reforms as they might be needed.[49] Still Pergen refused to give up. He followed up his conversation with the empress with a long memorandum in which he did not hesitate to point out the inconsistencies in her actions: she had assured him that his strictures on the nature of the existing system were both just and accurate, yet she objected to his suggestions for improving it, suggestions which, if he might be so bold as to say so himself, represented the sole possible means of bringing about a beneficial change. Obliquely, but for all that, unmistakably, he went on to blame her unfavorable decision on the agitation of the Viennese clergy, which had somehow gotten wind of his intentions and had not hesitated to do everything in its power to attack and revile him.

In these circumstances, he continued, he failed to see how he could continue to remain active in this endeavor, believing as he did that the one most necessary condition for bringing about the realization of his, no less than the empress's, intentions had been discarded. Indeed, were Maria Theresa to remain inflexible on the point of using lay teachers exclusively, his advice was to leave things as they were. In that case he would at least be able to console himself with the reflection that, in God's inscrutable wisdom, the time for change had not yet come. He would, however, not be so remiss in his duty as to keep from expressing his fear that things could get even worse than they were at present. Now that the monks had smelled danger, they would surely hasten to suppress all vestiges of reform in the schools as a threat to their staying in control of the educational system. Given these considerations, he regretfully would be unable to serve in the capacity of head of the directory, as Maria Theresa had asked him to do. And finally, he asked to be relieved of the duties of overseer of the Oriental Academy, with the proviso that the official gazette publish the explanation that this was being done at his own request, so as to avoid giving the impression that he had in any way incurred the imperial displeasure.[50]

Fortunately for Pergen, who, after this intemperate outburst, might well have found himself permanently unemployed, Kaunitz now made good on his promise to find another suitable post for him in the capital. At the end of 1771 he was confirmed in the position of coadjutor to Trautson, with implied rights of succession. Even better, he was to retain his title of minister of state, along with the emoluments of that position, in addition to what he would be paid in his new post, while being excused from attending the meetings of the *Staatsrat*.[51] Thus, paradoxically, in the aftermath of his second failed major assignment en suite (his performance, of necessity, was thus viewed by both sovereigns), Pergen at last had what he had sought to achieve for himself for the last dozen years or so, an income allowing him to live like a *grand seigneur*. To be sure, he was paying for this by being shunted into a branch of government in which he was unlikely to play an important political role, but perhaps something could, over the long run, be made of the position of *Landmarschall* of Lower Austria, as, and the circumstance did not escape Pergen's attention, in those days Vienna was an administrative part of that province. And, as chief administrator of the capital, Pergen might well yet find a way of drawing the attention of the sovereigns to himself.

Pergen's venture into the area of school reform had a bizarre conclusion. For reasons best known to himself he failed to inform Birkenstock that the entire operation had been aborted, so that this good man continued to traverse all of North Germany through the first four months of 1772, submitting enthusiastic reports about the various innovations he encountered, whose good qualities he attributed largely to the fact that the prejudices and preconceptions that ruled in the monarchy were, for the most part, absent there. Birkenstock made literally dozens of recommendations to appoint various individuals to positions that—Pergen never bothered to inform him—no longer existed. It was not until May 1772 that Pergen recalled him, still without offering the least explanation.[52]

When the *Staatsrat* at last did turn to an official consideration of Pergen's proposals in July, not only the personnel but the entire spirit of that body had undergone a drastic transformation. With Joseph in the chair, it voted overwhelmingly against employing any German Protestants, a decision that in effect disposed of Pergen's plan for good.[53]

Many years later the affair had a brief epilogue. Shortly before Maria Theresa's death, Joseph asked Pergen to send him a copy of his original proposal, so that he could study it with the goal in mind of implementing some of its provisions.[54] Pergen hastened to oblige, sending along not just the original plan but also a very thick file of the correspondence it had generated as well. The emperor duly thanked him, adding that he felt sure that, somewhere in that mass of material, he would discover many useful suggestions for the improvement of the school system.[55] The educational reforms of the 1780s suggest that this may very well have been the case.

NOTES

1. C. V. Hock & H. Bidermann, *Der österreichische Staatsrath (1760–1848)* (Vienna, 1879), passim; F. Walter, "Kaunitz' Eintritt in die innere Politik," *Mitteilungen des Instituts für österreichische Geschischtsforschung,* XLVI (1932).

2. A. v. Arneth, *Geschichte Maria Theresias,* 10 vols. (Vienna), 1863–79, VII, 10, 300–301; cf. Maria Theresa to Kaunitz, 4 June 1766, in A. Beer, *Joseph II, Leopold II, und Kaunitz: Ihr Briefwechsel* (Vienna, 1873), 501.

3. Arneth, *Geschichte Maria Theresias,* VII, 305.

4. *Ibid.,* 310–11.

5. *Ibid.,* 316.

6. *Ibid.,* IX, 244. At one time Kaunitz had envisaged sending Pergen to Florence to replace Botta d'Adorno as principal adviser to Archduke Leopold but had changed his mind upon learning that Pergen's Italian was poor. Cf. A. v. Arneth, *Briefe der Kaiserin Maria Theresia an ihre Kinder und Freunde,* 4 vols. (Vienna, 1881), IV, 58. Pergen's appointment to the *Staatsrath,* which coincided with that of Starhemberg, was made possible by the vacancies created by the deaths of Haugwitz and Daun. Hock & Bidermann, 21; F. Walter, *Die österreichische Zentral-Verwaltung in der Zeit Maria Theresias* (Vienna, 1938), II/1/1, 493–94.

7. F. Walter, *Zentral-Verwaltung*, II/1/1, 493–94.

8. Pergen's report, 31 March 1762, V.A., Nachlass Pergen (hereafter N.P.).

9. Pergen's report, 8 March 1765, V.A., N.P.

10. Stadion to Pergen, 24 January 1767; Pergen to Stadion, 20 February 1767, S.A., G.C. 401.

11. K. Schönemann, *Österreichs Bevölkerungspolitik unter Maria Theresia* (Berlin, n.d.), I, 238–42.

12. Arneth, *Maria Theresia K&F*, IV, 256.

13. A. Ellemunter, *Antonio Eugenio Visconti und die Anfänge des Josephinismus* (Graz & Cologne, 1963), 53.

14. Kaunitz to Pergen, 12 July 1767, S.A., G.C. 406.

15. Pergen to Kaunitz, 5 September 1767, S.A., G.C. 405.

16. Kaunitz to Pergen, 10 September 1769, S.A., G.C. 405.

17. Walter, *Zentral-Verwaltung*, II/1/1, 434.

18. Pergen to Kaunitz, 1 March 1770, S.A., G.C. 406.

19. Walter, *Zentral-Verwaltung*, II/1/1, 434.

20. Arneth, *Maria Theresia*, IX, 227; cf. K. A. Roider, Jr., "The Oriental Academy in the Theresienzeit," *Topic*, XXXIV (1980), 23–24. The relevant documentation in S.A., Interiora (hereafter I.), 55. I am indebted to Professor Roider for calling my attention to this collection in this context.

21. Pergen's report, January 1770, S.A., I. 55.

22. Helfert, *Schulsystem*, 195–96. Well over a century ago Helfert complained that he had been unable to locate the original of this plan in any of the most likely places and thus had been reduced to working from an unauthenticated copy in the S.A. The original has still not turned up.

23. *Ibid.*, 196–201.

24. *Ibid.*, 207. Pergen's blanket condemnation of the Austrian school system was probably not unreasonable. A few years later the English traveler Nathaniel Wraxall had nothing good whatever to say about the educational level of the Austrians he had met, after all not only peasants but also members of Vienna's aristocracy. Wraxall compared the intellectual accomplishments of the Austrian haut monde extremely unfavorably with those of the burghers of almost any German town. N. W. Wraxall, *Memoirs of the Courts of Berlin, Dresden, Warsaw, and Vienna*, 2 vols., 3rd ed. (London, 1806), II, 257.

25. The following document in V.A., N.P., n.d., but on the basis of internal evidence, probably mid-1770.

26. For Gebler, cf. P. P. Bernard, "The Philosophe as Public Servant: Tobias Philip Gebler," *East European Quarterly*, VII/1 (1973).

27. Helfert, *Schulsystem*, 208–11.

28. *Ibid.*, 211–12.

29. *Ibid.*, 213–14. The suggestion to use the Oriental Academy as a trial ground, when this was perhaps the one school in the whole of the monarchy not in need of drastic reform, was of course grotesque, but for Pergen to take

exception to this would have been to gag on a sardine, having swallowed a whale.

30. *Ibid.,* 214.

31. Pergen's report, 16 July 1771, V.A., N.P.

32. G. Klingenstein, "Akademikerüberschuss als soziales Problem," G. Klingenstein et al., eds., *Bildung, Politik und Gesellschaft* (Munich, 1978), 180.

33. G. Strakosch-Grassmann, *Geschichte des österreichischen Unterrichts-wesens* (Vienna, 1905), 87.

34. Van Swieten to Maria Theresa, 2 August 1771, V.A., N.P. It should not be forgotten that van Swieten sympathized with the Jansenists in their wholesale condemnation of the Society of Jesus.

35. Helfert, *Schulsystem,* 230.

36. Pergen to Maria Theresa, 12 October 1771, V.A., N.P.

37. Helfert, *Schulsystem,* 232.

38. Van Swieten to Pergen, 7 October 1771, V.A., N.P.

39. Helfert, *Schulsystem,* 232.

40. *Ibid.*

41. Maria Theresa to Pergen; Maria Theresa to Hatzfeld, 9 November 1771, V.A., N.P.

42. Helfert, *Schulsystem,* 236–37.

43. Pergen to Maria Theresa, 22 November 1771, V.A., N.P.

44. Helfert, *Schulsystem,* 237–38.

45. *Ibid.,* 240. As a sop to Pergen, Kressel suggested that, should the teaching orders refuse to go along with the changes he was suggesting, he would then recommend their complete removal from the schools. Cf. J. Schmidt, *Entwicklung der katholischen Schule in Österreich* (Vienna, 1958), 191–92. It was hardly likely that the orders would risk so adamant a refusal, since what Kressel was proposing left them substantially in control.

46. Pergen to Maria Theresa, 20 December 1771, V.A., N.P. Pergen may well not have been quite so innocent as he was claiming, as he now hastened to submit his plan to an old acquaintance in Mainz, who indeed warned him that it was in no way suitable for a Catholic country. Mantzall to Pergen, 10 January 1772, V.A., N.P. Klingenstein, "Akademikerüberschuss," 180, suggests that concern about the growing number of freethinkers and the spread of superstition in the cities was, in large part, behind the push for educational reform, and quotes this document in support of her hypothesis. Perhaps, but it seems as least as likely that Pergen, having convinced himself that only desperate measures were capable of saving his plan, decided to make use of the one argument that might yet sway Maria Theresa.

47. E. Guglia, *Maria Theresia,* 2 vols. (Munich & Berlin, 1917), II, 326–28.

48. Maria Theresa's resolution, 15 January 1772, V.A., N.P.

49. Helfert, *Schulsystem,* 241.

50. Pergen to Maria Theresa, 31 January 1772, V.A., N.P.

51. Walter, *Zentral-Verwaltung,* II/1/1, 440.

52. Birkenstock to Pergen, 7, 13 February, 28 March, and 1 May 1772, V.A., N.P.

53. Hock & Bidermann, *Der österreichische Staatsrath,* 114.

54. Joseph to Pergen, 18 January 1781, V.A., N.P.

55. Pergen to Joseph, 19 January 1781, V.A., N.P.

4

Governor of Galicia

O N 19 FEBRUARY 1772, the governments of Austria, Prussia, and Russia agreed in principle on a partition of the kingdom of Poland. By May, Austrian troops had begun their occupation of the areas allocated to the monarchy, essentially the principalities of Galicia and Lodomeria.[1] With events moving so rapidly, they outstripped Austrian planning. No decision had yet been made on how the newly acquired territories were to be governed. The invading troops were accompanied by two political commissioners, one from the Hungarian chancery, the other from the Transylvanian, but they had been instructed only to prepare the way for a permanent governing body. How this would be constituted, to what agencies it would be responsible, from what bodies the personnel were to be chosen were all questions no one had even considered. The trouble was that once Joseph and Kaunitz had at last overcome Maria Theresa's by no means unreasonable objections to partitioning the territory of a friendly neighboring state, and thereby removing a useful buffer between themselves and the Russians, they acted with such unseemly haste in getting the partition under way that one has the distinct impression that they were afraid she would change her mind.[2]

At first it seemed as if, for want of a better solution, Austrian Poland would simply be added to the already long list of territories administered directly by the state chancery, such as Lombardy and the Austrian Netherlands, to become, not to put too fine a point on it, an appanage of Kaunitz's. Maria Theresa saw no objections to such an arrangement, and in fact promised the chancellor that, at least for an initial period of not less than two years, the principalities would be placed directly under his ministry. Joseph, however, while he continued to think of

Kaunitz as the one irreplaceable man in the government, had long since ceased to look upon the chancellor as uncritically as his mother did, and was to do until the end of her life. Unwilling to see Kaunitz's influence yet again increased, he raised various objections. Some of these were so pointed that Baron Binder, the chancellor's closest adviser, felt that there was no alternative to the prince's backing down on the excuse that the state of his health would not permit him to assume such onerous additional duties. Kaunitz, however, was reluctant to acquiesce in this matter, fearing that unless he was in control, he would soon be deprived of any influence over events in the principalities.

It soon occurred to Kaunitz, however, that there was more than one way to of skinning the Polish cat. Even if Galicia and Lodomeria were not to be subject directly to the state chancery, the same effect could be achieved by indirect means. What now followed was, on the surface, an arrangement of almost baroque complexity, but was simple enough when regarded as nothing more than a device meant to insure that Kaunitz would have the last word in deciding future events in the newly acquired territories.

Kaunitz first proposed that Count Hadik, the commander of the Austrian occupying forces, be named governor, but added that he would report to a separate Galician chancery in Vienna, on the model of the Transylvanian chancery, which, as it happened, was administratively a part of the chancellor's bailiwick. As head of this new ministry he proposed Pergen. There is no doubt whatever that, had Joseph accepted this arrangement, Kaunitz would have determined the course of events in Galicia. The emperor, however, was by this time too wary to be taken in by such a transparent stratagem, and objected that Pergen's talents, which he had no wish to denigrate—they were considerable—were not well suited to the task at hand.[3]

After protracted additional wrangling, it became clear to all the principals that further delay would be extremely unwise. The situation in Galicia, according to daily reports from a distraught Hadik, was threatening to dissolve into chaos. The only certainty that could be ascribed to the situation there was that Hadik was not the man to combine the functions of military commander with those of governor. He had a difficult time just attending to the needs of the army. The occupiers had immediately, after entering the country, found to their dismay that effective organization at the local level, for the purpose of collecting supplies for the army, just did not exist, and were forced to import everything they consumed from their own depots in Upper Silesia. Although Hadik could hardly be blamed for all of the difficulties that the Austrian troops were encountering, neither was he giving an impressive display of sangfroid.[4]

Since, also, it hardly seemed likely that the complicated and delicate task of imposing Austrian rule while disturbing Polish institutions as little as possible could be accomplished from far-off Vienna—the transition would require hundreds if not thousands of decisions, most of them extremely minor but likely to stir up passions if not tactfully arrived at—Joseph finally gave way. He now approved a revised version of Kaunitz's plan in which Pergen himself would be named governor, reporting directly to the *Staatskanzlei*.

As soon as Pergen's appointment had been decided on, the usual squabble about salary and travel expenses broke out. This time Kaunitz was firmly on Pergen's side. He pointed out to Joseph that the new governor would have to maintain two households, since it could not be expected of him to expose his family to the rigors of Galicia, at least not until the situation there had settled considerably; and since as governor, Pergen would have to entertain on a lavish scale, one would not want him to cut a bad figure in a country where display counted for so much. He suggested that Pergen be allowed to retain his salaries as Lower Austrian coadjutor and as minister of state and, in addition, be given a monthly supplement of 2,000 florins. As for his moving expenses, he would have to transport a good part of his possessions to Lemberg; it was most unlikely that anything suitable could be found there. In fairness he should be granted 20,000 florins for the purpose—at the very least 15,000.[5]

However much Kaunitz may have been pleased at winning what was clearly a tactical victory over Joseph, Pergen himself harbored no illusions about the nature of the job now facing him. Instead of biding his time until the rapidly aging and often unwell Trautson should decide to retire, and then emerging as the unexpectedly energetic governor of the monarchy's central province, he would be taking on a task of inestimable difficulty. Polish administration on all levels had long ago degenerated into a bad joke, and it would be necessary to reconstitute the governmental apparatus from the bottom up. He would have to try to make a centralized administration palatable to people who had not known anything except feudal anarchy for well over a century. Worst of all, he would have to accomplish this in the full knowledge that Joseph had been opposed to his appointment from the outset, and would undoubtedly cast a jaundiced eye on whatever he did.[6] It speaks volumes for Pergen's trust in Kaunitz that he refrained from seizing whatever opportunity came his way, plausible or not, to decline the appointment.

Even so, Pergen tried to cover his flanks as best he could by asking Kaunitz to supply him with infinitely detailed instructions, covering every conceivable eventuality, so that he would not be in danger of acting contrary to the *"allerhöchste Willensmeinung."* He also recited a long litany of the difficulties he would be encountering so that no one in Vienna would expect swift and brilliant results of him. Among the many obstacles he cited was the circumstance that, at the first rumors of the Austrian occupation, the most productive elements of the population had fled in panic to the areas that had remained Polish, and it was by no means clear to him how he should go about trying to coax them back. The inhabitants who had stayed behind were, on the whole, a sorry lot. The vast privileges that had over the centuries accrued to the first two estates, clergy and nobility, had placed practically all of the arable land in the provinces in their hands. As a result, no such thing as a class of peasant proprietors (*bonis rusticalibus*) existed. The ordinary peasant was far too poor to pay taxes, and the privileged orders would doubtless refuse to, taking a stand on their ancient liberties. The towns, such as they were, were overrun with Jews who, except in one or two of the very largest, actually outnumbered the Christians. The Jews, possessed of the full rights of citizenship, not only dictated the course of events in the urban areas, but virtually monopolized all commerce in the countryside, including the all-important trade in foodstuffs.[7] The Poles had virtually forgotten how to fend for themselves.

In Pergen's opinion these inherited evils could be corrected only gradually, if at all. To avoid later misunderstandings, he now went on to explain in detail how he intended to proceed. First, as it had now been decided that he would be responsible to Kaunitz, through the state chancery, he underlined that he did not propose to send reports to any other branch of the government. To do so would only create confusion and lead to interminable delays. Then, he wanted it clearly understood that he would be responsible only for the direction of civil affairs. He did not propose to concern himself at all with the needs of the Austrian troops stationed in the principalities. Otherwise he would be inviting endless conflicts with the ministry of war.[8]

Pergen also addressed himself to Kaunitz for detailed instructions on the following matters that were, in his view, crucial to his mission:

a) Should he follow the traditional Polish practice of negotiating with the clergy and the nobility as separate entities through the estates?

b) He had been told that one of his first official acts would have to be a major reallocation of the tax burden on a more equitable basis. Should the details of this reform be left to various local assemblies to work out, or would it be preferable to dictate the changes from above?

c) Should the absolute tax immunity of the privileged orders, anchored in the old Polish constitution, be abrogated?

d) Should serfdom be abolished; and, if this were to be the case, in what manner were the privileged orders to be compensated for their loss?

e) Should the old crown lands, long since parceled out to the *szlachta* by the pitifully weak Polish monarchy, now be confiscated?

f) Should he allocate pensions to the multitude of local officials who would inevitably now be replaced by members of the new administration?

g) All important mines and salt works, formerly the property of the crown, were now in nobiliary hands. Should he expropriate these?

h) Since public offices were regarded as a form of property in Poland, very much as was the case in France, would every dismissed officeholder be entitled to a monetary compensation?

i) Would it be useful to create a central fisc, into which all the money collected in the principalities, whatever its source, would flow?

j) Should he establish a separate agency for overseeing the activities of all teachers, both clerical and lay, who were the real molders of opinion—particularly in the countryside?

k) His own view of the matter was that, wherever possible, local officials should be native Poles familiar with existing conditions. Did the chancellor agree?

l) In order to make it easier for the Poles to reconcile themselves quickly to their loss of national independence, would it not be wise to allow them, barring serious jurisdictional conflicts, to retain their customs and traditions, along with—at a minimum in civil cases— their own courts of law?

m) Would it not be highly desirable to retain Polish as the language of administration?

Following these questions with broader implications, a host of minor ones were then posed, mostly having to do with what personnel Pergen would be able to count on. And finally he inquired whether, given the entirely desolate state of the economy, one should be prepared right from the outset to collect all taxes in kind.[9]

Kaunitz's answer, while it was couched in the most complimentary terms, commending the speed and thoroughness with which he had familiarized himself with the details of his new position, could hardly have been much of a comfort to Pergen. The chancellor said in essence that all questions dealing with matters of local administration were to be referred directly to the *Staatskanzlei.* As Pergen had every reason to know, the scribbling that would necessarily result from such a procedure would by far surpass even his astonishing capacity for putting things on paper. As for consulting various local elements, Kaunitz maintained that Austria was not in any fashion bound *de jure* to respect local institutions. Pergen was free to introduce any changes he thought would prove useful. While strictly speaking this might be true, Pergen, from his experience in administering the conquered territories in the *Reich* during the last war, knew very well that such arbitrariness was an infallible recipe for generating trouble, and, as will emerge presently, did not propose to follow this advice. In answering what was certainly the question with the broadest policy implications, the chancellor expressed the opinion that the Galician peasantry should probably be brought up to the economic level of the Hungarian and Upper Silesian peasants. This would, he realized, result inevitably in a considerable loss to the landowners, who would have to be compensated. It was, however, up to Pergen to find the funds for this. Finally, Kaunitz agreed with Pergen that Polish officials should be used wherever possible in the ranks of the lower administration, but only as window dressing; no important decisions were to be left to them.[10]

Maria Theresa added some thoughts of her own to Kaunitz's comments. She told Pergen that, although this might seem petty to him, it was her will that within a year no Pole be seen in public wearing the national costume, the peasants excepted. This was important not merely in order to thwart any explicit identification of the politically influential classes with their co-nationals in what remained of the Polish state after the partitions, but also for hygienic reasons. In addition, she would insist that all public business be transacted either in German or in Latin. Polish was to disappear as a language of administration. As far as the Galician Jews were concerned, they were a completely unproductive race, eternal parasites on the labors of the Christian population. If Pergen had any doubts on the matter, let him consult the publications of the abbé Petansky. There, he could inform himself thoroughly on this subject. While it would hardly be possible to eliminate all the Galician Jews, particularly as the Christian population seemed to be so heavily in debt to them, Pergen was to do his utmost to reduce their numbers. The Greek Orthodox population, and members of various Protestant sects, were not to be interfered with in any way. As for what was, by common agreement, the worst problem Pergen would be facing, the utter economic misery of large segments of the populace, that could be blamed largely on the Jews and would be alleviated once this pest had been radically cut back.[11]

Thus armed with complex and by no means always consistent orders, Pergen set out for Lemberg, where he arrived safely on 29 September 1772.[12] It took him hardly any time at all to confirm his worst suspicions about the totally impractical nature of his instructions. He arrived at a crucial decision right at the outset of his mission. Rather than engage in endless wrangling at all levels, which attempting to follow his orders in a strict sense would have entailed, he chose instead to resolve the most urgent problems facing him in whatever manner seemed to offer some hope of success. Kaunitz was left with no choice but to put as good a face as possible on Pergen's arbitrary methods, telling Maria Theresa that it would be ungracious to judge his conduct by any standards other than those of compelling necessity. Also, he reassured her, everything that Pergen was doing in the early stages of his administration was merely of a provisional nature, in no way committing Austrian policy for the future.[13]

It was as well for Pergen that Kaunitz suppressed all knowledge of his activities in Vienna, because, had Maria Theresa been aware of what he was actually doing in Galicia, her wrath would undoubtedly have descended upon him in full measure. First, on no authority but his own, he granted a general amnesty to all the members of the Polish nobility who, upon approach of the Austrian occupying forces, had fled the country. Maria Theresa had given him specific instructions that such individuals were to be dispossessed without further ado; but, realizing that such a step would merely exacerbate the organizational chaos already existing in the province, Pergen decided to let bygones be bygones. Kaunitz was left with the task of convincing the empress of the wisdom of sanctioning this measure. The argument he used was that every returnee would be required to submit to the authorities a letter outlining good and sufficient reasons for his absence. The delinquent noblemen, knowing that paper is patient, were happy to avail themselves of this opportunity, and Maria Theresa seems to have been satisfied to accept the most transparently fictional excuses, so long as an excuse was being offered at all.[14]

Next, Pergen had been instructed to void all existing Polish land grants. Maria Theresa, fully aware of the degree to which the Polish Monarchy had lost its powers in the course of the last century and a half, believed with good reason that the greater portion of the huge nobiliary estates had been acquired, not by royal charter, but much more simply by pure theft from the royal domain. As successor to the kings of Poland, she now proposed to reacquire all the lands for which their owners could not show indisputable legal title. Pergen, however, now argued that whatever the legal niceties of the case might be, such a step would lead at once—if not to a general revolt of the *szlachta*—at the very least to the immediate pauperization of a large portion of the nobility, and thus to the ruin of the whole province. Kaunitz saw the force of this argument, but did not quite dare to oppose the empress in a matter that so directly affected her pocketbook. He suggested a compromise: where a title was questionable, the estate involved should, for the time being at least, be left in possession of its supposed owner. However, for the period in which the case was not resolved in the owner's favor, one-third of the income from it would be turned over to the treasury. As Kaunitz told Pergen, this expedient had the additional advantage of keeping a large portion of the *szlachta* suspended between fear and hope. This, better than any other measure he could think of, would assure their loyalty.[15]

Third, Pergen blatantly ignored Maria Theresa's expressed wish that a majority of the members of his administration be drawn from a pool of names recommended to him by the court. Instead, he chose almost exclusively Polish nationals. Without actually dotting the *i*, Kaunitz tried to make this piece of disobedience palatable to the empress by pointing out that, whatever advantage there might be in using the Galician administration as a kind of pork barrel for rewarding her deserving subjects, such people would inevitably be resented as grasping interlopers by the local population. The monarchy could gain far more from bestowing its rewards upon locals, who could not only be expected to have a detailed knowledge of obtaining conditions, but whose loyalties would thus be purchased.[16]

Finally, Pergen, on his own initiative, negotiated an agreement with the government of rump Poland, regulating the commerce in Galician salt. Kaunitz was now left with no alternative but to argue that, as salt exports constituted a very considerable proportion of Galicia's commercial wealth, it would have been highly unrealistic for Pergen to cut off the flow of income from this trade merely for the sake of consulting Vienna about the particulars of an agreement, which, in any case, would have had to be made.[17]

But matters did not rest there. As Pergen had feared would be the case, Joseph began to take a lively interest in Galician affairs. Before long he was bombarding Pergen with memoranda on every aspect of Austrian policy. So far as the *starostie,* the former crown lands whose titles were in dispute, were concerned, he felt that their owners should be made to pay half, not a third, of their revenues to the state. Moreover, even this was to be only a lifetime concession; on the death of the owners these lands were to revert to the crown without possibility of testamentary disposition. It would do no good for Pergen to point out that such a provision would alienate the *szlachta* just as much as outright confiscation. The emperor remained adamant on the point. As for staffing various governmental positions mostly with Poles, Joseph

Beeler ?!

argued that the best should not be allowed to become the enemy of the
good. As he saw it, every district would require at least one highly
placed official who could be depended upon to carry out orders. It was
unrealistic to expect absolute loyalty from the Poles, many of whom
bitterly resented the partition. As Pergen himself would come to realize,
it would eventually be necessary to use mostly Czechs in this capacity.
And Joseph urged Pergen to appoint General Prince Poniatowski as his
principal aide, the prince having been the only prominent Polish *grand
seigneur* known to have expressed any pro-Austrian sentiments.[18]

It was only with great difficulty that Kaunitz was able to persuade
Maria Theresa that, in the interest of domestic tranquility in the Polish
territories, it was best not to interfere with Pergen's dispositions, based
as they were on firsthand observations of the situation.[19] In spite of the
chancellor's support, Pergen soon found himself in a most unpleasant
situation: while faced with the necessity of having continually to explain
to Vienna why various centralizing measures urged on him were being
postponed, he found himself dealing daily with one crisis after the
other, all of them rooted in the circumstance that the Galician economy
was on the point of collapse. He was increasingly being made aware
that, were such a collapse to be avoided, a whole series of ad hoc
decisions would have to be made quickly, without reference to some sort
of theoretical ideal. Thus he pointed out to Kaunitz that, although he
had no quarrel whatever with Maria Theresa's stated intention to dimin-
ish the role played by Jewish merchants in the distribution of foodstuffs,
it would first be necessary to come up with a workable replacement for
this regrettable system.[20]

Furthermore, Pergen complained, if he were to obey to the letter his
instructions concerning how he should collect various contributions
in kind from the peasants, this would lead without fail to the utter ruin
of a large proportion of Her Majesty's new subjects. The exactions
traditionally made by the nobility in their capacity as feudal overlords
were in themselves so elevated that the peasants would be unable to
survive if they were forced to deliver taxes at the rate Vienna wanted
him to collect. At the moment, he had to employ the full range of his
persuasive powers to convince the peasants in the poorer areas to go
ahead with the planting of their crops of winter wheat, because they
maintained that, should the announced tax rates in fact be enforced, it
would simply not be worth their trouble to plant and harvest a crop. In
order to prevent a terrible catastrophe, it would be necessary to exempt—at
the very least—the poorest districts from the announced taxes entirely.[21]

Perhaps, with Kaunitz's continued support, Pergen might have pulled
it off, although it would have taken a minor miracle for his empirical

measures to succeed quickly and impressively enough in turning the situation around to make Maria Theresa and Joseph overlook his independent spirit, not to say downright disobedience; but such miracles, based on spectacular successes, are not entirely unknown. Pergen's situation, however, became untenable when he found himself increasingly in open opposition to the policies dear to Kaunitz himself. As we have seen, the chancellor had convinced Maria Theresa that the most promising avenue for initiating the changes she desired for Galicia was to govern the province through the *Staatskanzlei.* Pergen would report directly—and only—to him. The difficulty with this arrangement was not so much that Pergen objected to working directly under Kaunitz's orders; he had, after all, done this throughout his post in the *Reich* and had learned long since how best to please the chancellor, while still, in large measure, pursuing his own goals. The trouble was rather that, as was becoming all too clear, Kaunitz intended the Polish territories to be governed in accordance with the system in use in the other territories directly subject to the *Staatskanzlei,* namely the Austrian Netherlands and the Milanese. And, as Pergen correctly perceived, this made no sense. Those provinces were among the richest and politically most progressive in the whole of the monarchy. Galicia, in contrast, was hopelessly backward. The methods that Kaunitz wanted to use could not possibly work there, and their inevitable failure would result in the disgrace not of himself, as he was by definition never mistaken, but of Pergen. The only positive element in this bleak picture was that Pergen's doubts about the feasibility of Kaunitz's plans were shared in large measure by Joseph. To be sure, the emperor was not so much motivated by a skepticism about the practicality of what Kaunitz proposed as by a strong inclination to resist a further extension of the prince's already vast powers; but, from Pergen's vantage point this was all the same: one could be played off against the other.[22]

Still, while making common cause with Joseph against Kaunitz might well appear to be the only course open to him, Pergen was not prepared to break with his long-time patron and friend. For once he was careful not to commit himself irrevocably to either side. This turned out to have been just as well for him, as Kaunitz, once more resorting to his favorite weapon in difficult times—the threat of his resignation—prevailed over Joseph. Maria Theresa put aside the co-regent's objections and assured Kaunitz that, at least for the time being, the Polish territories would, as originally decided, be administered directly by the *Staatskanzlei.*[23] Of course, there was no ready means of establishing what "for the time being" might mean in this context, but Pergen was on notice that he would have to proceed with extreme caution in disregarding Kaunitz's wishes as well as those of the sovereigns.

At the heart of the system that Kaunitz had employed with a considerable measure of success in Lombardy and the Netherlands was the principle of cooperation with various assemblies of local notables. Nobles and urban patricians had been wooed by him with the argument that, in spite of what any reasonable man would be bound to assume, their class interests would be favored rather than hurt by their acquiescence in the various centralizing measures he introduced. Perhaps, ultimately, this argument was the equivalent of squaring the circle, but in practice it had worked out well enough, as there was a sufficient economic margin in these places to enable the chancellor to bestow certain advantages upon those who cooperated with him. Any attempt to introduce this practice into the Polish lands, however, was bound to result in a spectacular fiasco as the *szlachta* would interpret any concessions of that nature as a sign that nothing had changed in its basic relations with the crown. Very much aware of this, Pergen attempted to resolve his difficulties by dealing not with the corporate bodies of the nobility but rather with individual magnates, who, unsupported by an institutional framework, might prove more pliable.[24] This method, while capable of producing immediate results in any number of pressing matters, had the considerable disadvantage of leading, over the long run, to an administrative tangle matching in complexity the Byzantine chaos that had prevailed before the partition.

Kaunitz was not the man to be fooled for any length of time by such devices. But, in part because he could not help seeing the force of Pergen's arguments, probably as well because he had no desire to be embroiled in endless disputes with Maria Theresa and Joseph, he now adopted a curious tactic for dealing with his troublesome subordinate. With great earnestness he would relay to him the latest instructions from Their Imperial Majesties, down to the minutest detail, while tacitly (and, on occasion, overtly) approving of measures Pergen had taken that ran directly counter to his instructions. From Kaunitz's point of view, this technique had the additional advantage of letting him disclaim all responsibility, should things go badly in Galicia—he had, after all, faithfully forwarded the emperor's instructions. It was not his fault that Pergen had chosen to disregard them. And, for the moment, Pergen had a free hand to test out his methods. If they worked, so much the better; the chancellor would see to it that the lion's share of the credit went to his ministry.

Thus Kaunitz, while pointing out in practically every letter that Maria Theresa, now just as much as before, wanted to see members of the Bohemian, Moravian, and Silesian nobilities appointed to the higher positions in Pergen's administration, informed him that he, personally, fully approved of his intention to appoint Poles. No doubt a great many urgent decisions needed to be made on all levels, and he could quite see that Galicia could not go ungoverned while Pergen waited for these carpetbaggers to show up in sufficient numbers. The only measure with which Kaunitz disagreed in principle was Pergen's decision, doubtless a consequence of his lifelong admiration of English ways, to introduce a strict separation of judicial and executive powers. The chancellor, familiar with the French rather than the English model, saw nothing but inconvenience and delay resulting from so cumbersome a system.[25]

While thus in effect giving Pergen his head, Kaunitz, nevertheless, protected his flank by informing Joseph in great detail about every one of Pergen's official acts, in that manner shifting the burden of approval or disapproval from himself to the emperor. Joseph had voiced the desire to visit the new provinces as soon as he had acquired them, and Kaunitz lost no opportunity to reassure him that, whatever measures Pergen might have taken as governor, these were to be considered as no more than a temporary expedient until the time of his arrival. At that point, the All Highest himself would decide what needed to be done for the long run. Everything, including the question of whether Pergen was to be retained in his post, would depend solely on his decision, which he himself would certainly not presume to influence.[26]

In the meantime, Pergen continued to settle a variety of local matters in whatever way appeared to him to promote the smooth functioning of his administration. Thus he raised no objections when one of the two or three greatest landowners in the provinces, Count Potocki, having heard that Vienna would repossess all former royal domains as lapsed fiefs upon the death of their owners, simply transferred the title of his lands to his infant son.[27] Inasmuch as this action represented a precedent that, if it were allowed to stand, was bound to find imitators, both Maria Theresa and Joseph now descended upon Kaunitz with loud complaints, not only about the case in question but about the entire spirit of Pergen's conduct of affairs. At that point the chancellor seems to have realized that some sort of apology for his difficult protégé was in order. He hastened to assure Their Majesties that, it went without saying, he would long ago have dismissed a subordinate who took so cavalier an attitude toward their expressed wishes, were it not for the fact that in his opinion there were compelling reasons behind Pergen's actions. He now took the liberty of spelling these out:

a) Their Majesties had ordered Polish law replaced entirely by that of the Czech lands bordering the provinces. Given the confused state of affairs in the territories, such a measure appeared to be highly desirable in theory. In practice, however, one could not get around the fact that, in the length and breadth of Galicia and Lodomeria, not a single individual learned in Czech law was to be found. All efforts to bring in a sufficient number of such persons from the rest of the monarchy had gone for naught because the incentives being offered were evidently insufficient to attract well-situated legal scholars to the Galician service. Moreover, even if this obstacle could be surmounted, it seemed clear to him that to introduce so many foreigners into the provinces would chiefly have the effect of driving a deep wedge between populace and administration. The continued orderly government of the province seemed to demand a transitional period in which local talent was made use of, while the lawyers needed to staff the new system were being trained within Galicia itself.

b) As for Joseph's command that "Pergen was not to concern himself in the least with what existing Polish laws might be, but rather to put Galicia on the same footing as Moravia in the least possible time," Kaunitz begged leave to ask whether this was really the emperor's intention. If so, one would first have to find out a lot more than was presently known about existing conditions there, in order to decide what changes needed to be made. In the meantime, there was no alternative to allowing Pergen to work as best he could within the existing legal framework.

c) Finally, in all humility, Kaunitz put Joseph on notice that the best interests of the state forced him to oppose his intention to replace the entire church hierarchy in Galicia without bothering in the least about what the papacy might have to say on the matter. As Maria Theresa would undoubtedly remember, if Joseph did not, throughout his long career in public service he had never been known as a man who had the least hesitation about supporting the crown against the exaggerated claims of Rome. In the present circumstances, however, he saw no alternative to supporting Pergen's claim that Joseph had no choice except to come to terms with the Polish hierarchy, which was not only interconnected with the most influential noble families in the country, but which also enjoyed great popularity among the humble people. To dismiss them as Joseph wanted would be to invite rebellion.[28]

It might be added that Pergen's opposition to replacing the Polish legal system with something that actually worked was by no means one of principle. It had not taken him long to notice that Galician law consisted mainly of a hopeless tangle of Polish, German, and Russian codes of widely differing periods of origin. These laws as often as not canceled one another so that quite frequently it proved impossible to bring a litigation to a conclusion acceptable to any of the parties. Moreover, the few trained legal scholars in the province held Austrian law in high esteem and would presumably not object to its introduction. But, as Pergen was most keenly aware, the transition would take considerable time if the result were not to be yet another piece of patchwork, and time was precisely the commodity in shortest supply.[29] In the end even the enthusiasts in various ministries realized this, and Kaunitz was able to persuade Maria Theresa that one could only slowly introduce really fundamental legal changes. It was preferable to allow Pergen to proceed on the strength of his on-the-spot observations.[30]

While wholly engaged in trying to reconcile Vienna's elaborate plans for Galicia with the political realities in the province, Pergen was confronted with a recurring difficulty. However the propertied classes might view the recent change of regimes—and there was a wide variety of opinion there—all were agreed on one point: the general confusion and the multiple administrative breakdowns resulting from the recent political changes were to be exploited in every possible way. In particular, although various bureaucrats in Vienna were developing elaborate schemes for tripling or even quadrupling the (admittedly inadequate) tax revenues from the province, in actual fact payment of even the few existing taxes had virtually come to a halt. The Jews, who, even if they were mostly poor as individuals, collectively controlled a substantial portion of Galicia's wealth, had almost entirely stopped paying the special assessments levied on them, the so-called *Kopfgelder* and *Quarten*. By the end of 1772, these were in arrears by some 2 million florins. At that point Pergen inquired whether he should make every effort to collect these delinquent payments. On the one hand, he saw no other way of getting his hands on a sum of money large enough to pay for the implementation of the various changes and reforms that Vienna wanted him to introduce. On the other, as these exactions were so blatantly discriminatory, even the rudiments of a humane administrative practice demanded their abolition. Should he just write off the amounts owed? As for the considerable quantities of *naturalia* owed by the Polish landowners, he proposed a payments moratorium to run until September 1773, when the new harvest would be in. And as for demanding that the Poles pay their taxes in cash, he could not refrain from pointing out the utter inanity of such a suggestion. They simply did not have it.[31]

In the meantime, of course, Pergen himself was desperately short of cash as Vienna, on principle, refused to send any ready money into the province: it was meant to be a source of additional income, not a burden on the treasury. Whatever money he was unable to raise locally was simply not available to him. This circumstance alone goes a long way toward explaining why, throughout his tenure as governor, he was so anxious to maintain good relations with the Poles.

Pergen's reports, sent off regularly at least twice weekly, more often whenever he addressed an issue of some importance, while bespeaking the tensions inevitably present when an envoy is at odds with the policies of his government, also go well beyond this. In fact, they reveal in every particular the most serious shortcomings of Austrian administrative practice. At the same time that he was essentially ignoring Vienna's broad policy lines (whether for good or bad is not at issue here), he evidently thought it necessary to consult Kaunitz on the disposition of the most trivial issues. In his turn the chancellor, without fail, submitted these questions to Maria Theresa for final decision. The empress must have been drowning in a sea of trivia, and the fact that she made no objection is a good indication that these were by no means unusual conditions. Thus in February 1773 alone, Pergen wanted to know which side to support in a jurisdictional dispute between two neighboring districts; what relative value to assign to the numerous coinages circulating in the province; requested directions on how best to manage salt distribution to the towns; inquired if he might stop the payment of a pension amounting to 130 florins annually, because its recipient had recently died; asked permission for allowing a local council secretary in Sandomierz to retire from his post; and respectfully begged for the emperor's permission to appoint an apothecary in the town of Wiliczka.[32]

The impression all this gives is that Pergen, probably only to draw attention away from his various departures from the court's policies, was doing his best to appear to Vienna as a sort of *Kreishauptmann*, who needed to be given elaborate instructions at every turn. What is truly mind-boggling is that Kaunitz and Maria Theresa, instead of telling him once and for all to leave such petty details to his subordinates, did not hesitate themselves to spill large quantities of ink over these matters. How far Pergen was willing to play this game is shown by his elaborate report to Kaunitz about an incident involving the theft of a cart belonging to a local dignitary, to which he appended a page-long inventory of the stolen goods. The chancellor duly passed this information on to the empress, who then initialed the document.[33] It seems not to have occurred to any of the principals that it is simply not possible to govern a province, much less an empire, in this fashion.

It would be inexact to imply that Pergen dealt only in trivia in this period. Insofar as he was able, he tried to address himself to problems of greater magnitude. Among these was the religious situation in the predominantly Eastern Orthodox areas. As he saw matters—and there was something to be said in favor of this opinion—the chief evils were the credulity and the overwhelming ignorance, shading into stupidity, of a considerable portion of the rural population. These were not only tolerated but actually abetted by the clergy, which, at the lower levels, was intellectually very little better off than their parishioners, and at the upper ones was universally lazy and corrupt. The archbishop and the bishops he characterized as being, without exception, *bon vivants* and worldly intriguers who took no interest whatever in the welfare of their flocks. As a result of this condition, practically no money had been made available for generations to improve the quality of the seminaries. This, in turn, since practically all teachers were priests, had had a disastrous effect on the level of instruction in the schools. To make matters worse, education seemed to be largely the concern of the monasteries, of which there were so many in these districts that, so far, he had not even succeeded in identifying them all.[34] One is, of course, at this point forcefully reminded of Pergen's recent misadventures in the area of educational reform, but he must have concluded that Maria Theresa was not nearly as apt to intervene in behalf of the Orthodox clergy as of the Catholic.

Pergen's most frequently repeated complaint in his reports, doubtless fully justified, was that he had been allowed neither an adequate staff to carry out the ambitious measures expected of him, nor sufficient funds to employ local people, assuming that there were qualified individuals available. For example, he pointed out that he needed at least one chief deputy in every one of the districts making up the provinces. He had been alloted a maximum of 2,000 florins annually for each of these positions. Because this sum was well below the minimum amount needed by a gentleman to live on, not surprisingly he had been unable to fill the vacancies. The only advice Kaunitz had to offer was that whenever Pergen came up with a qualified candidate he should appoint him at the same time to the court of appeals. The man would be drawing two salaries and could thus afford to live decently. The chancellor did not address the question of how these people would simultaneously carry out the duties of two full-time jobs.[35]

In March Kaunitz passed on the disturbing news that Joseph himself would no longer be deterred from visiting Galicia. The emperor believed enough time had now passed for that province to have been fully integrated into the rest of the monarchy, and he wished to gather firsthand observations on what had been accomplished toward that end. Joseph's numerous inspection trips were even then notorious for leaving in their wake whole staffs of disgraced officials who had in some manner failed to live up to his high expectations. All too aware of this, Pergen now looked frantically for some tangible accomplishments that might be brought to Joseph's attention before he arrived on his doorstep, to counteract the unfavorable impression that he was bound to come away with otherwise. There was not much to show him, and a cursory inspection might miss that little altogether. Pergen dwelt in some detail on his ongoing efforts to confiscate at least a part of the huge landholdings of the bishop of Cracow—an arch reactionary and a notorious enemy of Austria—and to distribute this among prelates friendly to the monarchy. But so far this project was only in the planning stages; he had not yet succeeded in uncovering a mechanism to accomplish this within the bounds of legality.[36]

Pergen was able to report with considerable pride that the Galician postal service had been completely overhauled, and the mail now arrived with the same punctuality that people in the rest of the monarchy had come to expect. And, he announced, he was at the point of implementing the instructions he had been given concerning the Jews. Within the month he would be introducing an edict requiring all Jews to secure government permission before they could marry, and all Jewish beggars would presently be deported to rump Poland.[37] All this was of course very thin beer in comparison to the major policies that Pergen had failed to implement, neglected, or flatly contravened, and one may reasonably assume that he breathed a huge sigh of relief when Joseph let it be known in April that he would confine his inspection trip to Hungary and Transylvania, on which he actually set out in May in the company of his friends, Counts Pellegrini and Nostiz.[38]

Pergen's respite, however, turned out to be extremely brief. By mid-June Joseph and his small retinue were in Kaschau, and the emperor was less than edified by what he had seen. Finding himself so close to the Galician border, he decided that at least he would not pass up this opportunity to look over his new province. Since Maria Theresa had expressed certain reservations earlier in the year when he had expressed the desire to travel to Galicia, saying, not unreasonably, that such a visit would be premature, and that the new administration had to be given sufficient time to take hold, Joseph now let it be known that the purpose of his visit was merely to reassure himself that the border defenses were in a state of satisfactory readiness. To underline the military nature of the journey, he ordered Field Marshal Laudon to accompany him.[39] It hardly needs to be said that, once in Galicia, Joseph did not confine himself to looking at military installations. Nor, obviously, had he ever intended to, since he arrived bearing a document encompassing 154 separate questions dealing with the civilian administration, to which he wanted Pergen's answers.[40]

As was only to be expected on such an occasion, all persons with any kind of grievance now availed themselves of the unique opportunity to present their complaints directly to the emperor. The lamentations a number of prominent Poles now engaged in could be dismissed as the special pleading of interested parties. These people had suffered losses of power, influence, or money, not necessarily as the direct result of what Pergen had done, or failed to do, but rather because the Austrian government made greater demands on its subjects than the weak Polish Monarchy had done. On the whole, Joseph seems to have taken these considerations into account. Far more damning for Pergen were the numerous complaints registered by his own staff. Foremost were those advanced by Hofrat Kozian, who had been in charge of organizing the local administration at the *Kreis* level. He charged that, although Pergen had dispatched lengthy reports to Vienna, describing in great detail everything he intended to accomplish, in fact nothing had been done. Nor was this exclusively the consequence of various difficulties that had been encountered. The evil lay, rather, in the governor's work habits. He consented to deal with official business only between nine and twelve in the morning; his afternoons as well as his evenings were given over entirely to the pursuit of various pleasures.[41]

While this last accusation may have come as quite a surprise to Joseph, who was aware of Pergen's not undeserved reputation of having been addicted to work in his previous posts, he was all too willing to believe it. In the report he sent off to Maria Theresa, he found very little good to say about Pergen's performance of his duties.[42] This lengthy document opened with the rueful observation that, apart from some preliminary steps taken to establish a new high court, not a single one of their intentions that had been relayed to Pergen had even begun to be realized, although the province had now been in Austrian hands for an entire year. Worse, he had found it impossible to elicit exact information about anything from anyone. Everyone seemed to be groping in the dark. This was the case in political affairs, for which Pergen was responsible, as well as in militaria which were subject to Hadik. The emperor informed his mother that he had seen no alternative but to inform Kaunitz about the true state of affairs, impressing on the chancellor the absolute necessity of implementing the desired changes at the earliest possible moment.

The most crucial unresolved questions, in Joseph's eyes, were the following:

a) Should the Galician nobility, which had not been organized in a corporate body of its own, but had always attended the meetings of the

Polish Diet, now be gathered into an estate, like the nobles in the hereditary provinces?

b) Should the Polish nobles who, like their Russian neighbors, had no titles be assigned these, and would such titles be granted the *Inkolat* (equivalency) in the rest of the monarchy?

c) What steps might be taken immediately to reform the local clergy, which was as ignorant as it was influential with the people?

d) What practical steps might be taken to increase the amount of revenue generated by the province? At the very least, the land tax would have to yield a quarter more than it was presently bringing in.

e) Should local governmental agencies, since these would be established little by little, continue to report to the *Staatskanzlei,* or would it not be more efficient to put them directly under the various concerned ministries in Vienna?

The only even remotely positive thing that Joseph found to say about Pergen was that it had been obvious to him that the majority of the individuals who had been sent to him from Vienna lacked all administrative talent. The rest were totally useless because of their reluctance to engage in honest work (an obvious allusion to the carpetbaggers with whom Maria Theresa had saddled Pergen). Things would go far better if the whole crew were to be recalled.[43] There was another indication that the emperor was willing to accept mitigating circumstances for Pergen's failure to carry out his instructions in an aside he made, to the effect that Pergen had been working under the considerable handicap of not ever being able to count on clear instructions from Vienna (an indirect criticism of Kaunitz). But the overall tone of the report hardly augured well for Pergen. Joseph asked Maria Theresa pointedly if it was her intention to keep Pergen at his post. If so, he had better be informed that he had found a position with lifetime tenure; there was so much that needed to be done in Galicia that, at Pergen's present pace, decades would not suffice to complete the work. If Her Majesty were to seek his advice, however, he would suggest that Hadik, who in any case was too old for a field command, should be appointed chancellor of both Galicia and Transylvania, and that this combined office should be removed entirely from the control of the *Staatskanzlei.* As for Pergen, one could give him the choice of staying on as governor under Hadik, or of requesting a transfer to another post. In the former case, it would not be an unreasonable expectation that he would perform his duties in a more satisfactory manner, working, as he would be, under the direction of another man. Such an arrangement would have the further advantage of benefitting from Pergen's undeniable talent for making himself popular among the local *Honoratioren* (elite). This would unquestionably facilitate Hadik's task by eliminating a good deal of the built-in opposition to change, which was so great an obstacle to good government.[44]

In the wake of Joseph's visit, Pergen found himself face to face with a virtual mutiny on the part of his subordinates. Half a dozen of his *Gubernialräte,* the chief administrative officers in the districts, took the unusual step of going over his head with a complaint addressed to Kaunitz. The gravamina of this document were, first, that Pergen refused ever to convene a plenum of his subordinates, each of them being forced to work in isolation without any notion of what the others might be up to; second, that he systematically ignored whatever advice they gave him; third, that he would not spend any time with them in discussing the proposals they submitted to him, but at the same time insisted that even the most insignificant document coming out of their respective offices be submitted to him for his approval; fourth that whenever they had important questions about how to proceed in a given matter, he refused an answer, or, at best, took such an interminable time in giving one that the issue had long since resolved itself by the time they received it; and finally, that he would never pass on to them important information that he received from Vienna, including even the text of imperial rescripts.[45]

These complaints, when combined with the impressions Joseph had gained during his tour of inspection, were enough to settle the matter. The emperor was now determined that Pergen would have to go. At that point, though, the question became entangled in the twisted strands of Viennese policy-making. Joseph had in mind the creation of a separate ministerial department for Galicia, which would result in taking the provincial administration out of Kaunitz's hands. The latter put on a display of calculated indifference, telling Maria Theresa that he was, even without having to worry about Galicia, badly overworked, his health could not hold up under the strain very much longer. But the empress knew better, correctly discerning that Kaunitz was deeply hurt, as Joseph's tactless insistence that Galicia was being misgoverned from top to bottom struck out not only at Pergen but at him as well. Maria Theresa, concerned also that the familiar storm signals of references to his health were a prelude to new threats of Kaunitz's resignation, did all in her power to postpone a decision. After all, it was always possible that Joseph's attention would be diverted elsewhere, as had frequently happened before, and then, by the time he concerned himself about Galicia again, he might well not remember that his advice had been swept under the rug.

As a result, Pergen was left in his post for another six months. The empress's hand was finally forced when she received an anonymous denunciation (as it later turned out, from the hand of a prominent Jewish merchant) citing chapter and verse about how Pergen was consistently meting out favorable treatment to various Polish aristocrats in disputes over crown lands in their possession.[46] Hearing of the matter, Joseph returned to the attack, and in these circumstances Maria Theresa felt that she could no longer oppose herself to his wishes. In December 1773, she agreed to the formation of a special Galician chancery under Count Wrbna, whom Joseph had had in mind for such a position all along. And as Joseph had also been urging, Hadik was named as Pergen's replacement.[47]

What emerges only from the letters exchanged between mother and son about these changes in personnel is that Pergen had originally been intended for a position very like that which Wrbna would now occupy, and had instead been sent to Galicia as governor only because he himself had insisted that he could not possibly decide what needed to be done without being there.[48] Ironically, Joseph was to be even more dissatisfied with his own solution for Galicia than he was with what Kaunitz and Pergen had been able to accomplish. By 1776 he was complaining that Wrbna, whom he had repeatedly described as being both hard-working and conscious of what he wanted to accomplish when he was proposing him as Galician chancellor, was hopelessly disorganized as well as irredeemably lazy.[49] Perhaps there was something about the Galician political climate that defeated the best efforts of even the ablest of Austrian administrators.

At any rate, in January 1774 Pergen was relieved of all his duties and recalled to Vienna. When the news became known, a committee composed of the most prominent members of the nobility, as well as of various important merchants, was formed to organize a gala dinner in honor of the departing governor. During the festivities the committee handed over to Pergen a farewell gift of no less than 6,000 gold ducats (24,000 florins), a truly princely sum.[50] The generosity of this present caused considerable astonishment in Vienna. Instead of asking herself why the Poles, generally conceded to be an impoverished nation, should have been so openhanded toward Pergen, Maria Theresa merely concluded that she had made a mistake. If, as it now turned out, Pergen had really been so popular a governor, she must have maligned him by giving in to Joseph's insistent urgings for his dismissal. In consequence, to console him for the loss of his post, she granted him an additional 6,000 ducats from her private purse and let him know that a suitable job would be found for him as soon as possible.[51] As a result of all this,

Pergen came home with the equivalent of nearly three years' salary in his pocket. As he was still drawing the pay of a minister of state, and would be returning to his old job in the provincial administration, he could well afford to wait for the empress to make good on her promise.

NOTES

1. For the background of the first partition, see A. Beer, *Die erste Theilung Polens*, 3 vols. (Vienna), as well as the more recent but not always reliable G. Kaplan, *The First Partition of Poland* (New York); also Arneth, *Maria Theresia*, VIII, 383 ff.

2. Arneth, *Maria Theresia*, X, 76–77.

3. *Ibid.*, VIII, 416–17; Walter, *Zentral-Verwaltung*, II/1/1, 474; cf. Binder to Maria Theresa, 11 September 1772, S.A., Staatskanzlei, Vorträge (hereafter SK.V.), 109. Maria Theresa relied so heavily on Kaunitz's opinions that she solicited his comments on the proper size and shape of the oriental fish basins being put in at Schönbrunn: *"Dans les petites choses comme dans les grandes je n'ai pas de tranquilité que quand j'ai votre opinion."* Arneth, *Maria Theresia*, X, 752.

4. Arneth, *Maria Theresia*, X, 77. The lack of effective preparation for the occupation of Galicia was best brought out by the circumstance that the Austrian military command was reduced to begging for practically all the supplies needed for the operation from the commanders of various depots in Upper Silesia. Cf. Seilern to Kaunitz, 8 May 1772, S.A., SK.V. 109.

5. Kaunitz to Maria Theresa, 17 May 1772, S.A., SK.V. 109.

6. Arneth, *Maria Theresia*, X, 77.

7. Pergen to Kaunitz, 30 April 1772, V.A., Hofkanzlei, Galizien (hereafter H.G.), II/A/6.

8. *Ibid.*

9. *Ibid.*

10. *Ibid.*

11. *Ibid.,* The census of 1773 registered 224,981 Jewish inhabitants in Galicia. Three years later this number had dropped to 144,200, but one may safely assume that the voluntary, if illegal, movement of the Galician Jews to other parts of the monarchy had more to do with this reduction than did Theresian policy. A further caveat is that, for tax reasons, the Galician Jews profited by underreporting the size of their families, so that their total numbers may well have been higher. Cf. W. Häusler, *Das galizische Judentum in der Habsburger Monarchie* (Munich, 1979), 18. Joseph concurred with his mother on the question of the wearing of national costumes, ordaining that it was to be prohibited, except on national holidays. He also cautioned Pergen about being overly deferential to local custom. Cf. S. Schnür-Peplowski, *Z Przeslosci Galúczi 1772–1862* (Lwów, 1895), 6. For a detailed account of Jewish participation in the economic life of the region, see G. Hundert, "The implications of Jewish economic activities for Christian-Jewish relations in the Polish Commonwealth," in C. Abramsky et al., *The Jews in Poland* (Oxford, 1986).

12. Kaunitz to Maria Theresa, 12 October 1772, S.A., SK.V. 110. The only useful account of Pergen's activities in Galicia is to be found in H. Glassl, *Das österreichische Einrichtungswerk in Galizien, 1772–1790* (Wiesbaden, 1975), 59 ff., which goes into considerable detail but is less good on the larger context. M. Yurenko, *Galicia-Halychyna from Separation to Unity* (New York, 1967), is superficial and tendentious.

13. Kaunitz to Maria Theresa, 11 November 1772, S.A., SK.V. 110.

14. Pergen's reports for October 1772 seem no longer to be extant but are quoted at length in Kaunitz's *Vortrag* of 17 November 1772, S.A., SK.V. 110.

15. Kaunitz to Maria Theresa, 11 November 1772, S.A., SK.V. 110.

16. *Ibid.*

17. *Ibid.*

18. Joseph to Kaunitz, 13 November 1772, S.A., SK.V. 110.

19. Kaunitz to Maria Theresa, 18 November 1772, S.A., SK.V. 110.

20. Pergen to Kaunitz, 1 November 1772, S.A., SK.V. 110. The erpress's formulation read: *"um die Judenschaft in die gehörige Schranken zu bringen."*

21. Kaunitz to Maria Theresa, 18 November 1772, S.A., SK.V. 110. The fact that, in contrast to Joseph, Pergen made a serious effort to mediate between Austrian interests and the realities of Polish life is appreciated by present-day Polish historiography. Cf. S. Grodziski, *W kràlestwie Galicyi i Lodomerii* (Krakòw, 1976), 43 ff.

22. Glassl, *Einrichtungswerk*, 56–57.

23. *Ibid.*

24. *Ibid.*, 58–59.

25. Kaunitz to Maria Theresa, 18 November 1772, S.A., SK.V. 110.

26. Kaunitz to Joseph, 21 November 1772, S.A., Sk.V. 110.

27. Kaunitz to Maria Theresa, 20 November 1772, S.A., SK.V. 110. This is but one of many examples of Pergen's policies favoring the local nobility. Cumulatively, these must raise serious questions about Glassl's blanket judgment that his administration was a political disaster for the *szlachta*, depriving it of all its ancient privileges. Cf. Glassl, *Einrichtungswerk*, 61.

28. Kaunitz to Maria Theresa, 2 December 1772, S.A., SK.V. 110.

29. Pergen to Kaunitz, 18 December 1772, V.A., H.G. II/A/6.

30. Kaunitz to Maria Theresa, 29 January, 12 and 18 February 1773, S.A., SK.V. 111.

31. Kaunitz to Maria Theresa, 2 January 1773, S.A., SK.V. 111.

32. Kaunitz to Maria Theresa, 21 February 1773, S.A., SK.V. 111.

33. Pergen to Kaunitz, 25 July 1773, V.A., H.G. II/A/6.

34. Pergen to Kaunitz, 25 January 1773, S.A., SK.V. 111. These various strictures, couched in language very similar to that which Pergen had used in advocating his educational reforms, developed a number of arguments which Joseph would later resort to in order to justify his attack on the Austrian religious establishment.

35. Kaunitz to Maria Theresa, 7 March 1773, S.A., SK.V. 111; cf. Glassl, *Einrichtungswerk*, 61.

36. Kaunitz to Maria Theresa, 12 March 1773, S.A., SK.V. 111. Kaunitz vetoed this suggestion because he rightly assumed that the bishop of Cracow would be supported by the large majority of Poles in the province.

37. Kaunitz to Maria Theresa, 21 March 1773, S.A., SK.V. 111.

38. Grassl, *Einrichtungswerk*, 69.

39. S.A., Hofreisen (hereafter HR.) V/1.

40. Glassl, *Einrichtungswerk*, 70.

41. *Ibid.*, 71.

42. Joseph to Maria Theresa, 9 August 1773, S.A., SK.V. 112.

43. *Ibid.*

44. *Ibid.* Glassl, *Einrichtungswerk*, 72, is mistaken in his assertion that Joseph criticizes Pergen only indirectly, by failing to give even the least praise to his performance as governor. The explicit criticisms contained in Joseph's report are not to be missed.

45. *Ibid.*

46. These allegations are recapitulated in Mathias Lipski to Kaunitz, 26 March 1776, V.A., H.G. II/A/6.

47. Walter, *Zentral-Verwaltung*, II/3, 296–97.

48. Arneth, *Maria Theresia*, VIII, 416–17.

49. Walter, *Zentral-Verwaltung*, II/3, 298–300. Joseph now decided to dissolve the Galician chancellery and to divide the administration of the province between the combined Austro-Bohemian chancellery and the ministry of finance. As might have been expected, this separation between the political and the financial affairs of the province did not prove to be a happy solution.

50. Glassl, *Einrichtungswerk*, 75.

51. *Ibid.*, 75–76.

5

The Making of a Police Force

P ERGEN'S RETURN TO Vienna was somewhat less than triumphant.
If he had expected to be put up at once for another high position, he
was to be badly disappointed. Nothing came his way for almost two
years. Perhaps nothing suitable turned up; or Maria Theresa, her promise notwithstanding, was unwilling to risk an argument with Joseph
over the employment of a man whom the emperor had evidently dismissed
as unreliable. So Pergen went back to being *Landesverweser*, representing
Trautson on various ceremonial occasions, far removed from the centers
of power. The only real business he found himself transacting during
this stage of his career arose whenever some nobleman, overcome by
feelings of nostalgia for a not so distant past, rose to his feet during a
meeting of the estates and called for the reintroduction of some point of
lost nobiliary privilege. Invariably, such demands would throw Pergen
into a tizzy. It was not so much that he was caught up in a conflict of
loyalties—however he may have felt about his own prerogatives, deep
down he had long since identified himself with the interests of the
state over those of his class—but rather that he hated having to
give offense. After all, however archaic in their political sentiments
these troublemakers might be, they were, as often as not, influential
and highly placed. They might find themselves in opposition to the
will of the monarch on a given issue, but on another day they might
be sitting at his right hand. And they all had notoriously long
memories.

Hofrat Greiner, whose responsibilities included shepherding the decisions of the *Staatsrat* through the estates, went so far as to complain to
the empress that nothing would ease his task so much as a little
courage on the part of Pergen. Every minor dispute, he wrote, left the
Landesverweser trembling like a leaf and moaning like a woman in

labor. One example will have to suffice. What appeared to be a relatively straightforward matter, the introduction of a tax on alcoholic beverages—which had already proven successful in Bohemia—was bogged down for over a year in the Lower Austrian estates, principally because Pergen did not dare ride roughshod over the opposition put up by several abbots, all of them members of prominent noble families.[1]

At long last, in October 1775, Trautson, whose health had been failing for some time, asked to be relieved of his duties.[2] As was only to be expected, this news set off a scramble among a number of would-be successors to his position, so that Pergen's elevation was anything but a foregone conclusion. Foremost among the candidates was Count Sigmund Khevenhüller-Metsch, whose father, as Maria Theresa's master of ceremonial, had every opportunity to approach the empress on personal matters. The elder Khevenhüller did not fail to make strong representations on behalf of his son, but, after thinking the business over, Maria Theresa decided that, as Pergen had been told that he would replace Trautson when he had accepted his present post, it would be extremely awkward to deny him the succession now.[3]

Thus on 12 November 1775, Pergen was named *Landmarschall*, with the understanding that he would be allowed to retain the designation of minister of state, but in an honorary capacity only. It need hardly be added that there now ensued the by now traditional tug-of-war over his salary. As Trautson's assistant, he had been drawing his old minister of state's salary of 12,000 florins, supplemented of course by his pension of 6,000 florins. Now the pay of a provincial governor was fixed at 10,000 florins, so that it appeared his promotion would in effect cost him 2,000 florins yearly. Pergen protested piteously, and Maria Theresa saw the justice of his case. Still, to give him the increase he desired would lead to similar demands by all the other provincial governors, something that the empress plainly wished to avoid. Therefore, to compensate Pergen for the financial loss he would be accepting, she doubled his pension, so that altogether he would now be drawing 22,000 florins.[4] From Pergen's perspective this solution had everything to recommend it, since he would be taking his pension with him wherever he went, whereas a highly inflated salary might not be matched in his next post.

Pergen was formally installed in his new position on 21 November, but this was anything but a happy occasion for him. Most of the heads of the great noble families, who had made no secret of their opposition to the empress's choice, chose to stay away from the ceremony. It can be safely assumed that many of them held grudges against Pergen related to his equivocal conduct in matters that had come before the estates; all of them, without question, were envious of the unequaled financial generosity with which he had been treated.[5] But as they could not well afford to make these sentiments public, they found a more accept-able explanation for their conduct: Pergen, they alleged, whose reputa-tion as an administrator was anything but impeccable, would become the first governor of the province in all of its history who was not a member of the old, distinguished *Herrenstand.* Indeed, his great-grandfather had been nothing but a court physician — a very able one to be sure (he had been ennobled for his outstanding services), but a commoner nevertheless.[6]

Nor would Pergen have been overjoyed, had he learned of Joseph's reaction to the more than generous treatment he had received from Maria Theresa. On the day the heads of the various ministries were to report to him in his capacity of co-regent, the emperor asked Count Kollowrat, the president of the *Hofkammer* — the office responsible for all disbursements — what Pergen's income would be. Upon being told, Joseph then asked how this figure compared to what various other top civil servants were getting. When Kollowrat answered that Pergen would be receiving one-and-a-half times the compensation of the next highest paid minister, with the sole exception of Kaunitz, Joseph commented that it was a good thing indeed that he who had the least to do was to get the most. Not satisfied with this sarcasm, the emperor inquired if it were true, as had come to his attention lately, that Pergen had been granted the incredible gift of 24,000 florins on his return from Galicia. As Kollowrat, greatly embarassed, was trying to compose an answer, Maria Theresa interrupted him, saying that, although this was perfectly true, there had been entirely reasonable grounds for her generosity: Pergen had owned no place that he could really call his own; he had been forced to live in rented quarters in Vienna, surely a disgrace for someone occupying the second highest post in the provincial administration. The money had enabled him to buy an estate in Pottenbrunn that was compatible with his high rank. Joseph's rejoinder was that one certainly ought to give the widest possible publicity to Her Majesty's intention to make such large gifts of money to persons desir-ing to purchase estates; he did not doubt that a number of candidates for such largesse might come forward in fairly quick order.[7]

But even the empress's proverbial generosity had its limits. It now emerged that Trautson, as an adjunct to his duties as governor, had received the title of Lower Austrian steward. This was an unsalaried dignity, but with it went a house in the Herrengasse in Vienna's inner city, a wing of which had actually been occupied by Pergen before he had gone off to Galicia. Maria Theresa now decided to bestow this dignity not upon Pergen but rather upon the senior Khevenhüller-

Metsch. As a result, Pergen would not have the use of the house, which would have provided him with more spacious town accommodations than those he currently occupied.[8] Basing his actions on this circumstance, Pergen now petitioned the empress once more: as governor he would have far greater representational duties than before; he would be forced to maintain a much more lavish house. As Her Majesty had been so gracious to allow him to retain the title of Minister of state, would she now grant him the salary that had gone with it as well? Apparently Maria Theresa had a bad conscience about the town house, as she now, *mirabile dictu,* informed Kollowrat that, at least for the present, Pergen's old salary was to be continued.[9] At the rate he was going, Pergen alone would soon be siphoning off a major portion of the monarchy's budget.

Joseph's remark that Pergen would not find his new duties overly burdensome was accurate enough, so far as the traditional functions of a provincial governor went. What it overlooked was Pergen's talent—latent in Galicia, but by no means dead—for generating make-work projects whose main purpose was to enhance the importance of whatever position he was occupying. Nor had Pergen neglected to cultivate the network of old friends who had served as his informants in the old Mainz days, so that he was very well informed about what went on at court. It could hardly have escaped his notice that, as Maria Theresa felt the advance of old age, her determination to limit Joseph's influence over questions of internal policy was waning. Joseph's powers were clearly increasing from day to day, and an ambitious public servant would do well to keep in his good graces.[10]

Demonstrating his potential usefulness to the emperor manifestly would be anything but easy for Pergen, given not only the relative distance of his position from the centers of power but also Joseph's unflattering opinion of his abilities. Casting about desperately for some means of winning Joseph over, Pergen eventually hit upon a useful if not precisely original stratagem: everyone was aware that Joseph had great plans for reforming the church, once his mother's protective hand was no longer extended over it. For many years Joseph had been urging Maria Theresa to do something about the baroque length and complexity of divine services in their dominions. Not only did these services habitually extend beyond the limits of tolerance of even the most devout worshippers, but also they lacked the barest rudiments of uniformity. The liturgy varied from church to church, depending on the whims of the officiating priest; Joseph, however, felt that when one went to church one should know what to expect. Pergen, drawing upon his familiarity with the Protestant service, worked out a standardized order of worship that was simplified, shortened, and above all uniform.

Sending this to Joseph, he suggested that it would be a relatively simple matter for him to impose it in all churches of Vienna and Lower Austria. The emperor, favorably impressed, ordered the archiepiscopal authorities to implement these changes at once.[11]

In this manner Pergen succeeded at the very least in mitigating the highly unfavorable opinion that Joseph had formed of him; but to convince the emperor that he was a man who deserved to be plucked from the wilderness of provincial government was quite another matter. This feat would require considerably more than submitting a plan that Joseph liked because it corresponded to his views. Pergen knew this, and the easiest thing in the world for him would have been to imitate all but a very few of his predecessors and treat his position as a sinecure that allowed him to participate in the social life of the capital and court. He certainly was being paid enough to cut a very handsome figure there. His duties, apart from requiring him to preside over the rare meetings of the diet, involved only taking the chair one afternoon a week when the diet's steering committee met to discuss whatever business had come before it, which was generally very little. Here, surely, was the ideal post for a man looking for an honorable and lucrative retirement. But retirement was the last thing on Pergen's mind. Not yet fifty, he was deeply convinced that his lack of success in public life had resulted entirely from various unfortunate circumstances. It never once occurred to him to question his own abilities. As he saw things, it was only a matter of finding the right vehicle for his talents; once he had discovered it, he firmly believed, he would rise to the top.

What Pergen eventually hit upon, which, in a relatively short time, would make him indispensable, had been under his nose all along. One of the responsibilities of his new office, a responsibility that had albeit been neglected by his predecessors, was to oversee the bodies in charge of maintaining law and order in both the province and the capital city. The provincial governors had not made much of this, not so much out of laziness (although in a number of cases that was undoubtedly a contributing factor), but rather because it never seemed to be a matter of great urgency. Vienna, whose population then hovered around two hundred thousand, although a considerable urban agglomeration by the standards of the time, lagged far behind such genuine metropolises as London and Paris, with populations well in excess of half a million. Moreover, a substantial proportion of Vienna's inhabitants consisted of servants in noble households whose heads were both willing and able to enforce discipline among the *Gesinde.* There was not as yet much of a wealthy bourgeoisie, the class that, par excellence, was rich enough to require protection but not sufficiently powerful to see to this by itself.

Thus there had been no great impetus toward the establishment of an effective constabulary such as already existed in the French and English capitals.

In the countryside law enforcement mainly continued to be the responsibility of the estates. In practice, this meant that a general tax on the nobility paid for what was essentially a remnant of the old feudal levy. This was commanded by the more important nobles of the districts, who were careful to protect their own interests—but were not always as scrupulous about safeguarding those of others.

What Pergen now found himself in charge of as *Landmarschall* was the socalled *Rumor-, Tag- und Nachtwache,* founded in 1646 to replace the even more archaic *Stadtguardia.* This was a subsidiary organ of the municipal court, which in turn was responsible to the provincial government. Because this force had never functioned reliably, an attempt had been made in 1749, as part of the general Haugwitzian reform, to improve upon the situation. This resulted in a veritable masterpiece of Austro-bureaucracy in that it combined the maximum imaginable concentration of administrative agencies with the least possible actual substance. An impressively titled *Polizei-Hofkommission* would now report directly to the central government. This commission would work together with the provincial government, cooperating with the even more grandly named *Kommission für Sicherheits-, Armen-, Verpflegs- und Schubsachen.* Yet a third body, the *Mittelstelle,* would act as liaison between these two commissions. But, although all of these agencies were duly established and staffed, no one ever thought to create an actual police force for them to supervise. When this oversight was at last noticed (in 1753), a new administrative organ, the *Unterkommission aus der Wiener Bürgerschaft,* was founded, which in fact proceeded to take the unusual step of putting together a flesh-and-blood force. However, due to monetary constraints, this was limited to 188 men, who, spread out over the six administrative districts of the capital, were unable to improve the safety of the Viennese burghers to a noticeable degree.

This modest constabulary, which under the best of circumstances could barely keep up with its duty of policing the capital, was hopelessly overburdened at the outset, when Maria Theresa decided it should also be required to suppress mendicancy. The police were to round up the numerous beggars who infested the streets of Vienna, transport them to specially created *Armen- und Wohlfahrtsanstalten* (detention centers), and exercise a supervisory function over these, making sure that the detainees performed an acceptable amount of useful labor. As if that were not enough, the police were additionally responsible for the *Meldepflicht*—the registration of all strangers in the capital—making sure that they reported their arrivals and departures, but also keeping them under close surveillance lest they engage in activities harmful to the state or to religion. Finally, the empress ordered that the police be made responsible for carrying out the decrees of the *Sitten- und Keuschheitskommission,* which she had founded in 1751 to suppress prostitution and general immorality. In these circumstances it should come as no surprise that the police, who in any case were awarded only the most miserly of stipends, chronically neglected all of their duties, and that, if folk tradition is to be trusted, its members could be encountered far more often drinking beer in Vienna's numerous taverns than on the streets.[12]

Another attempt to improve the situation was made in 1767 when the *Staatsrat* considered an anonymous proposal to establish a central police directory for the whole of Vienna. This, however, was blocked by the *Hofkanzlei,* whose more conservative membership was unwilling to approve a proposal that, in effect, would have made the capital into an administrative unit separate from the rest of the province, and consequently no longer even marginally subject to the authority of the estates. Thereupon Maria Theresa, convinced that reform was imperative, instructed Justi and Sonnenfels to produce an alternate plan. They introduced a concept so vast and so utterly unworkable that we must now devote some space to explain what they actually had in mind.

By the mid-eighteenth century, the notion that the state was directly responsible for monitoring the behavior of its subjects was already well-established—the whole idea of royal absolutism would have been unthinkable without this—but the modern concept of a police force, charged specifically with the prevention of crime, while it had undoubtedly emerged, was still rather nebulous. The term police was already in use, and *Polizeiwissenschaft* was even being taught in various universities (Sonnenfels lectured on the subject in Vienna), but this had a much broader meaning than it would to us. Functions such as the enforcement of a variety of economic controls; the provision of basic social services such as hospital care; the provisioning of the populace in times of scarcity; and censorship of press, theater, and books were all subsumed under it. These responsibilities were so far-reaching and diffuse that, in practice, they exceeded the competence of any one agency. It is by no means clear that a body capable of administering all of these areas could ever have existed; at the very least, its personnel would have had to be numbered in the tens of thousands. The inevitable consequence of this great disparity between the ideal and the possible was that all notions of policing society in a more effective way remained largely on paper, and that police work, insofar as it was accomplished at all, continued to be done in the old way.[13]

In the event, what Justi and Sonnenfels now submitted was an even more ambitious plan for extending police control to a whole gamut of public activities. Since it was by then generally recognized that something on this order could not be made to work, the plan was quickly shelved. The various regulatory activities with which its authors had intended to saddle the police were parceled out to a number of branches of the provisional government, and still another supervisory agency, the *Polizeiamt,* was created. Under this agency the number of police agents was increased to 250, but more important, it was empowered to employ an unspecified number of secret agents to assist it in its work by ferreting out any potentially dangerous activity on the part of the population, following the example of the notorious Parisian *mouches.*[14]

Still, the inadequacy of this force was so evident that, in 1771 and again in 1773, the *Hofkanzlei* submitted alarmist reports to the empress, arguing that, particularly in times of great economic hardship among the general populace, to neglect the all-important state function of protecting citizens' property constituted a false economy.[15] In the wake of these reports yet another reorganization of the urban police followed, which, like all its predecessors, remained largely on paper. There was, however, an important aspect of this latest attempt at reform which was to have a direct effect on Pergen. Once and for all, the Lower Austrian government had been made solely responsible for policing the capital. It was now to exercise a supervisory function over the formerly independent *Stadtgerichte* (municipal courts), which in turn oversaw the activities of the *Stadtguardia;* also over the *Magistrat* (mayor's court), which was responsible for enforcing various city ordinances and had its own executive personnel for this purpose; and finally over the *Grundwächter,* who combined the duties of a town crier with those of a public watchman. In addition, the governor would now appoint the director of the *Polizeiamt,* who would report directly to him.[16]

By the time that this latest round of changes was implemented, Pergen was provincial governor. He welcomed the reforms as an urgently necessary rationalisation of the police system, but insisted that they only represented a first step. Before any change at the administrative level could bear fruit, decisive changes would first have to be introduced below. What seemed to him critical was to alter the procedures of recruiting members of the force. Hereafter, policemen would have to be drawn from a different milieu than had up to then been the practice, as most of the agents he had inherited upon assuming his new post seemed to be ex-convicts of one sort or another. He recommended that a new force of at least three hundred men be recruited, consisting entirely of men of the highest moral character. Former prisoners were to be disqualified on principle. At least four new police stations were to be built in different quarters of the city, so that no citizen should have to travel too great a distance in search of aid. These proposals received Maria Theresa's *placet,* but the *Hofkanzlei,* for economic reasons, cut the number of the force back to the originally projected 250 men and vetoed the new police stations. Even this reduced program was deferred until 1776, when a further administrative reshuffle took place, with the city now being divided into a dozen districts, each with a supervisor responsible for police protection.[17] But these measures too remained largely unimplemented as both the central government, through the *Hofkanzlei,* and the provincial administration were each convinced that the costs of introducing these changes should be borne by the other.

In the short run, nothing came of Pergen's efforts to increase the size and improve the quality of the police force at his disposal. Nevertheless, the fruitless efforts he spent in trying to break through the wall of parsimony and indifference that surrounded the court, whenever there was a question of expending funds on some branch of provincial government, at least served to focus his attention on the subject. And— this had by now become a pronounced character trait—once he had expended large quantities of time and energy on a matter, it underwent a series of transformations until it emerged as an idée fixe, from which he was not to be separated except by main force.

As he immersed himself in the substance of police work, pursuing the subject for its own sake rather than considering it merely a useful device for extracting a little additional power and money from the court, he came to a conclusion that must have suggested itself irresistibly to any administrator with considerable practical experience. It seemed obvious to him that the everyday routines of police work, necessary though they were given the fairly rapid level of economic expansion, were also dull and grubby. They had as much chance of capturing the interest of the powerful and highly placed as, say, the details of their own digestive processes: a vital function, certainly, but not one they wished to discuss at any length. The aspect of police work that *was,* at least potentially, of considerable interest to the great, even to the sovereign, was what had become a specialty of the French police: spying on the population. It could, after all, be maintained with a good deal of plausibility that this kind of activity, in spite of its unsavory aspects, enabled the government to save the people from any number of grave dangers by taking timely preventive action. Pergen now proposed that, in imitation of the French example, he be empowered to employ a large number of clandestine agents to report on everything that was happening in Vienna. Curiously it was the conservative *Hofkanzlei* that objected, in part because it was known that in France the *mouches* cost the government horrendous sums, but also because such measures, in its view, were incompatible with *Bürgerliche Freiheit* (civic liberty).[18] For the moment Pergen had to abandon this idea, but, as we shall presently see, he did not forget it.

While there can be little doubt that Pergen was developing a fascination for police work in these years, on the basis of the available evidence, it is unknown if, and to what extent, he succeeded in converting Joseph to these tastes. His opportunities for accomplishing this would have been severely limited. In the last years of the co-regency, the emperor, while maintaining close contacts with the leading figures in the central administration, with practically all senior military commanders, with the more important court officials, and, to a lesser extent, with members of the *Reich* administration, seems to have taken very little interest in what the people who were governing his capital were up to.[19] Pergen, not without reason, felt that he had been banished to a wilderness from which there was no emerging.

How, then, did he succeed in drawing Joseph's attention to his schemes for vastly expanding the activities of the police? Mostly, it would seem, through pure good luck. What had consistently eluded him in his professional dealings with his sovereign fell into his lap in a purely social context. Joseph, after the death of his much beloved first wife, Isabella of Parma, had become something of a recluse. Insofar as was consonant with his duties, he avoided large official functions, preferring to spend his evenings in a small circle of ladies of the high aristocracy, conversing about literature and the arts, without—as he would have inevitably done in male company—talking shop. It may well be that he chose to entertain himself in this manner because these get-togethers provided him with an acceptable excuse for seeing as much as possible of Eleonora Liechstenstein, a lady whom he greatly admired, but who, unfortunately, was happily married to one of his generals. As the emperor could not see himself in the role of King David, these soirees would have provided the only means for him to be regularly in her company. Be that as it may, a permanent member of this *Damenkranz* was Countess Wilhelmine Thun, the best friend of Countess Pergen.

The Pergens and the Thuns frequently entertained one another. The Pergens specialized in arranging musicales featuring whatever new talent had been lately discovered in that age, which was just beginning to make a cult object of musical geniuses. Occasionally at Countess Wilhelmine's invitation, Joseph would be present at such an evening chez Pergen. Eventually finding the company congenial, he fell into the habit of dropping in for a chat when no performances were scheduled. These visits soon became so much a routine that the assembled company would not even interrupt its card games at his appearance. A chair would be drawn up for him and several ladies would gather around, engaging him in animated conversation.[20] Inevitably, Pergen himself would from time to time be present at his wife's soirees and on those occasions Joseph came to know him as a genial host and an always well-informed patron of music. This interest was no concession to his wife's tastes on Pergen's part; already in his bachelor days in Mainz he had taken a keen interest in music. He liked to tell the story of his having been instrumental in making little Wolfi Mozart's first German tour a success by giving Leopold Mozart introductions to various princely houses.[21]

But as Pergen soon found out, being on friendly terms with Joseph was one thing, becoming part of his political retinue quite another. As far as can be judged from the record, which is extremely sparse for these years, Pergen's activities as *Landmarschall* continued to engage only a small portion of his energies. While negative evidence can never be conclusive, Pergen, before 1773, had habitually generated enormous quantities of reports, memoranda, official letters, unsolicited critiques of other people's reports, as well as generalized musings about the great questions of the day, whether they concerned him directly or not. He would do so again after 1782. That practically no such documents survive from this decade is perhaps an indication that, for once in his life, he was not taking his responsibilities with full seriousness.[22]

On the one occasion when Pergen did emerge from the relative obscurity of the *Herrengasse* in these years, he cannot be said to have crowned himself with glory. Early in 1780, Maria Theresa, in view of the continuing financial crisis that, despite her best efforts to economize, showed no signs of abating, decided that the only way to avoid national bankruptcy would be to legislate new taxes. The question was, a tax on what? The traditional levies were already being collected at a rate that, in those less hardened times, was thought to be the very maximum people would put up with. At that point someone suggested that a tax on alcoholic beverages, which were consumed in great quantities in the monarchy, would raise a lot of money; furthermore, it would not have to be set very high, making up for its low rate in volume. In the *Staatsrat,* Greiner was instructed to work out a proposal acceptable to the various governments that would have to approve it. In his capacity of president of the combined Bohemian-Austrian chancery, Blümegen now appointed an ad hoc committee made up of Counts Kollowrat, Sinzendorf, and Pergen to draw up a feasability study in the matter. The work of this committee was conducted in such a way that Greiner was soon complaining to the empress that, although it was possible, with considerable skill, to get a soap bubble to float on the surface of a body of water, if one insisted on attaching two heavy weights to it (Sinzendorf and Pergen), it would inevitably sink to the bottom.[23] A little later Greiner was again wringing his hands over Pergen, "the prisoner of a thousand doubts," all of which he insisted on expressing, down to the last detail. If the governor could not bring himself to help matters along, could he not at least be persuaded to keep his doubts to himself? Otherwise the proposed new tax would never come out of committee.[24]

Indeed it would seem that Pergen, by then well into his fifties, had been undergoing something of a personality change. Even in his younger days he had rarely rushed into things blindly, preferring to take innumerable soundings before committing himself to a course of action. But this trait had now become so pronounced that it was all but pathological. The simplest explanation for this may well be that, having suffered Joseph's reproaches for what the emperor had perceived as his dilettantism in Galicia, Pergen was determined never again to give anyone cause for such a criticism. While this may have been a commendable attitude in an administrator, the practical consequence of this was that every public pronouncement or official report of Pergen's was so hedged in by qualifications, lists of hypothetical objections, general asides, and endless repetitions as to make it sheer torture for those who heard or read it. It seems as if Pergen was now determined that, no matter what might later go wrong with some proposal about which he had been consulted, he would be able to say that he had foreseen the problem well ahead of time.

Pergen's chance for promotion seemed at last to have come in 1780, when the post of governor of the Austrian Netherlands became vacant. Maria Theresa intended to fill it by appointing her daughter, Marie Christine, and her son-in-law, Duke Albert of Sachsen-Teschen, as joint *Stadthalter;* but since they would not be able to assume their new duties for at least half a year, an interim appointment would have to be made. It was generally supposed that the royal pair would prove more decorative than useful, therefore whoever was appointed to the temporary post would likely stay on as governor in all but name. Memory tends to be selective, and what the empress remembered at this point was not so much that Pergen's mission to Galicia had proven a failure, but rather that she had chosen to give him a rich reward upon his return. Hence, she informed him that she had decided to give him the Netherlands appointment. Unfortunately for Pergen, Joseph's recollection was more accurate and, as a result of his objection, Prince Georg Adam Starhemberg was appointed instead.[25]

When Maria Theresa died at the end of November 1780, after forty years on the throne, it was clear to everyone that there would now be major changes made. During the last five years or so of the co-regency, Joseph had increasingly been showing signs of impatience and frustration with the empress's adamant refusal to accept the innovations that he thought were necessary for the welfare of the monarchy. By the mid 1770s at the very latest, he had developed a very clear idea of what he wanted to accomplish and of the changes in internal administration this progress would require. Not on every occasion, but all too often, his mother had chosen to heed the advice of the conservatives around her and had turned aside his often impetuous demands for change. Upon her death the only real questions were what changes would have priority, and whom Joseph would pick to carry them out. There could be no doubt in the minds of the politically ambitious that the big rewards would go henceforth to those who succeeded in becoming identified in the emperor's mind with one or the other of his pet projects.

In this race Pergen's placement was anything but ideal. Joseph had never taken much of an interest in provincial government. The power of the estates had been substantially broken early in Maria Theresa's reign, so that there was no longer a real danger that the nobility as a class could put up successful opposition to government policy. As for the rest, Joseph was content to ignore the provincial administrations so long as these prevented the sort of internal breakdown that might hamper the activities of the central administration in a serious way. If that happened, the responsible officials were dismissed. Pergen of course knew all this. If he were to find a place among those whose careers would flourish in the new reign, it would be up to him to interest the emperor in some aspect of his domain.

It cannot be said with any degree of certainty whether, acting upon such reflections, Pergen set out deliberately to draw Joseph's attention to the police—the only area under him that offered at least some chance of interesting the emperor—or whether this was a purely serendipitous discovery of his. The documents, imperfectly preserved for the period in question, are silent. All that can be established definitely is that, in April 1782, there was yet another major reshuffling of the Lower Austrian administration, as the result of which what remained of the old estates was merged with the provincial government, Pergen assuming the direction of the combined apparatus with the new title of *Regierungspräsident*. As part of this reorganization, at Pergen's insistence a substantive rather than merely pro forma reorganization of the police took place. The basis of this was a long report of Pergen's, arguing that to bring about any kind of improvement in the work of the police, the narrow law-and-order aspects of police work would have to be separated from the broader concept of *Polizeiwissenschaft*. In addition, Pergen had maintained, the *Stadthauptmann* of Vienna, the official directly concerned with police matters, was so overburdened with other duties that it was totally unrealistic to expect him to exercise effective control over the police.

Joseph accepted Pergen's report and decreed that police work in the narrower sense of the term should become the responsibility of the *Polizei-Direktion* under Franz Anton von Beer. This office had been created some time earlier by Pergen, apparently in the hope of putting some order in all the administrative duplication surrounding the police. Indeed, it is almost certain that Pergen's 1782 report was taken almost verbatim from a proposal that von Beer had submitted to him, but this would hardly have been the first time a superior appropriated the work of his subordinate.[26]

In the spirit of this proposal, Pergen now attempted to define the spheres of responsibility of the various police agencies subject to him. The broader police functions, such as the supervision of a variety of norms, including the size and quality of loaves of bread offered for sale, maintenance of streets and country roads, the assignment of market booths to those who applied for them, the running of soup kitchens for the destitute, and the maintenance and repair of Sonnenfels' pride—Vienna's spanking new network of street lamps—remained within the province of the *Stadthauptmann*, who was to report to the municipal court, as before. Von Beer's office, aside from being in charge of the maintenance of public safety and the suppression of prostitution, was to concern itself with a variety of secret tasks—chiefly, the gathering of information about the conduct and opinions of public servants and other prominent persons. Of particular importance for the course of events later on was that von Beer would now report directly to Pergen, instead of, as had previously been the case, to the municipal court.[27] Actual police work was thus once and for all separated from the broader aspects of municipal administration. At the other end of the spectrum, Pergen also took care to seal off the police from any interference by other organs of the government, getting Joseph to agree that henceforth he would report to him directly on all police matters, without first having to submit his reports to the *Hofkanzlei*.[18]

What Pergen thus succeeded in creating was a seamless web. Hereafter, only the emperor would be in the position of disputing his actions. In effect, if not in name, he had established an independent ministry of police, which was limited in its powers only insofar as its area of

Very little about not. larger nol.
background of B's police system - only f was
THE MAKING OF A POLICE FORCE   129   *an attractive*
to JIT

competence did not extend beyond the capital and Lower Austria. But such an extension would soon follow.

None of this should be taken to imply that either Joseph or Pergen were, at that point, aware of the implications of what they had done. Pergen just may have been; almost certainly Joseph was not. In fact, he continued to take so little interest in police matters that Pergen was forced to be on the continual lookout for some way of reminding the emperor of what he was doing. To accomplish this task he hit upon an ingenious device. Having experienced its effects very directly and painfully while in Galicia, he had a lively awareness of Joseph's unquenchable appetite for information of all kinds. Knowing about everything in great detail was the main thing for him, so much so that at times he gave the impression of not caring one way or another if something was done about a given situation so long as all its minutest details were known. Banking upon this knowledge, Pergen dropped repeated hints to Joseph that an aspect of the Haugwitzian reform, the *Meldepflicht,* could easily yield much more information than it was doing. He proposed that the system be expanded to take in the whole of the monarchy. In that fashion the police would be able to keep track of all known criminal elements even when the capital had been made thoroughly uncongenial for them; and it would, under cover of this system, be easily possible to keep track of all foreigners and suspicious individuals without incurring the condemnation of such critical voices as were always being raised against similar measures in Paris.[29]

Elaborating upon a further proposal of von Beer's, Pergen, in November 1782, urged Joseph to consider a vastly enlarged realm of police activity, whose most important function, he all but literally said, would be to keep track of what virtually everyone in the monarchy was doing at any given time.[30] This was just the thing to appeal to Joseph, who was at that moment working out a system under which all civil servants were encouraged to spy upon one another and to turn in to him reports of their observations—the notorious *Conduitenlisten;* and who also was sending agents to attend Sunday masses in order that they might report to him what was being said in the *Predigerkritiken, précis of* the sermons.[31]

One of Pergen's innovations, full of implications for the future, was to create a wholly new identity for the prisoners under his jurisdiction. Hereafter they would be *Sträflinge,* no longer to be casually confined under loose supervision, idling away their time, as often as not seizing one of the many opportunities for escape. Instead, anyone condemned to a term of more than six months imprisonment would have his hair shorn and be dressed in prison uniform; moreover, all felons physically able to work were now to be employed in various public-works projects.[32]

Soon gangs of prisoners could be seen cleaning out stopped-up drainage canals in Vienna's *Prater*, or cleaning the city's streets with brooms and water.[33] But activity of this kind, although doubtless useful, did not strike Joseph in any way as appropriate punishment for serious crimes. Complaining that this was at best "light" work, which, in addition, the prison inmates were required to perform only in good weather, he insisted that Pergen devise more suitable activities for the social outcasts in his prisons.[34]

One of the emperor's suggestions was meant to accomplish this end as well as to relieve the perennial overcrowding, which soon came to be a chief characteristic of the main prisons. This worried Joseph, since it seemed to him undisputable that the more crowded a prison was the easier it would be for its inmates to escape. Would it not be possible, he wanted to know, to remove all felons convicted of lesser crimes, and thus presumably less dangerous individuals, from the prisons altogether? They could be employed in digging the new Danube-Theiss canal, which, as it traversed extensive areas of notoriously unsalubrious marshland, was claiming numerous lives among the workers employed on it. But Joseph did not overlook the possibility that unconfined prisoners would be even more likely to escape than when they had been kept behind bars. He demanded that if Pergen were to adopt this suggestion, all felons so employed must be kept in irons by day and chained by the neck to the decks of the barges in which they slept at night.[35] It should come as no surprise to anyone that these men, forced to perform the hardest of labor in these conditions, died like flies. It was of course paradoxical that, as a result of this imperial whim, men with light sentences were in effect often condemned to death, while the really serious criminals could at least expect to remain alive in prison. But as we shall see, this was not the only occasion on which this happened.

In part to prevent petty offenders from being swept up in such a massacre, Pergen now convinced Joseph that it was necessary to segregate these people from serious criminals. To this end he divided the main prison into two sections. The *Polizeihaus* would be used for the confinement of convicted felons. The *Arbeitshaus* would harbor the transient population of the capital's riffraff—drunks, petty miscreants, prostitutes, and those who had been repeatedly picked up by the police for lounging about in the streets, without being able to produce any evidence that they were pursuing any lawful trade or occupation in Vienna. These people were to be employed in various public-works projects in the city and its environs until they had thoroughly learned to adhere to a work ethic. Most of the inmates of the *Arbeitshaus*, as it turned out, were persons convicted of misdemeanors not by the courts but by the *Magistrat*, which could impose terms of imprisonment up to a year, but Pergen succeeded in publicizing his hopes for the *Arbeitshaus* as an instrument of social redemption in such glowing terms that numerous individuals had themselves voluntarily committcd there in the expectation that they would be taught a useful trade. Soon, however, it became all too evident that conditions in the *Arbeitshaus* corresponded closely enough to penal standards, but in no way met the expectations of those who hoped for social redemption. The chorus of complaint grew so loud that Joseph was moved to institute a commission of inquiry, under the presidency of Count Johann Buquoy, who had distinguished himself in reforming the system of relief to the poor.[36]

The Buquoy Commission eventually absolved Pergen of all charges of wrongdoing and maladministration. That in fact the blame for the experiment's dismal failure should be laid not entirely at Pergen's door but also at Joseph's can be deduced plainly from the minister's first-year report.[37] For a change, what was at fault in this instance was not the emperor's habitual parsimony, but its opposite. Determined that the experiment should succeed, Joseph had given orders that the inmates of the *Arbeitshaus*, for the most part employed as spinners, should be paid a stipend of six kreuzer a day, which was a little more than half of what similar work earned a man in the private sector. This was fair, as the inmates also were housed and fed at state expense. But, as Pergen pointed out, the system incorporated the worst of both worlds. Paying that kind of wage, his expenses were such that he was unable to turn a profit, as he had assured Joseph he would do; at the same time, the inmates, comparing their money wage to that of workmen on the outside, were sullen and resentful, and worked accordingly. Inordinate quantities of material were spoiled as a result, so that Pergen had no option but to dock the pay of those responsible, which in turn exacerbated the already awful work climate. Reflecting on all this, Pergen saw the solution of the problem not in the abandonment of the experiment, which so clearly was not working and in all probability could never be made to work, but in its expansion. He begged Joseph to allow him to round up every last one of Vienna's thousands of beggars and idlers and place them all in the *Arbeitshaus*. To be sure, such a step would make his financial problem utterly hopeless; he could never even dream of running the place at a profit, but it would be well worth it. The great social problem of *Müßiggang* (public idleness), which was the chief cause of crime in the capital, would have been solved once and for all. Joseph, however, seemed unwilling to push the experiment to these limits.

As for the *Polizeihaus*, Pergen was on more solid ground. It was with considerable pride that he was able to report that his measures had resulted in the all but hermetic isolation of the prisoners. While previously their meals had been brought in from the nearby taverns—a condition that had inevitably led to continual contacts between them and the delivery personnel, and thus to the massive smuggling of letters and other contraband in and out of the prison—he had now had a kitchen installed on the premises, thereby putting an end to these "intolerable" conditions.

Throughout all this, Joseph kept giving Pergen detailed advice on how better to run his prisons, and the minister, it goes without saying, treated every one of these for the most part hackneyed proposals as inspirations of the purest genius. But the emperor's interest in Pergen's work was by no means confined to the prison system. Having discovered the delights of modern policing, he proceeded to interfere in all of its many aspects. Through his considerable network of spies and informers he often learned of alleged transgressions of which the police were unaware. Thereupon he would hasten to inform Pergen of the facts, demanding instant action by the police. No charge was too petty to slip through the imperial nets. Thus Joseph wrote that he had learned that a certain Jewess named Neuhauser had come into possession of a silver bar of dubious origin. Joseph himself had organized a search that led to the seizure of the object in question, and Pergen was now to round up the woman's accomplices.[38] Pergen only too gladly fell in with the game and was soon outstripping Joseph in his ardor to turn up crimes on every street corner. In over three folio pages he informed the emperor that, in a series of four protracted hearings, over all of which he had personally presided, he had established without possibility of doubt that one Elizabeth Eberlein had offered a quantity of overripe beans for sale on the Neuer Markt. Instead of returning this document to Pergen with an indignant question about the minister confusing him with some under secretary of the *Magistrat*, Joseph noted his pleasure at Pergen's zeal in the margin.[39]

If this was a curious way for an emperor and his chief of police to occupy their time, these were at least relatively harmless pursuits; worse would come. Given Joseph's constant encouragement, not to say prodding, it is hardly astonishing that Pergen occasionally overshot the mark. In the autumn of 1784, Joseph promulgated a decree aimed at the numerous procurers who made their living off the swarm of prostitutes plying their trade in the capital. Having convinced himself that if procuring were to be punishable prostitution itself must clearly also be a crime, Pergen promptly ordered the police to arrest over five hundred Viennese prostitutes. An instant and clamorous outcry arose, not so much from the women in question, for they retained few illusions about what they might expect in this world, but rather from their customers, who suddenly found themselves deprived of their services. This was accompanied by various apocalyptic prophecies predicting that, once the safety valve of prostitution had been shut down, no respectable woman would be safe from attack on Vienna's streets. Not wishing to be thought responsible for such a catastrophe, and perhaps feeling a certain amount of sympathy for the members of a profession of whose services he was said to avail himself occasionally, Joseph ordered Pergen to release the prostitutes.[40]

Joseph's apparent willingness to distinguish between the activities of the madams and those of their girls, always difficult to enforce in practice, turned out to be short-lived. By 1785 he seems to have made up his mind that prostitution was a general social *Unwesen* (evil) that must be eradicated. He thereupon ordered the police, along with the forces of the *Magistrat* (who were, however, to be kept in the dark about the nature of the mission until the last possible moment), to mount a *razzia* upon all of Vienna's known brothels. All persons seized upon the premises were to be examined for venereal diseases and suitably treated if found to be infected. Everyone engaged in the trade in one fashion or another was then to be put under arrest and given the maximum term permissible under the *Magistrat's* jurisdiction, one year in jail. Lest Pergen be in any doubt about where to dispatch his men, Joseph supplied him with a complete list of all of the city's establishments.[41]

The suppression of the houses did not, as anyone not endowed with Joseph's almost childlike belief in the efficacy of decrees would have known, lead to the disappearance of prostitution from Vienna: the prostitutes, many of whom had escaped the *razzia* in spite of all precautions (the *Magistrat,* seemingly, having turned out not to be the only source of leaks in the administrative apparatus), simply took to the streets. Before long it had to be conceded that these new conditions made it significantly more difficult than before to control the spread of venereal disease. By 1787 the government was considering a proposal by an expert in these matters from the *Reich,* who advised that the most practical course would be to establish state-run bordellos in Vienna. Joseph's initial reaction was that it would be far cheaper just to put a roof over the whole city, but, after further consideration, he seems to have taken to the notion. Pergen, however, supported by his staff, objected that, whatever conditions might be in Germany, it would not be possible to run such establishments profitably in Vienna. The acquisitive instincts of the prostitutes were so strongly developed that, without violent methods quite unworthy of the state, it would never prove possible to separate them from a significant fraction of the money they took in.[42] Thus the girls remained on the streets, and every year or so, when Joseph once again complained that nothing was being done to suppress the evil, a few dozen would be rounded up and deported to whatever villages they had come from.[43]

From Pergen's point of view, the most important issue brought to light by these various misadventures was the continuing insistence on the part of the *Magistrat* to interfere in what he regarded to be exclusively police business. As early as 1782 von Beer had objected to instances of this intrusion, demanding that any investigation concerned with matters of security, either public or private, be handled exclusively by the police. In a sense, this was of course merely a continuation of von Beer's ongoing campaign to separate police activities from the more general housekeeping concerns of the urban administration—a question that had been settled in favor of the police in theory, but which kept reemerging in practice. Pergen supported von Beer insofar as he dared. He had to proceed with caution as Joseph was all too prone to develop sudden enthusiasms for questions that Pergen considered to be far beneath the dignity of a chief of police, much less an emperor; but in private, he hardly bothered to conceal his annoyance at having constantly to deal with what he dismissed contemptuously as *"Hurensachen."* Finally, in August 1783, the city administration was made solely responsible for overseeing the day-to-day routine of life, including, after much wrangling, the supervision of the capital's beggars and prostitutes.[44] However, as we have seen, this was at best a partial victory for Pergen's views, as Joseph would repeatedly insist that the police lend support to the *Magistrat* in dealing with these affairs.

Still, Pergen and von Beer were now free to concentrate their attention on what they deemed far more important matters. As they saw it, no institution of any sort could function, be it well or badly, in the absence of a healthy state. Thus it followed that, were the security of the latter to be threatened in any way, such a threat must take precedence over all other police concerns.[45]

Having defined the spheres of police activity to his satisfaction, Pergen dreamed of other worlds to conquer. He had succeeded in ridding himself of various responsibilities that he regarded as undesirable and had at least begun to convince Joseph of the necessity of expanding others that he viewed as crucial, but his mandate was still severely circumscribed. Ultimately, he derived his powers from his position as governor of Lower Austria, and in consequence he could exercise no control of any sort over the police in the rest of the monarchy; but it was precisely such a position to which he aspired. He began his campaign by urging Joseph to establish police forces, modeled on the one that he and von Beer had created in Vienna, in all of the provincial capitals. The operative part of this proposal was to be found in a codicil: the heads of these newly established police bureaus were to report not to the various provincial governors, as long-standing practice would have dictated, but directly to him. He justified this novel suggestion with the argument that the highest, most fundamental duty of the police, beyond even safeguarding the persons and property of His Majesty's subjects, was to protect the sacred person of the emperor himself. If the safety of the ruler were not guaranteed, the state itself might well crumble. Hence no obstacle of any sort must be put in the path of the police, who alone were capable of performing this most important of all conceivable roles.[46]

Had Joseph given way in all these particulars, Pergen would doubtless have ended in creating an organization with vast and unprecedented powers. But it may very well have struck Joseph that the sacred person of the ruler had been safe enough throughout the centuries in which, to all intents and purposes, there had been no police. Moreover, Joseph tended to react with nothing short of outrage whenever someone was incautious enough to attempt to convince him that he was threatened by some danger. It was almost as if the mere suggestion of such a possibility questioned his personal courage. Even more, he looked on such speculation as something that undermined the absolute primacy of his position: no one is rash enough to try to kill a god. More concretely, the *Hofkanzlei*, doubtless prodded by various provincial governors, all of whom regarded Pergen's proposed incursion into their domains as a monumental piece of effrontery, expressed the gravest reservations about his plan.[47]

Aware that he had stirred up a hornet's nest, Pergen now tried to retreat to safer ground. He attempted to justify his demand for a centralized police command with the technical argument that, being in charge of policing the capital, he was forced to deal with by far the greatest number of crimes in the whole of the monarchy. His task, difficult enough under ideal circumstances, was made all but impossible if a felon, discovering that the Viennese police were on his trail, merely needed to leave Pergen's jurisdiction in order to be virtually safe from arrest. After all, experience had taught that it was all but hopeless to expect that a criminal wanted by the police in Vienna would be picked up by the authorities in other provinces: the state of the police forces there was not even up to the primitive level that he had encountered upon first assuming his present office.[48]

Such arguments, aside from making Pergen few friends, availed him little. The *Hofkanzlei* dug in its heels, and its chief, Count Kollowrat, repeatedly appealed to Joseph in the name of all the provincial governors. The end result was, as so often before, a pallid compromise. Pergen would be responsible for directing and collating the activities of the *geheimer Dienst* (the secret police) throughout the monarchy, and the governors were not to interfere with the activities of this service in any way. In all other police matters, though, the chiefs of police, insofar as there were any, would report to the governors. And, as it turned out, when it came to creating effective police agencies in the provinces, Joseph decided to economize at the last moment. For the time being, these were to be instituted only in Prague and Brno, as a kind of experiment. If this were to prove successful, other agencies might eventually follow.[49]

The resulting situation was not devoid of an element of paradox. Pergen had aspired to become something very much like what, in later days, would be called a minister of the interior. Now he had to come to terms with the fact that his unlimited powers were confined to secret police matters. Not astonishly, he began to concentrate his interests increasingly in this area. In contrast Joseph, who had refused Pergen's request for full control over the police, continued to pester him with matters of police routine that seemed to interest him as much, if not more, than clandestine operations. Not before another four or five years had passed would Pergen succeed in winning over the emperor to his own view of the absolute primacy of his secret police.

NOTES

1. Arneth, *Maria Theresia,* X, 12–14.

2. H. Schlitter et al., eds., *Aus der Zeit Maria Theresias: Tagebuch des Fürsten Johann Josef Khevenhüller-Metsch,* 10 vols. (Vienna, 1907–72) (hereafter *Khevenhüller-Metsch*), VIII, 105. Although Pergen performed most of the official duties of Trautson's position, he carefully avoided representing him at purely ceremonial occasions so as not to give the impression that he had been appointed coadjutor.

3. *Khevenhüller-Metsch,* VIII, 113.

4. *Ibid.,* 117.

5. Apart from ambassadors in notoriously expensive posts such as Versailles and Madrid, only Kaunitz received a higher salary. H. C. Ehalt, *Ausdrucksformen absolutistischer Herrschaft* (Munich, 1980), 61–62.

6. *Ibid.* These objections coming from the great nobles were not merely invidious but were, in fact, based on incorrect information. The Pergens, although not members of the *Herrenstand* before the early eighteenth century, had been ennobled for some 250 years.

7. *Khevenhüller-Metsch,* VIII, 118.

8. *Ibid.,* 119.

9. *Ibid.,* 256–57.

10. Walter, *Zentral-Verwaltung,* II/1/1, 485.

11. Hock & Bidermann, *Staatsrath,* 513; H. Hollerweger, "Tendenzen der liturgischen Reformen unter Maria Theresia und Joseph II.," in E. Kovàcs, ed., *Katholische Aufklärung und Josephinismus* (Munich, 1979), 298.

12. J. Kallbrunner, "Die Wiener Polizei im Zeitalter Maria Theresias," in *Monatsblatt des Altertumsverein zu Wien,* XI, 237–39; cf. H. Conrad, *Deutsche Rechtsgeschichte,* 2 vols. (Wiesbaden, 1954), II, 257–60.

13. For the development of the concept of *Polizeywissenchaft* see M. Raeff, *The Well-Ordered Police State* (New Haven, 1983), 167, and Conrad, *Deutsche Rechtsgeschichte,* II, 257 ff. For Sonnenfels's contributions, see K.-H. Osterloh, *Joseph von Sonnenfels und die österreichische Reformbewegung im Zeitalter des aufgeklärten Absolutismus* (Lübeck & Hamburg, 1970); cf. L. Bodi, "Enlightened Despotism and Literature of Enlightenment," *German Life and Letters,* XXII (1968–69), 325; and E. Wangermann, "Deutscher Patriotismus und österreichischer Reformabsolutismus im Zeitalter Josephs II.," in H. Lutz & H. Rumpler, eds., *Österreich und die deutsche Frage im 19. und 20. Jahrhundert* (Munich, 1982), 63. F. Walter, "Die Organisierung der staatlichen Polizei unter Kaiser Joseph II.," in *Mitteilungen des Vereins für Geschichte der Stadt Wien,* VII (1927), and H. Benna, "Organisierung und Personalstand der Polizeihofstelle (1793–1848)," in *Mitteilungen des österreichischen Staatsarchivs,* VI (1953) (based on Benna's 1941 Vienna dissertation, "Die Polizeihofstelle") do not have much to say about the pre-Pergen period. As late as 1757, J. H. G. Justi, at work on his *Grundriß, der Polizeywissenschaft,* which would appear two years later, was urging Maria Theresa to create a "police agency" to oversee practically all state affairs outside of war and diplomacy. These sentiments were echoed by Sonnenfels, whose third edition of his own *Grundriß,* published in 1770, went almost as far.

14. Kallbrunner, "Wiener Polizei," 239–40.

15. V. Bibl, *Die Wiener Polizei: Eine kulturhistorische Studie* (Leipzig, 1927), 216.

16. *Ibid.,* 217.

17. *Ibid.,* 218–21.

18. *Ibid.,* 223.

19. K. Gutkas, "Der Kaiser und seine Mitarbeiter," in K. Gutkas, ed., *Österreich zur Zeit Kaiser Josephs II.* (Vienna, 1980).

20. D. E. Emerson, *Metternich and the Political Police* (The Hague, 1968), 9; E. Schenk, *Mozart and His Times* (New York, 1959), 43; Sir R. M. Keith, *Memoirs and Correspondence,* 2 vols. (London, 1849), II, 192–93; Wraxall, *Memoirs,* II, 249. According to Wraxall, the intellectual niveau of the Viennese ladies, practically all of whom had been educated in cloisters, was so abysmally low that Joseph found himself severely restricted in his search for intelligent female company. Thus he returned again and again to the few salons where this was to be found.

21. Schenk, *Mozart*, 55.

22. It is, of course, arguable that Pergen at this time was working on a lower level of the administration where documents were less likely to be preserved for the ages, but this does not seem to have been the case. The holdings of the Niederösterreichisches Landesarchiv for this period are considerable and include protocols of all meetings of the provincial government. These protocols contain summaries of the discussions and report of Pergen, with very few exceptions, merely that he occupied the chair. Even that was often not the case.

23. Arneth, *Maria Theresia*, X, 14–16.

24. *Ibid.*, 18. Pergen's doubts were not without foundation.

25. *Ibid.*, 713; H. Schlitter, *Die Regierung Josephs II. in den österreichischen Niederlanden* (Vienna, 1900), 11.

26. Bibl, *Wiener Polizei*, 225–26; Benna, "Polizeihofstelle," 291–93; Walter, "Organisierung," 4–5. In view of the opinions that Pergen would later hold on on this subject, it is of some importance to note that already in 1782 he argued that the performance of police duties in the narrower sense were bound to improve dramatically from ridding the police of responsibility for the larger sphere of governmental regulation. Pergen to Joseph, 3 December 1782, V.A., P.A., XVIII/A, 85. See also Joseph's resolution of 20 March 1782, V.A., N.P.

27. Walter, *Zentral-Verwaltung*, IV/1, 54.

28. *Ibid.*, 55.

29. Bibl, *Wiener Polizei*, 227–29. H. Oberhummer, *Die Wiener Polizei*, 2 vols. (Vienna, 1938), I, 49; Emerson, *Metternich*, 10.

30. Pergen's report is reproduced in Oberhummer, *Wiener Polizei*, II, 136–37.

31. Joseph needed little convincing from Pergen in this area. On his own initiative he ordered that all details of the police reorganization be kept rigorously secret, thus going a step further than Pergen had requested. Cf. Pergen to Joseph, 3 December 1782, V.A., P.A. III. It may be that, as Bibl, *Wiener Polizei*, 229, argues, Joseph and Pergen intended primarily to avoid giving alarm to the traditionally conservative Viennese populace by threatening their accustomed way of life. Nevertheless, the end result was to establish a pattern of secrecy, and ultimately to remove all control over the police from any level below that of the emperor himself.

32. Joseph's resolution, 10 August 1782, V.A., P.A. III.

33. Gameval to Joseph, 14 December 1782; Joseph to Pergen, 14 December 1782, V.A., P.A. III.

34. Joseph to Pergen, 22 January 1783, V.A., P.A. III.

35. Joseph to Pergen, 29 March 1783, V.A., P.A. III.

36. Bouquoy to Joseph, 23 September 1784, V.A., P.A. I, sect. V. One of Vienna's most acute observers of the social scene, Johann Friedel, commented openly on the disparity between appearance and reality in Pergen's efforts to solve the capital's unemployment problem in this manner. J. Friedel, *Freye Bemerkungen und Zweifel über das Armeninstitut in Wien* (Vienna, 1785).

37. Pergen to Joseph, 11 October 1784, V.A., P.A. I, sect. V.

38. Joseph to Pergen, 7 April 1783, V.A., P.A. IV.

39. Pergen to Joseph, 31 December 1784, V.A., P.A. IV.

40. Joseph to Pergen, 9 September 1784; Pergen to Joseph, 12 September 1784, V.A., P.A. IV.

41. Joseph to Pergen, 1 April 1785, V.A., P.A. IV. The houses in question were located at Naglergasse #157, 184; Lieben Frauen Stiege #398; Sieben Körbengasse #1095; Neugasse #432, 436; Neuwiess #125; Florianigasse #164; Kohlmarkt #170; Schottenbastei #1304; Tiefer Graben #321; Judenplatz #272; Franziskanerplatz #450; and Weihburggasse #938. It will be seen that, with few exceptions, the trade seems to have been concentrated in the inner city.

42. Von Beer to Pergen, 7 February 1787, V.A., P.A. VI. The author of this plan, one Theodor Reiser, suggested a large number of smaller houses with eight ladies in each. He calculated that on average each of them should earn 5,450 florins yearly. The expenses of the establishment, including fixed salaries for the principals, he projected at 42,378 florins. Thus each house would turn a miniscule yearly profit (224 florins), as well as producing a great deal of social advantage. Pergen and von Beer objected—not unreasonably—that these fanciful calculations completely disregarded the basic acquisitive instincts of prostitutes, a fact that would make nonsense of these closely reasoned accounts.

43. The last of these razzias in Joseph's lifetime occurred in February 1789. Cf. V.A., P.A. VI/B. Thereafter Joseph was presumably too ill to apply the kind of consistent pressure it took to get Pergen to proceed against the *milieu*.

44. Oberhummer, *Wiener Polizei*, I, 49–50; Walter, *Zentral-Verwaltung*, II/4, 55–56; Bibl, *Wiener Polizei*, 231–32.

45. Pergen formulated this proposition explicitly in 1785: *"Nur durch gut eingeleitete Polizeyanstalten kann die innere Ruhe, Sicherheit und Wohlfart des Staates gegründet werden."* Walter, *Zentral-Verwaltung*, II/4, 54.

46. Pergen to Joseph, 22 April 1784, V.A., P.A. III.

47. Walter, *Zentral-Verwaltung*, II/4, 55–56.

48. Pergen to Joseph, 22 July 1784, V.A., P.A. IV.

49. Walter, *Zentral-Verwaltung*, II/4, 56.

6

Joseph II, Pergen, and
the Secret Police

A T TIMES PERGEN must have been convinced that he was performing all the labors of Sisyphus. Joseph refused to take any interest in
the various jurisdictional disputes that kept cropping up between the
police and the *Magistrat* in spite of the various decisions on behalf of
the latter, which he had himself laid down. Instead, he regularly
deluged Pergen with orders, suggestions, demands for information, and
complaints about matters that the minister had long since believed
were no longer his responsibility. Finally in 1786, in the most submis-
sive language imaginable, but to those in the know not without a heavy
dose of irony, Pergen submitted a memorandum listing the thirty-one
areas he believed properly to be the concern of the police in the widest
sense.[1]

Evidently Pergen hoped to convince the emperor that no single man,
nor any one agency, could expect to keep abreast of all of these concerns.
He argued that, in practice, one of two courses would have to be followed.
Either the boundaries separating the areas of police responsibility from
the concerns of the *Magistrat* would have to be not only more sharply
drawn but observed as well; or, as he seems still to have aspired to,
his own powers would have to be considerably expanded, with a
corresponding increase in his staff. In this Pergen would be disappointed.
While refusing to give him anything like the financial support he
wanted (indeed the next years were to witness an endless series of
squabbles about finances), Joseph nevertheless expected Pergen to keep
on top of everything that took place in Vienna, and to report to him
about it in detail on the same day at the latest. The examples of this that
follow are not meant to demonstrate the development of any particular

pattern in Joseph's interest in these matters—such a pattern seems to have been largely absent—but rather to give some indication of what working for Joseph must have been like.

By no means were they all petty responsibilities with which Pergen was saddled in consequence of the emperor's refusal to let him specialize in security matters. Thus the police had their hands full in the terrible winter of 1784—when the Danube overflowed its banks and flooded considerable portions of Vienna—evacuating the inhabitants of the low-lying areas and finding temporary shelter for them in the suburbs. Pergen, who did yeoman labor organizing the rescue, reported to Joseph on all its details, remembering to reassure the emperor that the new quarters were in all cases *standesgemäß*, appropriate to the station of their occupants; and he claimed whatever credit he could for himself and for his men. At the same time he could not hold himself back from reporting that in his view such activities, while a necessary evil and probably inevitable in the circumstances, did not constitute a central element of police work. It is difficult to escape the impression that Pergen is arguing here that his men, while engaged in saving the lives of a by no means negligible portion of the capital's population, had been distracted from going about their real business.[2]

If natural catastrophes constituted for the minister of police an unwelcome interruption of his duties, it is easy to imagine how he must have felt about a much more persistent source of interference with his work, namely Joseph's nearly irrepressible tendency to interfere with the most trivial details of police business whenever this impinged on a particular hobbyhorse of his. One such imperial fixation was suicide. This struck him as the most unforgivable of sins (we must not forget how good a Catholic Joseph was); equally reprehensible, someone who took his own life cheated the state of years of service. Thus in February 1785, Joseph wrote Pergen a furious letter, telling him that he had recently been informed that a sixteen-year-old merchant's son named Bocchini had killed himself. He had reason to believe this act had not been committed in the grip of a sudden attack of melancholia, as the death certificate asserted (This formulation was simply conventional, making it possible for suicides to receive a Catholic burial.) Rather, it had been reported to him that young Bocchini, a young man of notoriously dissolute habits, having been turned down by his father when he had asked for money to support his vices, killed himself in protest. Pergen should look into the matter thoroughly, make sure that the guilty were punished (although it was anything but clear what laws, if any, had been violated); he should prosecute the physicians Störck and Leber, who had signed the death certificate, for obstruction of justice; and above all he should make sure that all cases of suicide in the future would be investigated to the last detail.[3] Over the next five years Pergen would compose more than twenty such reports, each filling many folio pages, going into such extensive detail that they must have taken weeks of intensive police investigation to compile.[4]

Another category of misdeeds with which Joseph concerned himself whenever they occurred was that of unseemly behavior in church, something that shocked him to the depths of his being. Hearing that a young accounting clerk in a government office, Hörmann by name, had so far forgotten himself as to light his pipe during Christmas Eve services, and thereupon had been ejected from the church by his indignant fellow worshippers, the emperor demanded that Pergen take up the case at once. Not only did it involve openly blasphemous behavior on the part of young Hörmann, but this was the stuff of which riots were made. Öffentliche Ärgerniße, blatantly provocative behavior of this sort, might well lead to people taking the law into their own hands.[5] A major investigation now followed, which revealed that the incident, which had been dismissed by the participants as a bit of juvenilia, had never been reported to the police, consequently Pergen had not been aware of it. Nevertheless, he now apologized profusely for not having learned of it before it had been brought to the emperor's attention, and reported that his investigation confirmed what the emperor had learned in all particulars. At that point, Joseph decided that the miscreant would be summarily dismissed from government employment.[6]

A more serious transgression of a similar kind earned its perpetrator even more draconic punishment. A lady of quality reported that a young man had so far forgotten himself as to expose himself to her in one of Vienna's churches. The culprit had shortly afterward been apprehended and promptly admitted the transgression, excusing himself with the argument that he had been carried away in a moment of ungovernable passion. Joseph then decided that anyone capable of such disgusting behavior had no right to expect so much as a trial. The fellow was to be given twenty-five strokes on the posterior with a cane and subsequently inducted into the army, which would know how to deal with him.[7]

As we have already seen, Joseph also took a lively interest in the new prison system that Pergen was developing. He himself collaborated with Pergen and von Beer in redefining the status of the prisoners, who were now to be divided into no less than five categories: (1) those persons being held before trial, (2) those convicted of the most serious crimes,

(3) those condemned to less than ten years of imprisonment, (4) persons convicted for petty offenses such as disobedience to parents or supervisors, or for slander, or poaching, and (5) debtors. Joseph insisted that prisoners in the first and fourth categories be kept strictly separate from those in the second and third. They, the *Arrestanten,* would be confined in the *Polizeihaus,* while those in the second and third categories, the *Sträflinge,* would be held in the *Zuchthaus,* where security measures were much more stringent. Even there, they were not to be allowed to mingle with one another. Debtors were, insofar as possible, to be held in the jails, and were not to be made to perform any labor, nor to be punished in any way beyond being deprived of their liberty.[8]

One can readily appreciate that this system caused Pergen endless headaches, as these distinctions, so clear in theory, were not always easy to enforce in practice by overworked and undereducated personnel in overcrowded prisons. Nor did Joseph hesitate to shower Pergen with gratuitous advice on how the prison system might be improved. As he saw it, the perennial problem of overcrowding could be easily solved by the simple expedient of rearranging the furniture in the cells and in the work rooms, and by removing all superfluous pieces. Moreover, those inmates too old to perform useful labor should be *abgeschoben,* transferred to their birthplaces, where the local authorities would have to worry about how best to deal with them.[9]

There were frequent discussions of financial problems. It had been Joseph's idea from the outset that the penal institutions were to be selfsupporting. The profits would be wrung from the sweated labor of the inmates. This hope, however, would soon prove illusory. Pergen blamed the huge losses he was incurring on three circumstances: (1) the terms of incarceration of the majority of inmates were too short for them to learn a trade thoroughly; (2) most prisoners turned out to be indifferent workers, with a regrettable tendency to spoil the products they were supposed to turn out (could this fact really have taken him by surprise?); and (3) he did not dispose over sufficient funds to acquire the expensive machinery that would allow him to compete successfully against the products of private enterprise.[10]

When these explanations utterly failed to satisfy Joseph, Pergen began to resort to creative bookkeeping in order to balance his accounts. In 1787 Count Rothan, the director of the *Hofrechnungskommission,* the central accounting office, questioned some of these practices and insisted that Pergen submit detailed statements of his expenses. The minister objected that he could not open his books to anyone, not even to the official accountants, as they contained numerous state secrets. The employees of the accounting office, not having been sworn to absolute secrecy, as had the members of his police, could not be allowed to see these.[11] It is of considerable interest that Pergen had by then succeeded in convincing Joseph of the paramount importance of maintaining secrecy about police business to the extent of getting a favorable decision in this matter. The emperor decided that while, in principle, the police books had to be open for inspection like those of any other branch of the government, any item that Pergen designated as a security matter could be withheld from scrutiny. He would be accountable only to Joseph for these.[12] As, of course the emperor was not a trained accountant, this dispensation gave Pergen considerably more leeway in managing his finances than he might otherwise have enjoyed. He knew that he could rely on the knowledge that Joseph, while capable of interesting himself in the most trivial details, lacked the patience to pursue such matters in any systematic way. In practice Pergen continued to juggle his books to suit his own convenience.

Thus we should look with some skepticism on Pergen's claim that, once the initial difficulties had been overcome, the penal system operated at a considerable profit, which, as a dutiful public servant, he hastened to reinvest in government securities.[13] In a way Pergen can hardly be blamed for attempting to hide as large a share of his finances as he thought he could get away with, as he was forever being queried about the most minimal of expenditures. For example, Count Kollowrat, as head of the combined Bohemian-Austrian chancery, did not hesitate to question an item of 7 florins that had been included by the police in a bill for the transportation of an accused criminal to Lemberg for trial. Pergen was forced to point out that the expense in question had been incurred partly to get the accused's laundry out of hock, so that he could be transported in clean clothes; and partly to settle a small amount due on his room rent, since it would have been unjust to leave the man's landlord with an unrecoverable debt. All of this took five lengthy memoranda to resolve;[14] small wonder that Pergen preferred to transact his business in private.

There was no predicting what detail of penal administration Joseph would seize upon next. At one point he informed Pergen that, having once again inspected the *Zuchthaus,* he had been unpleasantly struck by the observation that many of the inmates suffered from some sort of eczema. Such persons, he decreed, were to be incarcerated separately and kept in quarters on the ground floor so that, with a minimum of disruption of prison routine, they could be taken to bathing establishments for treatment. Such baths, insofar as they did not already exist, were to be built in the vicinity of wells so that there would be plentiful fresh water, and near sewers so that the dirty water could be readily disposed of.[15] One cannot help wondering about what must have gone through Pergen's mind whenever he found himself in receipt of such a communication from the emperor.

Joseph also demanded to be informed about every personnel change, every replacement, every promotion in the whole penal system. He insisted on knowing what every man on the rolls was being paid, and whether his abilities justified the salary he was receiving.[16] Pergen soon found out that, if he wanted to avoid later arguments, it was in his own best interest to explain in advance every step he took. Although this paper chase was terribly time-consuming, it did have the advantage of giving Joseph the impression that he was in touch with the system down to its last detail, while allowing Pergen a certain latitude to do as he wished in matters that he considered crucial by fobbing off the emperor with a mass of administrative trivia.

Something which inevitably led to an explosion on Joseph's part was an escape from one of the prisons. Whenever Pergen was forced to report such an incident, heads would roll. When two female prisoners made good their escape from the *Zuchthaus* because they had not been subjected to the same rigid supervision as the males, Joseph insisted on the prison director's dismissal. Pergen tried to shield the man who had put in over thirty years of blameless service in government, but the emperor remained adamant.[17] On another occasion, when Pergen reported that two prisoners had escaped by making ropes of their bedsheets and lowering themselves to the street, Joseph commented: "If these felons had been kept in subterranean cells, where ruffians of that stripe belong, this could never have happened."[18]

The emperor kept a sharp eye out for the least violation of the capital's many ordinances governing the quality and distribution of foodstuffs. Thus in 1788, he ordered Pergen to look into a report from the general hospital to the effect that several people had been admitted there with raw, swollen mouths. An investigation revealed that all the victims had been drinking wine at the same tavern, whose landlord admitted to having adulterated his rather too-sour vintage with lead carbonate.[19] *Plus ça change. . . .*

Inevitably, Joseph's sallies were sometimes well off the mark. Thus, he informed Pergen that three employees of the municipal street-lighting service had been observed while seizing a man on the street and forcing him into a cart, evidently a case of kidnapping that had escaped the notice of the police. After investigating, Pergen was able to reply that something of a very different nature had occurred. The men in question had, while engaged in the pursuit of their duties, encountered an intinerant Italian workman named Nardini, who, roaring drunk, had been making offensive and obscene remarks to passers-by. Thereupon they had decided to take matters into their own hands and had bundled off the culprit to the *Magistrat*. There, however, owing to the habitual disorganization that obtained in that branch, instead of being charged and put under arrest, Nardini had merely been pushed back out on the street. It was difficult to decide what to do with the lamplighters. On one hand, they had behaved as responsible citizens, quelling a public disturbance; on the other, they had acted in an unauthorized manner, taking the law into their own hands, and would have done far better had they hunted up a policeman instead. His recommendation was to leave things as they were, letting all concerned off with a stern warning.[20]

Pergen, of course, had no option but to follow up every one of Joseph's harebrained notions, even at an enormous cost of time and energy. After all, it was only prudent on his part to give Joseph the impression that, hardworking as he might be, he ultimately depended on the inspiration supplied by the emperor himself really to excel at his job. This was by far the best and easiest way of encouraging Joseph to identify himself closely with the work of the police. It cost Pergen nothing to encourage Joseph to believe that, in the last analysis, the entire system depended upon large infusions of imperial genius; the increase in police powers that resulted from Joseph's satisfaction benefitted not the emperor but himself. But even Pergen's obsequiousness had its limits. By 1789 his patience had been so far tried that he ventured to suggest that, while he was, of course, always inexpressibly grateful for whatever hints Joseph deigned to give him, it would facilitate the task of the police immeasurably if the emperor would be so gracious as to reveal to him the sources of his information.[21]

In all fairness it must be noted that, whenever he dared, Pergen attempted to mitigate the severity of some of Joseph's most impetuous inspirations. Thus, when the emperor decided that hereafter felons performing hard labor would be fed the standard army bread ration and nothing more, Pergen pointed out that this constituted only a portion of a soldier's daily food intake, and that it was entirely unrealistic to expect men doing heavy work to subsist on bread alone.[22] And once more, Pergen went so far as to request that Joseph agree to lift the anonymity of his many informers. In consequence of their accusations, many innocent citizens were disturbed in their tranquility, on occasion even arrested and deprived of honor and reputation for offenses that, upon thorough police investigation, turned out to have nothing to do with them. Perhaps if these fellows had been forced to stand behind their accusations, they would not have been so quick to make them.[23]

Not surprisingly, however, these were rare occasions. For the most part, Pergen seems to have believed the better part of valor to consist in abetting Joseph in his arbitrary behavior. This he did not only because he had no great desire to bring the imperial wrath down upon himself, but also out of the consideration that, once Joseph had become accustomed always to look to the police to enforce his will, he would be much more amenable to a project that had grown very close to Pergen's heart. The minister had conceived of the notion of transforming the police into something that by far transcended its initially envisaged functions. The role of the police was to assist in the maintenance of public order and to guarantee the safety of the lives and property of the citizens; no one any longer disputed that. But as already noted, Pergen deemed the protection of the emperor's sacred person to be not only a part of his duties but the paramount one: to protect the emperor was to preserve the state. To this end, all other concerns must be subjugated. It might be, of course, although Pergen tactfully refrained from saying so outright, that the state would ultimately survive the assassination of an emperor; but the point was that, once so dreadful a precedent had been set, a pattern of violence and disruption would inexorably lead to an apocalyptic end.

In practice, the conclusion which Pergen derived from this premise was that his chief duty consisted in preventing harm from coming to the ruler, rather than in merely being in the position of punishing those who would have perpetrated it. Furthermore, if he were expected to give satisfaction in the performance of this supreme task, it would be essential for him to ferret out all manner of plots, cabals, conspiracies, and discontents before these could be translated into overt acts. To turn this dream into reality he would need not a motley horde of amateur informants, such as Joseph had assembled for his own purposes, but rather a much expanded force of trained and responsible professionals. In such considerations lies the nucleus of the secret police apparatus that Pergen created in Joseph's last years, and that, after a brief hiatus under Leopold, was expanded into a veritable army under Francis.

But Joseph was far too intelligent to be fooled by subterfuges for long. Pergen knew this only too well and realized that the only means of convincing him of the necessity of expanding police power to such an extent would be to involve him directly in police business. Only in those circumstances would he eventually reach the conclusions that Pergen desired. This scheme of Pergen's was by no means as outlandish as it may sound, given the emperor's well-known proclivity for concerning himself with all the minutiae of a subject that had succeeded in capturing his interest. Once Pergen had grasped this essential fact, he applied all his energies to finding elements of police work likely to catch Joseph's eye. As he quickly found, a surefire method of accomplishing his aim was to involve the emperor in discussions about the redemptive, versus the retributive, aspects of punishment, a subject that seemed to hold endless fascination for him. Thus Pergen argued for Joseph's benefit that the function of the *Polizeihaus* was chiefly the reeducation and social reclamation of minor offenders young enough to be considered redeemable, while the *Zuchthaus* was intended to remove hardened criminals from society for as long as possible.[24] In this manner, Joseph's intention of protecting the law-abiding majority of his subjects from the depradations of this gentry would be realized, while those who had merely strayed a single time from the paths of righteousness could be reclaimed for society in an environment in which they were not constantly being corrupted by those beyond all redemption. What Pergen did not bother to add was that, in practice, this distinction hardly existed, as prisoners were assigned to one or the other of these institutions on the basis of the room available at the moment of their sentencing.

The emperor's rapidly developing interest in the day-to-day details of police business must have exceeded even Pergen's most sanguine expectations. The result was often that the most banal episodes, normally dealt with by the duty sergeant, were elevated into affairs of state. A single example of Joseph's excesses of zeal in this direction will have to suffice here.

Pergen had included in his weekly *Vortrag* a report disclosing that in the course of some street-tunneling operations in Favoriten a shaft had collapsed, as the result of which a workman had lost his life. Joseph at once pointed out that such accidents were entirely preventable; the owner of the firm performing the work was responsible for the safety of his laborers, and should therefore be punished.[25] At that point Pergen thought it best to put together a commission of investigation. That body, made up of von Beer, the vice-mayor of Vienna, and several *Magistrat* officials, duly held a series of hearings and, after having met at least a half-dozen times, submitted a report a month later. This account established that the unfortunate victim had himself been largely to blame for his unfortunate accident because he had ignored a series of warnings from his foreman about the unstable nature of the ground through which he was tunneling, which had been made particularly hazardous by an accumulation of loose earth from previous digging operations. The man had been told to shore up the excavation in which he was working, but out of laziness had neglected to take this sensible precaution. When part of the surface he was attacking with his pick suddenly crumbled, the loose earth was dislodged, burying the unlucky fellow.[26]

Joseph was anything but satisfied with this explanation. With considerable pique he pointed out to Pergen that some three years earlier he had promulgated an ordinance requiring that loose earth be removed from all excavation sites as soon as it was turned over, in order to prevent just this sort of accident. Apparently, as the owner of the excavation firm disclaimed any knowlege of such an ordinance, this must never have been publicized, doubtless due to administrative *Schlamperei.*[27] At that point Pergen turned the entire matter over to a new commission, made up of prominent members of the Lower Austrian government. In good time that body submitted a report of its own. The gist of this was that the works foreman had not only been aware of the ordinance in question, but had instructed the victim to carry away the dirt he was excavating at least once a day, informing him about the possible consequences of neglecting this precaution. The man, however, had consistently failed to heed these warnings. Thereupon Pergen recommended that, since it was the foreman's responsibility to ensure safety on the job, and since it could be argued that he should have seen to it that the remiss victim took the necessary safety measures, the man be symbolically punished with twenty-four hours of detention in the *Polizeihaus.* On Joseph's insistence, this was increased to three days.[28]

This episode reveals not only Joseph's compulsiveness, which is at any rate already sufficiently well documented, but also the nether side of the system Pergen was forging. Regrettable as the perhaps avoidable death of the workman might have been, it hardly seems reasonable to occupy a large part of the attention and energies of the government of a great city with such a matter for well over a month.

Basically trivial incidents of the sort, no matter how much they might capture Joseph's attention for a brief span, would hardly provide an answer to the question of when, and in what circumstances, the emperor came around to accepting the validity of Pergen's arguments about the central importance of the police in governing the realm. Paradoxically, this seems to have come about as the result of a reorganization of the police which took place in September 1786, following upon the already mentioned differences of opinion in the government about the proper role of the police.

At first glance, Joseph's decision in the matter seemed to represent a defeat for Pergen. Instead of putting Pergen in charge of the police throughout the monarchy, Joseph decided that the newly designated police commissioners in the principal towns would report to the provincial estates. Pergen's powers would be limited to the area of Vienna and Lower Austria. However, to make up for this, a secret arm of the police was now created under Pergen's control. The rather grand name of *Geheime Staatspolizei* by which this agency was designated hardly seems appropriate for the modest body this was. Pergen planned to build up a network of secret agents who would report directly to him on matters of vital security to the state. In addition, the usual parttime informants would be paid for the occasional information they provided. But by March 1787, there were only three *Vertraute* and Pergen's budget for the secret police, 40,000 florins yearly, for which he was accountable to Joseph alone, while it might have been adequate to mount a considerable operation, had, as we shall see, to be stretched over another area that sopped up its greater part. At the time of the reorganization, the chief benefit that accrued to Pergen from the formation of a secret police was Joseph's decision that henceforth his chief of police would have access to his person at all times, without having to request an audience.[29] Here, obviously, there was an opportunity for gaining considerable influence over the monarch, if it were to be used with the circumspection consonant with the emperor's suspicious nature.

In this event, Joseph himself provided the opportunity Pergen had been seeking. By the beginning of 1788 various centralizing measures, dear to the emperor's heart, were encountering stiff resistance in various parts of the monarchy, particularly in Hungary and in the Netherlands. The Hungarian magnates were extremely restive and consequently greatly angered by Joseph's tactless insistence on removing their holiest relic, the Crown of St. Stephen, to Vienna; by the introduction of legislation making German the only language of administration in Hungary; and, above all, by what they perceived as the inevitable consequences of Joseph's land-reform program, namely the breakup of their vast estates.

This was a particularly unfortunate moment for Magyar unrest—always latent—to be activated, as Joseph's habitual impetuosity, in no way restricted to domestic affairs, had just then succeeded in bringing about an extremely dangerous situation for the monarchy. Worried lest the steady application of Russian pressure lead at last to the final dissolution of the Ottoman Empire, without any advantage to Austria therefrom, he decided that the time was now ripe to implement the nebulous plans for a division of the Ottoman possessions in Europe that the Empress Catherine had proposed some years before. The alliance he concluded with her in 1787, although deliberately couched in vague terms, clearly pointed at this.

Inasmuch as Prussia, because of self-evident geographical factors, would clearly be unable to profit from such an eventuality, a situation had arisen that was in many ways similar to that of 1772. This time, however, no one came forth to suggest a renewed partition of Poland as a substitute. As a result, Austro-Prussian relations, which had appeared to take a considerable turn for the better the year before, following upon Frederick the Great's death, quickly deteriorated once more. Soon the Prussians, determined to prevent Joseph from enriching himself at the expense of the Turks while they themselves would get nothing, hit upon the notion of fomenting rebellion in Hungary. Through intercepts Joseph learned that various dissident Magyar nobles were negotiating with the Prussian foreign ministry and rumors were circulating that a bargain had been struck. Soon after the outbreak of the clearly impending Austro-Turkish war, when the Austrian armies would be fully committed to operations against the Ottomans, there would be an uprising in Hungary. At that point, the magnates would depose the Habsburgs as kings of Hungary and elevate a Prussian prince to the throne.[30] Shortly after learning about these events Joseph related the whole story to Pergen and ordered him to keep a sharp lookout for evidence of further Magyar conspiracies.[31]

The activities of the Hungarian dissidents were clearly seditious, but unfortunately their meetings with the Prussians had been held in Weimar, and so hardly fell under Pergen's jurisdiction. It was by no means clear to him how to turn these events to his advantage until, in March 1788, he received a communication from Joseph, informing him that his spies had learned that various Hungarian malcontents were meeting with the Prussian resident, Jacobi, in Vienna itself.[32] As it appeared that these gentlemen intended to strike him in the rear the moment that he was fully engaged in the field, the joke had ceased to be funny. Pergen should use his police to ferret out the details of the conspiracy, taking great care that no word of these investigations was made public. The evil would be compounded, were it to become generally known that he had to contend with domestic as well as with foreign enemies.[33]

This was all that Pergen needed by way of encouragement. He soon produced a report of von Beer's, indicating that Hungarian separatism was indeed active in the capital itself. According to information given the police by a Hungarian tailor established in the city, a trio of his countrymen had entered his shop, without identifying themselves to him. He had, however, recognized them, as they were all three prominent members of Vienna's Magyar community, namely Count Istvan Erddy and Counts Franz and Ignaz Festetics. The latter, acting as spokesman, had told him that they required complete outfits, consisting of white fur jackets with golden epaulettes and buttons and contrasting collars of brown mink, and linings made of yellow lamb's wool; vests of yellow cloth, with red linings; and red trousers, with golden stripes running down the sides. After the tailor had jokingly remarked that the carnival season was over, what did the men require such outfits for, he was told that information was none of his business; he would find out in good time.[34] "With fear and trembling" Pergen now confirmed to Joseph the appearance of the dreaded Hungarian *Freiheitsschwärmerei* in the capital itself. Such people were capable of anything.[35]

It is unlikely that Joseph would have assumed that the above-named conspirators, suitably attired for the occasion, were proposing to take to the streets of Vienna in order to commit some unspeakable outrage. Still, he was sufficiently concerned about the possible damaging effects of the Prussian machinations so that he now expressed his appreciation to Pergen and von Beer for their labors and ordered them to keep up a close surveillance of the suspects. It was to be hoped that before long these too brightly plumed birds would be caged.[36]

This rather bizarre affair seems to have ended at that point, since there is no record of any ensuing arrests, but it apparently had consequences quite out of proportion to its importance. Persuaded that he was confronted by internal conspiracy, and strongly abetted in this belief by Pergen, who clearly saw his opportunity to make himself indispensable in these matters, Joseph now apparently began to cast about for a way of suppressing such cabals. Unfortunately, there is no extant record that would allow one to decide how much of what now followed was due to whom. What is certain is that, between them, Joseph and Pergen worked out a highly effective system for dealing with treason and internal dissent, which was all the more remarkable for the economy of means upon which it rested.

Joseph and Pergen were evidently in agreement about one fundamental proposition: whatever means might be used to discover actual or potential traitors and subversives, the existing judicial system was inadequate for dealing with them once they were caught. Cumbersome and antiquated as Austrian criminal justice might be (the Theresian reforms had not been anything like fundamental, and Joseph's were still for the most part unimplemented), it did guarantee certain basic rights to those individuals accused of serious crimes, and, worse, functioned more or less publicly. As Joseph and Pergen saw it, putting someone accused of treason on trial publicly was risking an acquittal because the prosecution, anxious to safeguard the anonymity of its sources of information, would be reluctant to present key pieces of evidence in open court. Alternately, so much in the way of highly secret information would be revealed in the course of such a trial that the enemies of the monarchy would profit far more than they would lose by the trial and conviction of their agents.[37]

As it happened, there was a readily available means of dealing with this problem. As early as 1782 Joseph and Pergen had created a category of criminal quite outside the ordinary course of the judicial system. These were the so-called *Staatsverbrecher:* persons whose transgressions were of so serious a nature that the fundamental interests of society were endangered by them. Joseph himself would decide not only by what procedures they would be tried but also on the nature and extent of their punishment. Prisoners falling into this category were to be held in special isolation cells, specially constructed in the new *Polizeihaus* and in several fortresses. All proceedings against them were to be held in secret and no word of their fate was ever to be made public.[38] This was of course the purest kind of *Kabinettsjustiz,* wholly incompatible with Joseph's expressed views about the equitable administration of justice, but in the emperor's eyes, as the famous Zahlheim case (a nobleman who had murdered his landlady for her savings and who was broken on the wheel on Joseph's orders) illustrates, there were crimes so awful that the normally applicable standards had to be suspended. And in all fairness it must be said that in the period 1782–88 there were, at most, a half-dozen individuals whose cases were disposed of in this arbitrary fashion. Almost without exception, these were people who had been caught red-handed taking part in espionage activities, but against whom, for one reason or another, it would have been either difficult or politically embarassing to make a public case.[39]

Joseph and Pergen now proceeded to extend the concept of *Staatsverbrecher* to include persons merely suspected of various kinds of subversive acts. It was a convenient mechanism for disposing of cases that threatened to become messy if handled in the normal way, but one must not assume that due process was now suspended on a wholesale basis in Austria. The number of persons classified as *Staatsverbrecher,* although increasing, hardly did so in dramatic fashion.

In the years 1788–89 altogether seven individuals were arrested, tried, and condemned in this fashion. First came the Piarist priest Remigius Fravo, who entertained grandiose notions of converting the King of Prussia to Catholicism and then placing him on the Hungarian throne.[40] Although clearly mentally deranged, Fravo, at Joseph's insistence, was condemned to a term of sixty years of fortress detention, during which he seems to have vanished.

Then there was Baron Karl Hompesch, a German convert to Magyar nationalism, who was suspected of plotting with Duke Karl August of Saxe-Weimar, the patron of the German Union and, in Joseph's eyes, the arch anti-Habsburg conspirator in the *Reich.* At the emperor's orders Hompesch was seized while on a visit to Vienna and interrogated in a secret underground cell for over two months. But nothing could be proven against Hompesch, and Pergen seems to have convinced himself of the man's innocence. At that point, in an unusual show of independence, he did not stop short of pleading the baron's case forcefully to Joseph and finally convinced the emperor to release him.[41]

Next came the case of Friedrich Justin and Karl Löw, who had tried to turn the war against the Turks into a good thing for themselves by peddling information about the strength of the Austrian forces to various foreign embassies. Pergen was soon able to establish that what they were peddling had nothing whatsoever in common with reality; they had made all of it up themselves. Upon learning the facts of the case from von Beer, Pergen suggested that the most expedient way of dealing with these culprits, both of whom were of foreign nationality, would be to expel them from the monarchy. Joseph, however, would not hear of this and insisted that they be classified as *Staatsverbrecher* and ordered them to be employed at hard labor in the fortress of Peterwardein. Some six months later Pergen again tried to intercede in behalf of the pair, but with no success. Löw died in prison and Justin was not released until, upon the accession of Leopold II, the cases of all *Staatsverbrecher* were reviewed.[42]

Pergen's actions in the case of Franz Rudolf Grossing were considerably more equivocal. This man who, some years before, had been expelled from Austria for immoral conduct, had taken up residence in Bavaria, where, it now came to Joseph's attention, he served as a contact person between local political radicals affiliated with the German Union and various Hungarian dissidents. Joseph now decided that he should be lured back upon Austrian territory, where he would be arrested and charged with having violated the terms of the *revers* that he had signed at the time of his expulsion, promising never to return. This plan was duly put into effect and soon Grossing was being interrogated in one of Pergen's underground cells.

Once he began to confess there was no putting an end to the revelations he made to the police. He eventually revealed the existence of a network of conspirators encompassing all the better-known German radicals, dozens of members of the Hungarian nobility, and, even more frightening, the greater part of the membership of various Masonic lodges in the monarchy. It was not entirely clear from these revelations exactly what this monstrous conspiracy hoped to accomplish, but from Pergen's point of view, whether or not he took everything that Grossing confessed at face value, information of this sort was worth its weight in gold. Confirming, as it did, Joseph's grimmest fears about internal disaffection, it could be used over and over again to plead the case of the secret police. Soon Pergen, while passing on the latest revelations from

Grossing, was begging the emperor not to reveal the details of these to anyone. If these disclosures were to become generally known, a terrible outbreak of panic would inevitably ensue throughout the monarchy; or, he might have added, but didn't, there would be no lack of scoffers among Joseph's other advisers.[43]

Pergen was eventually so favorably impressed with his star informant's performance that he took up the man's case. A man with such highly developed talents, he was soon telling Joseph, should be a cabinet minister, not a jailbird. Could not something be done for him? Evidently the emperor did not think that there could, because Grossing stayed where he was, in jail. Not even Leopold's amnesty worked in his favor and he ended his days as a *Staatsverbrecher.*[44]

Aside from providing this comparatively rare insight into Pergen's methods, the Grossing case is also revealing in another respect. The circumstances of the man's arrest were of course highly irregular, and would hardly withstand close scrutiny. In the normal course of events this might not have been much of a problem; after all, Grossing's past was sufficiently shady, and his social position so unremarkable, that even his total disappearance would not have caused much head-scratching. But, as luck would have it, an ambitious prefect in the little town to which Grossing had been lured took it into his head that, since the arrest had been made in his jurisdiction, the man should be tried there. The prefect was soon enough told in no uncertain terms not to meddle in affairs of state, but by then the matter had come to the attention of Count Leopold Kollowrat, the head of the Austro-Bohemian Chancery. Kollowrat had once before had a run-in with Pergen about what he regarded as arbitrary police methods and did not let this opportunity to renew the argument pass him by. He now claimed that the case should be tried where it had originated and wanted to know by whose authority Grossing had been spirited out of his jurisdiction.

When Kollowrat had challenged Pergen in the matter of a *Staatsverbrecher* some four years earlier, the latter had been forced to beat a hasty retreat. After all, in his official capacity Kollowrat worked directly under Kaunitz, and the state chancellor was the last man in the world with whom Pergen wanted to pick a quarrel. However he had felt personally about Kollowrat's untimely inquiries into police business, he had assured him that, had he but once mentioned Kaunitz's name, all the information he requested would have been made instantly available to him.[45] On this occasion Pergen's tone was markedly diferent. He informed Kollowrat that he owed no explanations in matters related to his official duties to anyone besides the emperor, and he had this from the emperor himself. Had Kollowrat approached him informally, as one ministerial colleague to another, he would, as a matter of common courtesy, have been given an explanation of what had happened to Grossing. As matters stood, he was welcome to lodge an official complaint with His Majesty.[46] The fact that Pergen was not afraid to occupy this high ground vis-à-vis Kollowrat is the best indication of how secure he felt, by this time, of Joseph's support.

The case of Josepha Willias has been blown entirely out of proportion by historians searching for a convenient stick with which to beat Pergen.[47] This was a lady with a rather shady past who, upon the departure for the front of her lover—an officer in the Austrian army— took up with one of his colleagues. This gentleman hit upon a scheme to enrich himself by offering to sell various military secrets to the Prussians, who took a very lively interest in Joseph's new military adventure. Frau Willias's new lover did not hesitate to use her in the role of courier. As it happened, she was stopped outside the Prussian embassy. The police had received a tip, and she was caught red-handed with various incriminating documents. Thereupon she was arrested. As this was a clear case of war-time espionage, Joseph decided to treat her as a *Staatsverbrecherin.* Although she denied all knowlege of the contents of the documents that she had been carrying, her case dragged on and, without being formally tried and convicted, she remained in custody until Leopold's accession. Pergen's role in these events was anything but that of the single-minded persecutor of the innocent—a role assigned to him by his detractors. He repeatedly informed Joseph of his doubts about the woman's guilt and, when these communications were ignored, did his best to make her imprisonment bearable. Willias's long incarceration was due, more than anything else, to the circumstance that the emperor was absent from his capital, at the head of his armies, and when he returned he proved to be too ill to attend to all but the most pressing business, and that no one, not even Pergen, dared to do anything in his absence about a case in which Joseph had taken a direct interest.[48]

Finally, there was the affair of Georg Philipp Wucherer, one of the more successful, as well as notorious, booksellers who flourished in Vienna as the result of the partial relaxation of the censorship that followed upon the death of Maria Theresa. I have dealt extensively with the episode elsewhere[49] so that I shall confine myself here to a brief discussion. Wucherer, a Swabian, had made a good business out of pirating foreign books that had hitherto been banned in Austria. This activity, while regarded as highly unsavory in the publishing trade, was not illegal under Austrian law. Thus Wucherer first came to the attention of the police by dealing in pornographic woodcuts, for which transgression, however, he does not seem to have been prosecuted. In spite of the fact that he routinely published the most scurrilous of pamphlets, notorious for the outlandish character of their attacks on the emperor even by the generous standards that prevailed in the *Broschürenflut* — that eruption of criticism which had followed upon Joseph's relaxation of the censorship — Wucherer was allowed to go about his business. It was not until Joseph learned that Wucherer had become the Austrian representative of Bahrdt's German Union that he decided to proceed against him. The decision seems to have been his exclusively, as Pergen was away from Vienna at the time on one of his infrequent holidays, and there is no record of any correspondence about the matter between the emperor and his chief of police.[50] At any rate, Joseph arranged with von Beer, who was acting for Pergen during the minister's absence from his post, to have Wucherer entrapped. He was tricked into selling a prohibited publication to an agent provocateur and then promptly arrested. Although the offense was a serious one, a public trial would undoubtedly have exposed the circumstances in which Wucherer had been led to commit it, a turn of events that would have been most unwelcome to Joseph. So he decided, instead, to classify Wucherer as a *Staatsverbrecher* and to prosecute him in camera.

Moreover, subsequent to Wucherer's arrest, a search had uncovered a large stock of radical and inflammatory pamphlets on his business premises. While technically this was no violation of the law, as the pamphlets in question had not so far been circulated, and Wucherer maintained that they were intended for sale outside of Austria, Joseph was now determined to rid himself of the man. In this decision he was abetted by Pergen, back at his post, who later explicitly justified the proceedings to Leopold, arguing that the works in question were of so dangerous a nature that the higher interest of the state demanded their suppression.[51] Wucherer's stocks were pulped and he himself was summarily expelled from Austria. When Kollowrat presumed to enquire about the reasons for the expulsion, Pergen summarily informed him that this decision was due to the fact that Wucherer had been guilty of selling prohibited and uncensored books (patently an untruth), and "for another extremely important secret reason known to His Majesty."[52] While Pergen was chiefly interested in demonstrating to his old antagonist how far he had risen above the necessity of having to justify his actions to him, the formulation he chose is nevertheless extremely unfortunate, evoking as it does the worst aspects of inquisitorial proceedings. It should be added that it is all but certain that Pergen was referring to Wucherer's membership in the German Union, an organization which both he and Joseph thought of as constituting a clear and present danger to the security of the state. It would have been better for his subsequent reputation had he simply stated this fact.

This tendency to overreact on the part both of Pergen and Joseph, like most such behavior falling just short of clinical paranoia, was partly based on nothing more mysterious than a bad conscience; but it rested also on the perception that Joseph's policies had, in fact, produced genuine opposition. Unfortunately the most radical of the Josephinian reforms coincided in the period of their implementation with the Turkish War that had begun in 1788. This conflict, whose conduct Joseph hopelessly bungled from its outset, by first monopolizing his energies and subsequently by ruining his health, served as a catalyst for a whole variety of discontents that had hitherto not been able to surface in the conditions of relatively rigid centralism that Joseph had succeeded in imposing. Conservative revolts were brewing in both the Netherlands and in Hungary, and worse, and more directly in Pergen's field of vision, domestic discontent threatened to go beyond the chronic nobiliary grumbling that Joseph had been determined to ignore from the outset of his reign. The war, by playing havoc with the monarchy's by no means overly abundant supply of transport, caused serious shortages of foodstuffs in Vienna, which inevitably led to painful price increases. The government attempted to master the situation by imposing a price maximum, whereupon the Viennese bakers closed their doors in protest. This action in turn led to some nasty incidents, with open talk of profiteering and some actual attacks by the populace on a number of bakeries.[53] The high price of bread, leading to urban disorders abetted by a resentful nobility, could constitute a nasty mixture, as events in France were shortly to reveal, and doubtless Pergen must have felt that there were good reasons to encourage Joseph in the belief that extreme measures were required to suppress the outbreak of any domestic revolt in its germinal stage.

In the midst of these various proceedings against individuals suspected of activities dangerous to the state there came yet another reorganization of the police system. In 1789 jurisdiction over the police was removed from the *Hofkanzlei* and police activities were placed directly under Pergen, who was now styled minister of police. Much has been made of this, although most of what has appeared in print about it is based upon a misunderstanding of the situation.[54] What seems to have taken place is that Pergen, increasingly troubled by an eye ailment that had become chronic, convinced Joseph that his duties would have to be lightened. Consequently, Pergen was relieved of all responsibility for the government of Lower Austria, as well as of the duty of attending *Staatsrat* meetings—which he had still been obliged to do on occasion—

and was henceforth to confine his activities entirely to the police sphere. That no functional change was intended is shown by the wording of Pergen's new instructions. The only substantial difference from the way things had been done in the past was that henceforth the provincial governors were to send their reports dealing with police matters to Pergen instead of, as earlier, to the *Hofkanzlei,* so that, in some measure, Pergen attained his long-standing goal of exercising a degree of centralized control over the police of all of the monarchy. But needless to say, he did not thereby acquire any control over what actions the provincial governors, in their wisdom, chose to take. Essentially, he could now read their reports and, if he disagreed with them, complain—for the most part without result. Nor was Pergen now in the position of greatly expanding the activities of the police, as the entire staff of his new ministry consisted of two secretaries taken over from the Lower Austrian administration.[55] His new post might well, were he to regain his health, allow Pergen to build up a substantial power base for himself; the potential was there. But this would still take considerable work on his part. A genuinely independent police power did not as yet exist.

We must now turn to the question of whether, and to what degree, Pergen aspired to this goal. It has been maintained that this was his ambition all along, and that he succeeded in convincing Joseph of the necessity of making the police essentially independent of all but the emperor's control, over the objections of Sonnenfels, who vainly sought to defend the proposition that the "organization and jurisdiction of all public authorities be based on agreed principles embodied in public law."[56] What is the evidence for such an assertion? Unfortunately the bulk of Pergen's arguments on the subject must have been presented to Joseph in audience and, because of the sensitive subject matter, were not incorporated in the frequent memoranda that Pergen was in the habit of sending the emperor. Thus one can only argue from inference.

In 1784, when he had first argued on behalf of a general expansion of secret police activity, Pergen had pointed out the utility of keeping track of the comings and goings of suspicious foreigners and, above all, had put his emphasis on the necessity of keeping abreast of the doings of state servants. The chief concern of the police would be whether these men performed their duties faithfully and to the satisfaction of the public, whether they took bribes, and whether they engaged in suspicious exchanges of letters with individuals in foreign lands. Unmistakably, Pergen was playing up to Joseph's sometimes paranoid—on other occasions justified—suspicions about the loyalty of the administrative personnel that he had, in large part, inherited from his mother. Furthermore, the police would report whether the clergy was duly loyal, or whether its sermons contained veiled criticisms of the monarch. Only in an aside, while mentioning the necessity of keeping track of public opinion in order to determine the extent to which the monarch's policies were popular or resented, did he refer to the desirability of identifying *Mißvergnügte oder gar Aufwiegler,* malcontents and conspirators.[57]

Considerably different was the tone of a document in which Pergen described the activities of the secret police to Leopold II, shortly after Joseph's death.[58] Here state security is assumed to be the paramount concern. Whereas previously only the Prussian and papal representatives had been the subject of police surveillance, this had now been extended to all the diplomats stationed in Vienna. Every publication even mildly critical of the government was traced to its source. All suspicious persons were kept under close observation and, if warranted, arrested by the secret police. At that point it was left up to the emperor whether they were to be turned over to the courts for prosecution, or if it was preferable to proceed against them in camera. All manifestations of popular discontent were reported, kept track of, and, whenever possible, smothered before they could produce serious harm. Finally, the secret police was engaged in various activities which, for the good of the service, Pergen would reveal to Leopold only face-to-face (the existence of the *Staatsverbrecher* system is what was meant here). We shall presently see how Leopold reacted to all this, but for the moment suffice it to say that, if Pergen's report is to be taken literally, a long road had been traveled in the years since 1784. Although at that time Pergen had described what was at most a system for extending normal police powers in times of great emergency, his 1790 statement seems to speak of a pervasive surveillance of the population all too familiar to our ears. Even if one takes into consideration that there had in the meantime been an open rebellion in the Netherlands, an incipient revolt in Hungary, an unpopular and inconclusive war that had brought about sharp increases in the price of foodstuffs, and a great revolution in France that was beginning to spill over that country's borders, the tone of Pergen's report to Leopold is nevertheless chilling. In all fairness, however, it must be pointed out that much of what he developed for the new emperor's instruction was the stuff of which dreams are made. There was simply no way for Pergen—given the meager resources that Joseph had put at his disposal—actually to do all the things he claimed to be doing.[59] The 1790 report represents an agenda, not an accurate description of existing conditions.

It is of considerable interest that in the matter of what at the time appeared to be the most worrisome of the crises facing the monarchy— the threatened uprising in Hungary—Pergen's role was anything but that of a blindly committed suppressor of the malcontents. Although, or perhaps because, he was so well informed of what was taking place in Hungary from the reports of the *Polizeistelle* in Ofen, knowing precisely who the leading conspirators were, he was not in favor of settling the matter by simply putting them under arrest. Instead, he was convinced that Magyar discontent ran so deep that mere repression would achieve nothing. Only substantive concessions, including the cancellation of Joseph's most unpopular reforms, would in his eyes prevent a general uprising. It would have been interesting but inconsequential if Pergen had merely harbored these opinions in private. But the fact is that, once convinced of the rightness of these views, he did not hesitate to state them unequivocally to Joseph, who could hardly be expected to receive this information with great pleasure. Indeed, Pergen would undoubtedly have earned himself one of the emperor's celebrated reproaches for his trouble, had it not been for the circumstance that this advice corresponded precisely with what Kaunitz had been telling Joseph for some time.[60]

As Pergen saw it, to persist on the course Joseph had embarked on would inevitably lead to a major uprising. It was no longer a question of mere formalities, but one of the vital interests of all the propertied classes in Hungary. Faced by the prospect of a significant diminution of their incomes, the Magyars would not be deterred from rebelling by even the prospect of the most brutal sort of repression. Moreover, it would prove possible to suppress such a rebellion only if the majority of the troops engaged in the war against the Turks could be detached for the purpose. As there was no immediate likelihood of such a resolution of the monarchy's difficulties, and as the Hungarian situation could no longer be ignored, Pergen made so bold as to offer his advice to Joseph in a matter that, while it might not have been directly his responsibility, was of so grave a nature that it must concern every loyal subject of the crown. It was absolutely necessary to convince at least those Magyars who had not as yet committed themselves irrevocably to the road of revolution that Joseph cared deeply about their situation. The only way to accomplish this would be to take a line that, while retaining all due respect for royal privilege, would nevertheless be characterized by the most generous possible spirit. Joseph would have to agree to allowing the Hungarian estates to meet in formal session; to at long last having himself crowned as king of Hungary; to receiving petitions from the various provincial authorities in Hungary, outlining their specific grievances; and, most important, to assure his Hungarian subjects that all attempts to alter their constitution in a manner inconsistent with their material advantage would be abandoned. If Joseph could see his way clear to making these concessions, there was no doubt in Pergen's mind that the Magyars would quickly enough rally to his cause, as they had not failed to do on many previous occasions. It was also, after all, very much in their interest to beat back the Turks.[61]

Joseph answered Pergen in a marginalium, assuring him that he was most grateful to him for his sincere and friendly counsel, and that he proposed to act upon it without delay. In fact, only two days thereafter, a communication to thirty-seven Hungarian districts went out, assuring them that only an unfortunate coming together of circumstances, forcing him to concentrate his attention entirely on the war, had prevented him from having himself crowned in Hungary and from summoning the diet. He proposed to remedy this at the earliest possible occasion, at which time all substantive differences between him and his Magyar subjects would be open to discussion.[62]

It would soon enough turn out that the Magyars were not to be pacified with mere promises, but for the time being Pergen had every reason to be pleased. As he saw it, not only had his intervention prevented the worst from happening, but, by accepting his advice in the matter, Joseph had in a sense elevated him from being merely minister of police to the far more important position of adviser on all important questions of state security. He did not hesitate to say so openly by thanking Joseph for the confidence he had shown him in a further note on the Hungarian question, in which he urged great restraint. Now that the decision had been taken to reach an accommodation with the Magyars, no action should be taken even against those persons who had been actively engaged in seditious activities.[63]

In less than a month Pergen saw himself forced to point out to Joseph that the promised concessions had failed to achieve their desired effect.[64] While making it clear that he was in no position to offer advice on questions of foreign policy—having not been in close touch with that branch of government for a quarter of a century—he felt it his duty to address himself to the internal problems of the monarchy in all their amplitude. Not only were the Magyars as intransigent as ever, but, as he now put it, throughout the monarchy Joseph's subjects regarded themselves as unfortunate in their lot in spite of all the measures that had been taken to promote their well-being. He would, as he boldly said, be remiss in his duty were he not to point out the reasons for this unhappy state of affairs. He would pass over in silence the reckless and hyperbolic tone that was being taken by Joseph's critics among the common people, but it was not possible to ignore the objections to his policies that were daily being made by sensible persons. These were as follows:

a) Once Joseph had convinced himself that a measure was desirable, he insisted on implementing it—often against the counsel of his most experienced advisers—in the belief that he was making his subjects happy.

b) Joseph appeared to proceed from the premise that only one system was the correct one, and that it had to be employed uniformly in all the provinces of a large and disparate state. But this was simply not possible without doing irreparable harm to the condition of many of his subjects, who were understandably attached to their own traditions.

c) Joseph seemed to be in the habit of introducing new legislation first and determining the lay of the land afterwards. As a result much of his legislation resulted in contradiction and confusion. Moreover, since the public remained unconvinced that Joseph had sought out the advice of his experts before deciding on various innovations, the impression that these were of a precipitate nature was impossible to eradicate.

d) There was a general conviction abroad that Joseph had gone out of his way to ignore the advice of the various provincial estates, indeed to eliminate whatever influence these bodies had retained. Nothing good could ever come out of the systematic repression of one class on behalf of another; the basic equilibrium of the state would ultimately be destroyed thereby. And it seemed obvious to all that Joseph was determined to suppress the nobility.

e) The proofs of this proposition that were generally cited were the following: Joseph's insistence on the introduction of the new tax legislation that was so unfavorable to the landowning nobility; and his stated intention to dissolve the remaining bonds that tied the peasantry to the nobles, which had impelled the peasants to cease paying attention to whatever demands the landlords might still legitimately make of them. These proposals had led to tumults and disorders in many places, which constituted a great danger to the state.

f) The most recent judicial reforms, both in civil and criminal law, had been carried out with unseemly haste, so that innumerable contradictions had been introduced into legal procedure, and many instances of unjustified deprivations of property had resulted. Much discontent had resulted from Joseph's habit of leaving the formulation of new laws to legal scholars who might be accomplished theoreticians, but who knew nothing of the practice of daily life. Such measures might well be accepted in those provinces accustomed to *Machtsprüche*, blind obedience to the will of the sovereign; they would unfailingly lead to revolution in the Netherlands and Hungary, and alienate Galicia.

g) Joseph's choice of personnel to carry out his reforms had been, to put it mildly, unfortunate. They were theoreticians who, upon finding that their proposals were out of touch with political realities, tended all too often to blame their failures upon the largely imaginary opposition of some of His Majesty's most loyal subjects.

h) Much harm had been done at the time of the dissolution of the monasteries, when the property that had belonged to these orders had been confiscated. Included in this now nationalized monastic wealth were sums of money owed by the monasteries to over twenty thousand individuals. These creditors had been promised indemnification by the state, but the promise had not been kept; thus Joseph had created that many enemies for himself at one stroke.

i) While it had been Joseph's most laudable intention to use the bulk of the confiscated monastic wealth for subsidizing the parish clergy through the *Religionsfonds,* it had not escaped the public's notice that the village priests were as poor as ever. The public suspected, by no means without reason, that the finance authorities had simply merged the funds taken from the monks into the general *Kasse.*

j) The decision to require all landowners to turn over immediately to the *Religionsfonds* all the sums they owed to the monasteries could not be complied with in many cases without bringing about the immediate ruin of those concerned.

k) The uncertain conditions resulting from the ongoing war had led interest rates to rise to unparalleled levels, threatening the economic ruin of many.

l) The new system of military conscription had led to the virtual depopulation of whole districts, so that in many cases it was all but impossible to find and to keep servants, whose wages had gone up so much that cultured life suffered therefrom.

m) As for the price inflation in Vienna, this had been so considerable, and had given rise to so much complaint, that he was devoting a separate memorandum to the subject.

This recital of the evils of the Josephinian system is followed by a good deal of flattery, whose main point is that Joseph, although his intentions have all along been the best, has been tragically misunderstood by his subjects; but that when confronted with such a misunderstanding, a loyal servant has no option but to tell his master the unvarnished truth. Misguided and misinformed as they might be, all classes in the monarchy have become dissatisfied. The nobles are justifiably unhappy because the new tax and judicial legislation have narrowed the gulf between themselves and the burghers and peasants to the vanishing point. The surviving clergy resent the considerable loss of income which resulted from the dissolution of the monasteries. The bourgeoisie feel threatened by those measures making it easier for artisans to rise into their class from the bottom, and are frightened by the evident lowering of status of the privileged orders, inasmuch as the bourgeoisie have reason to believe that their privileges will be the next to go. The peasants, who have been the chief beneficiaries of Joseph's reforms, instead of singing his praises to the skies, have become so arrogant that they refuse not merely all contributions to the landlords, but even to pay taxes to the state. Only a spark is lacking; as soon as the word "freedom" is heard in the countryside, a general uprising can be expected.

Under these circumstances it would be unrealistic to hope for a favorable outcome of the ongoing war, since the best that can be expected from the populace is footdragging, and the prospect of treason has to be constantly kept in mind. The example of the Netherlands is beginning to have an intoxicating effect on the rest of the monarchy. To calm spirits in the German-speaking lands it will be necessary to abolish the recent tax reforms. But even this drastic step will not suffice in Galicia and Hungary. The former province has been egregiously misgoverned for years: the fundamental interests of the propertied classes have been trampled underfoot; arbitrary measures, incompatible with the most basic traditions have been imposed from above. In spite of all its natural advantages, the province has failed to produce any economic advantage to the monarchy for two decades. Leading elements of the nobility are agitating for reunion with the rump Polish republic, or with Prussian Poland. If the loss of the province is to be averted, a minister plenipotentiary must be sent there at once to hear the grievances of the population and to come to terms with the dissidents.

As for Hungary, it is not just a question of preventing the outbreak of revolution there; the whole fate of the monarchy depends on being able to replace the present indifference reigning throughout that country with the enthusiastic support that the House of Habsburg once enjoyed there. While Joseph's intentions were doubtless the best, and no one would wish to deny the desirability of eliminating the dreadful backwardness—even barbarism—that still obtained in parts of that realm, his reforms had without exception been introduced with arbitrary disregard for the Hungarian constitution and the wishes of the greater part of the inhabitants. The result had been the alienation of nobility and clergy to the point where many of them were openly conspiring with representatives of the king of Prussia. Given the determined and warlike character of the Magyars, this represented a mortal danger to the continued existence of the monarchy. It would prove all but impossible to suppress an open rebellion in Hungary; many of the troops that would have to be used were themselves Magyars, and the likelihood that they would join the cause of the rebels was all too great.

Sadly, Joseph's concessions of the previous month, consisting as they did largely of assurances for the future, were insufficient to prevent the outbreak of revolution in Hungary. To achieve this end it would be essential to go further. Indeed, the worst would be avoided only if Joseph could see his way clear to issuing a declaration, whose text, in all due humility, he would now suggest: As it had come to His Majesty's attention that misguided elements of the population had made known their opposition to the progressive and useful task of surveying now in progress, this would be suspended until such a time as the question could be decided at a meeting of the Hungarian diet, which is to be convened no later than April. Second, all arbitrary requisitions for the army are to be halted. No time must be lost in issuing these orders. He would suggest that Joseph submit this memorandum to Kaunitz for his comments. The chancellor was in the best position to judge these matters.

This is certainly a remarkable document. Stripped of its formulaic courtly language, which one may assume the emperor registered only subliminally at any rate, it constitutes a merciless critique of some of Joseph's most cherished projects, and above all, of his habitual mode of governing. Even if one assumes, as the concluding sentence gives reason to, that it was drawn up only after extensive consultations with Kaunitz, open criticism of this sort was not what Joseph was accustomed to hearing from his ministers. The emperor, of course, was mortally ill, and Pergen may have been writing with an eye on Leopold, who was known to harbor reservations about Joseph's methods, but Joseph had recovered from similar crises before, and Pergen had no way of knowing that this would be the final one.

Of great interest too are the arguments that Pergen employs. If one leaves aside his comments on Galicia, which can be interpreted largely as an ex post facto justification of his own activities there, they represent almost without exception the viewpoint of an aggrieved landowning class. What he warns Joseph about is the imminent prospect of the outbreak of a nobiliary *fronde*, or, possibly, of a peasant jacquerie, which he regards as nothing more than the inevitable result of Joseph's disruption of the rural equilibrium. Nowhere does he mention the possibility of a generalized popular uprising. His cautionary examples are all drawn from the rebellion in the Netherlands; at no point does he mention the recent events in France. Yet, as minister of police, Pergen was in the best position to know about any possible echoes of the recent French penchant for egalitarianism. Did he feel that this was not a suitable argument to use on Joseph? Or were there none?

Apparently Pergen's memorandum, in spite of the harsh criticism it contained, was well received by Joseph. At any rate the emperor, notwithstanding the by then catastrophic state of his health, granted him an audience in which he developed his proposals for Hungary in further detail. These constitute the body of what was, as it turned out, Pergen's final communication to Joseph.[65] The points incorporated therein were rendered moot by the course of events. By the time Joseph received this document he had decided on the withdrawal of the great majority of his reforms in Hungary. On 29 January he turned over all the affairs of state to a regency council. In another three weeks he was dead. The exact extent to which Pergen's influence had been instrumental in persuading Joseph to cancel his reform program cannot be determined from the existing evidence; but at the least it seems to have been considerable.

NOTES

1. S.A., Familien Archiv, Sammelbände (hereafter F.A.S.), 67.

2. Pergen to Kaunitz, 28 March 1784, S.A., G.C. 405.

3. Joseph to Pergen, 19 February 1785, V.A., P.A. IV.

4. For example Pergen to Joseph, 8 May 1788, V.A., P.A. IV.

5. Joseph to Pergen, 7 January 1786, V.A., P.A. III.

6. Pergen to Joseph, 11 and 14 January 1786, V.A., P.A. III.

7. 13 May 1786, V.A., P.A. IV. Cf. P. P. Bernard, *The Limits of Enlightenment* (Urbana, Ill. 1979), 54–57.

8. Kaunitz to Pergen, 23 January 1784, S.A., G.C. 405.

9. Joseph to Pergen, 8 April 1785, V.A., P.A. I. Pergen to Joseph, 10 June 1785, V.A., P.A. III.

10. Pergen to Joseph, 2 May 1785, V.A., P.A. I.

11. Pergen to Rothan, 27 February 1787, V.A., P.A. I.

12. Joseph to Pergen, 1 March 1787, V.A., P.A. I.

13. Thus Pergen claimed that in 1786 the *Arbeitshaus* had generated a profit of 11,246 florins, 9,000 of which had been reinvested, the rest being spent to replace worn-out machinery. Pergen to Joseph, 9 March 1787, V.A., P.A. I. This seems highly suspicious, given Pergen's description of the desolate state of the institution's finances in the previous year.

14. Pergen to Kollowrat, 27 February 1787, V.A., P.A. IV. No wonder that Pergen preferred transacting his business in privacy.

15. Joseph to Pergen, 6 November 1787, V.A., P.A. III.

16. Cf. Pergen to Joseph, 15 February and 1 March 1787, V.A., P.A. III.

17. Pergen to Joseph, 14 February 1787, V.A., P.A. III. For a similar case a year later, see S.A., Handbillets-Protokolle (hereafter H.P.), 16 August 1788, and V.A., P.A. VI. Cf. Bernard, *Limits,* 70.

18. Von Beer to Joseph, 2 June 1789, V.A., P.A. IV.

19. Joseph to Pergen, 18 February 1788; Pergen to Joseph, 9 July 1788, V.A., P.A. III.

20. Von Beer's report, 16 May 1787, V.A., P.A. IV.

21. Pergen to Joseph, 7 February 1789, V.A., P.A. IV.

22. Pergen to Joseph, 4 June 1787, V.A., P.A. III.

23. Pergen to Joseph, 3 February 1789, V.A., P.A. IV.

24. Pergen to Joseph, 17 March 1787, V.A., P.A. I. Pergen's report, 14 May 1788, V.A., P.A. III.

25. Pergen to Joseph, 16 September 1787, V.A., P.A. III.

26. Pergen to Joseph, 17 October 1787, V.A., P.A. III.

27. Pergen to Joseph, 23 November 1787, V.A., P.A. III.

28. Pergen to Joseph, 1 December 1787, V.A., P.A. III.

29. Walter, *Zentral-Verwaltung*, II/1/2, 57–58; A. Fournier, "Joseph II. und der geheime Dienst," in *Historische Studien und Skizzen*, III (Vienna & Leipzig, 1912).

30. P. P. Bernard, "Joseph II's Last Turkish War Reconsidered," *Austrian History Yearbook*, XVII/1 (1988); and W. Weckebecker, *Von Maria Theresia zu Franz Joseph* (Berlin, 1929), 44 ff.

31. Joseph to Pergen, 29 March and 23 July 1788, S.A., F.A.S. 27.

32. Joseph to Pergen, 29 March 1788, S.A., F.A.S. 27.

33. Joseph to Pergen, 23 july 1788, S.A., F.A.S. 27.

34. Von Beer to Pergen, 2 October 1788, S.A., F.A.S. 27.

35. Pergen to Joseph, 15 october 1788, S.A., F.A.S. 27.

36. Joseph's Marginalium on above.

37. Pergen and Joseph were increasingly concerned about the negative consequences of public trials in espionage cases from the mid 1780s. Cf. Pergen's report on police responsibilities, dated 1786, S.A., F.A.S. 67.

38. For evident reasons, not much was ever put on paper about the genesis of this system. Its workings can be reconstructed from the reports Pergen made about it, both after Joseph's death and when he was recalled to office by Francis II. Cf. Pergen to Leopold, 24 February 1791, V.A., P.A. IX, and Pergen to Francis, 1793, V.A., P.A. V. See also Bernard, *Limits*, 86–87, and E. Wangermann, *From Joseph II to the Jacobin Trials*, 2nd ed. (Oxford, 1969), 91–93.

39. Pergen's report, 1786, V.A., P.A. VI; Joseph to Pergen, 2 December 1786, S.A., H.P. X.

40. Bernard, *Limits*, 87–88.

41. Bernard, *Limits*, 103–7; cf. E. Wertheimer, "Baron Hompesch und Joseph II.," in *Mitteilungen des Instituts für österreichische Geschichtsforschung*, Ergänzungsband VI, 1901.

42. Bernard, *Limits*, 114–16.

43. *Ibid.*, 110–14.

44. Archiv der Stadt Wien (hereafter A.S.W.), Annalen des Wiener Kriminal Gericht (hereafter A.W.K.), 4 April and 29 September 1794, A 68.

45. 18 January 1788, V.A., P.A. VII. Bernard, *Limits*, 100–101.

46. *Ibid.*

47. In particular, see Wangermann, *Jacobin Trials,* 91–94.

48. Bernard, *Limits,* 107–9.

49. *Ibid.,* 57–60.

50. Wangermann, *Jacobin Trials,* 41.

51. *Ibid.,* 42–43.

52. 2 October 1789, V.A., Präsidialakten (hereafter P.).

53. Benna, "Organisierung," seems confused on this point. See V.A., P.A., Personalien/1.

54. H. Reinalter, *Aufgeklärter Absolutismus und Revolution* (Vienna, Cologne, Graz, 1980), 67. To be sure, Reinalter, who is anxious to establish the existence of a broadly based movement of popular opposition, rather overshoots the mark when he writes *"1789 soll es sogar zu einer Massendemonstration in Wien gekommen sein, wo das Volk in Anwesenheit des Kaisers 'die Abschaffung der Kriegsteuer und den Frieden' forderte."* This is based on a nineteenth-century account that gives no source for this allegation. Cf. A. J. Groß-Hoffinger, *Joseph II, als Regent und Mensch* (Stuttgart, n.d.), 193.

55. Walter, "Organisierung," 17.

56. Wangermann, *Jacobin Trials,* 38.

57. Pergen to Joseph, 22 July 1784, V.A., P.A. XVIII.

58. Pergen to Leopold, 1 and 2 March 1790, V.A., P.A. XVIII.

59. Even in 1790 Pergen disposed over no more than eight full-time secret police agents. Most of his information still came from Joseph's *Vertraute,* who were notoriously unreliable and over whom Pergen exercised no control. Cf. V.A., P.A., Personalien/1.

60. Pergen to Joseph, 16 and 18 December 1789, V.A., P.A. X/A.

61. It had seemingly escaped Pergen's attention that the dissident Magyars were counting on Prussian influence with the Porte to secure for them the territories they coveted. See R. Gragger, *Preußen, Weimar und die ungarische Königskrone* (Berlin, 1923), and H. Haselsteiner, *Joseph II. und die Komitate Ungarns* (Vienna, Cologne, Graz, 1983), 196–97.

62. Cf. Joseph to Pergen, 21 December 1789, V.A., P.A. X/A.

63. Pergen to Joseph, 29 December 1789, V.A., P.A. X/A.

64. Pergen to Joseph, 13 January 1790, V.A., P.A. X/A.

65. Pergen to Joseph, 28 January 1790, V.A., P.A. X/A.

7

Leopold II Dismantles Pergen's System

A S JOSEPH LAY dying his minister of police was composing his epitaph in a long and heartfelt plaint to his old patron the state chancellor. The emperor, Pergen wrote Kaunitz, had throughout his reign been ruled by the desire to bring about the happiness of his subjects in as short a time as possible. But it had been precisely the contradictions inherent in this wish that had brought about the downfall of his well-meant plans. Radical changes in a body politic were always delicate and thorny matters, requiring careful preparation and much forethought. Unfortunately, there had been no lack of ambitious and self-serving individuals in Joseph's entourage who, in order to advance their own careers, had not hesitated to convince him that what he desired could be accomplished quickly. The result had been a series of ill-advised and hasty measures doing violence to ancient rights, privileges, and property. Hardly any class except the very lowest had been spared. He himself had often cautioned His Majesty about the dangers of proceeding in this manner, but although Joseph had listened to him graciously, in the end the advice of others had prevailed. As a result, the violent revolutions about which he had warned were on the point of breaking out in Hungary and Galicia, and he no longer knew what advice to give the emperor; it was all too evident that his eloquence had not been equal to the task of averting the catastrophe he had predicted, since Joseph had remained unconvinced. At this point a remedy could come only from Kaunitz, whose great wisdom and experience might yet find a way to avert the worst. Would the chancellor condescend to grant him a private interview?[1]

That Pergen was not solely concerned about the welfare of the state may be gathered from his additional comment that, while it had now been some twenty-three years since he had actively concerned himself with foreign policy, he had nevertheless—as far as had been consistent with his many onerous duties—kept a watchful eye on its development and hoped that he was still in the position to offer useful advice to those responsible for its conduct.[2] A change in the prevailing wind was imminent, and, as Pergen saw it, it was by no means clear that Joseph's heir, his brother Leopold, would wish to retain him in his present capacity.

Indeed, not much about the heir presumptive was known in Vienna, and what little there was, was contradictory. His administration of his Tuscan dominions was generally regarded as highly progressive in nature. He had introduced there many of the reforms that Joseph had labored over in the monarchy, and with much less fuss. Yet he also had the reputation of getting along with the local power structure, of being a man who did not swim against the stream. Furthermore, in twenty-five years in Florence he had built up a police force that easily matched that of Austria in its elaborateness and, by many accounts, surpassed it in efficiency.[3] It was difficult for Pergen to know what to expect of the new ruler.

If Pergen was in doubt about where he stood with Leopold, it did not take long for his doubts to be resolved. The new ruler clearly did not seem to take to his minister of police, and, from the outset, their personal relations were marked by a perceptible lack of warmth. Pergen did obtain from Leopold that he would continue to have free access to him at any time to ensure that no delay should occur in resolving important police matters such as the surveillance of potentially dangerous individuals, a practice that Leopold—no less than Joseph—regarded as essential to the security of the state.[4] This concession apart, however, Pergen had little reason to be pleased with the change of regime. Within a matter of weeks Leopold decreed that Pergen would be replaced as Lower Austrian *Landmarschall*. Pergen had neglected all but the most essential functions of this office for years, so there was no reason not to put it into the hands of a younger and more energetic man in the course of a general reorganization in the new reign. This step was explained to him as a concession to his continued poor state of health (his eyesight had, if anything, gotten worse), but it hardly augured well for the future.[5] Pergen's elevation to the post of minister of police in the previous year had, to be sure, removed control over the police from the Lower Austrian government, so that he had no reason to fear interference from that quarter, but being deprived of an old sinecure was not precisely a sign of imperial favor. While Leopold had decreed that Pergen would retain his principal post, and had even expanded his responsibilities by giving him the *Oberaufsicht,* general supervision of all the monarchy's prisons and jails,[6] it could hardly have escaped Pergen's attention that his actions were now being subjected to a far stricter scrutiny. His old enemies at the *Hofkanzlei,* Kollowrat in particular, were now quite openly criticizing his methods and seemed to be gaining Leopold's ear.[7] Pergen put as good a face on this as he could. Reporting to the Lower Austrian estates after having represented them at the oath of fealty to the new emperor in St. Stephen's Cathedral, he broke into tears, claiming that what had moved him so had been Leopold's declaration that he intended to work for the good and happiness of all his subjects, no matter how lowly their station in life. A great new age was dawning for Austria.[8]

Had Pergen been aware of Leopold's real opinion of the structure that he had so painstakingly built up under Joseph he might well have shed tears of rage instead. While the new emperor undoubtedly weighed the counsels of the various factions in the imperial government differently than his brother had, Pergen could argue, not without considerable truth, that the *Hofkanzlei* was merely jealous of his powers. He had, as everyone knew, expanded into areas that might originally have been in its purview, but that it had long neglected. Leopold had brought his own people with him from Florence, however, and their views counted most with him. In particular, a Major Stieber and a Hofrat Rühle were set, in secret, to analyzing Pergen's direction of his ministry. Their judgment, put in the form of a series of promemoria signed by Stieber, was devastating. They accused Pergen and von Beer not only of exceeding their by no means inconsiderable authority, but of doing so in an unsystematic, not to say a sloppy, manner.[9] It was not Leopold's way to procede hastily in important matters, he simply filed away these reports for future action, but it is fair to assume, from that time on, that Pergen's prospects for retaining his high level of influence were anything but brilliant.

For the time being, however, Pergen proceeded as if nothing had changed. In his initial report to Leopold he had given a lengthy justification of the principles governing the work of the police, and since these had not been queried, he had every right to assume that he was at liberty to go on as he always had.[10] What he had apparently been told was merely that the surveillance of suspicious and possibly dangerous individuals would continue; indeed, that it would be carried on even more systematically than before; but that greater efforts would have to be made to conceal these activities from the persons being observed and from the public at large.[11]

In one area, however, Leopold acted swiftly and decisively. Having decided that the entire concept of the *Staatsverbrecher* was incompatible with his views on justice, without abolishing the category, he nevertheless rendered it moot by ordering the release—for the most part coupled with expulsion from the territory of the monarchy—of the individuals who were being held as such.[12]

While Leopold proceeded in the sidling, cautious manner so typical of his administration in Italy (Pergen's reports were being laid aside without being acted upon—what can only be described as a hostile dossier on him was being assembled; but at the same time he was encouraged to believe that his services continued to be essential to state security), events in Hungary had unfolded at a much livelier pace. Ever since Joseph's decision in January to withdraw his reforms there the Hungarian State Chancery had pretty much done as it pleased. The representatives of the great magnates who controlled that body saw their opportunity to go well beyond the recall of the most unpopular aspects of the Josephinian system. They believed that their chance had come to bring about at least a partial dismantling of Habsburg centralism and did not hesitate to grasp it. Easily the most hated aspect of this had been Pergen's police. This force was now thoroughly dismantled with the justification that the municipal authorities in the major towns were more than capable of maintaining public order and that any police function going beyond this smacked of a political inquisition, incompatible with the Magyar constitution. As a result, the police was so thoroughly eliminated from the Hungarian scene that within three years banditry was out of control in the countryside, and the Hungarian diet had to meet in emergency session to discuss ways and means of combatting it. When a transcript of these discussions reached Vienna, Kaunitz observed, not without cause, that the Magyars were proposing measures that had existed for generations in all civilized countries.[13] In the meantime, however, Leopold found that he had been deprived of all practical means of influencing the Hungarian situation. Finally, he was reduced to making use of not just Pergen's methods but his personnel. The former head of Pergen's police in Pest, Franz Gotthardi, was commissioned by the emperor to recruit a body of agents among Magyars thought to be loyal to the monarchy to transmit reliable information to Vienna and, if possible, influence the Hungarian situation in a manner favorable to Habsburg policy. It was hardly fortuitous that a good portion of the undercover agents recruited by Gotthardi consisted of former members of Pergen's police.[14]

Anyone assuming that Leopold might have drawn a useful lesson from the Hungarian fiasco would have been quickly disabused of this notion. Instead, it almost seemed as if he were voluntarily setting out to accomplish throughout the monarchy what Magyar particularism had brought about in Hungary: the dismantlement of the apparatus of police surveillance and control built up by Pergen. Certainly, the emperor's motives were good. Kollowrat and his allies at the *Hofkanzlei* lost no opportunity to bring any and all irregularities in the judicial process to his attention, and Leopold was not the man to take such matters lightly. Thus, the *Hofkanzlei* was able to persuade Leopold that prisoners of the Jewish faith should be exempted from forced labor on Jewish holidays and that they should be provided with kosher food.[15] Pergen objected that such special treatment would be highly injurious to good order and that the morale of the non-Jewish majority of convicts would suffer greatly. He humbly requested that the emperor consult the high court of appeals in the matter, the justices would surely confirm his opinion. This motion, however, availed him nothing.[16]

Leopold seems also to have been even more parsimonious than Joseph in allocating money to Pergen for carrying out the various duties of the police. As early as July 1790 Pergen was complaining that it was all but impossible to maintain public order with the available resources. The Turkish War, still dragging on, had like all wars uprooted certain elements of the rural population, which had then drifted into the towns. In Vienna alone there were some eighteen hundred vagabonds, whom the existing police force could not possibly control. Since the emperor did not see fit to make additional funds available, Pergen saw no remedy but to ask for the creation of a *marechaussé,* a force detached from the active service army to maintain order. In his opinion four officers, a half-dozen noncommissioned officers, and thirty dragoons per *Kreis* would suffice.[17]

Although there were several hundred such administrative districts in the monarchy, Pergen must undoubtedly have felt that this proposal was unrealizable since it would be unthinkable to detach ten thousand or more men from active service in the midst of a war, and he hoped that Leopold would instead allow him the requested additional funds. The emperor, however, was not contemplating any further combat operations but rather awaiting a favorable opportunity to end the war, and promptly submitted Pergen's proposal to the war ministry. That body was of the opinion that nothing stood in the way of such a measure: the necessary troops could be put at the disposal of the various provincial governors; the per annum cost, billed to the provinces, would be roughly 9,000 florins per forty-man unit.[18] The Lower Austrian government now pointed out that these troops would have to be quartered in areas where the military was not as a rule stationed, which would give rise to further expense.[19] At that point the scheme was quietly dropped, but Pergen still did not get the money he had asked for.

For Pergen the point of no return arrived toward the end of 1790 when Leopold, once again prompted by the *Hofkanzlei,* took up the cases of Josepha Willias and Georg Philipp Wucherer. These individuals had been released under the terms of Leopold's amnesty for the *Staatsverbrecher* but were now appealing against their convictions and asking for damages.[20] After examining the dossiers in these two cases Leopold concluded that, although the plaintiffs had not succeeded in establishing the uncontested truth of their allegations about Pergen's arbitrary proceedings against them (Willias did eventually receive partial restitution for damage done to some of her belongings while she was in prison), enough evidence about some very dubious police procedures had been brought to light to warrant a fundamental overhaul of these. In February 1791 he decreed that henceforth a special governmental commission would interview all prisoners in the *Polizeihaus* at least once every three months to establish whether they were being treated in accordance with regulations, that no one would be held for more than three days without a warrant from the proper judicial instance, and that all individuals under arrest were to be examined in the presence of a representative from a court of justice.[21] Whatever Pergen may have thought about this latter provision, which in effect introduced the principle of habeas corpus into Austrian jurisprudence, he clearly could not accept a situation in which an imperial commission would be constantly interviewing the prisoners in his jail and, in effect, encouraging them to come up with complaints against the prison administration. This would inevitably bring about the end of all prison discipline. Pergen did not hesitate to lodge a detailed protest in which he pointed out that he could not run a penal system under those conditions, a protest that Leopold returned to him with the lapidary comment *"Dienet zur Nachricht"* (has been noted).[22] Pergen thereupon resubmitted his protest with an additional note in which he begged the emperor not to sacrifice the all-important institution of the police to those who would, for selfish reasons, destroy it.[23] As Leopold's answer in no way concerned itself with the gravamina Pergen had raised, the minister of police now saw no alternative to submitting his resignation. He did not hesitate to say that, in his view, Leopold's undermining of police authority would carry with it the gravest consequences. He rejected all criticisms of that institution, attributing it exclusively to the jealousy resulting from the circumstance that Joseph had insisted that no other branch of the government exercise any authority over it, and he concluded that, at his age he could no longer suffer continual humiliations without sustaining irreparable damage to his health.[24]

For the immediate future Leopold decided not to replace Pergen. His successor as governor of Lower Austria, Count Sauer, who, like Pergen before him, would have free access to the person of the emperor, was put in charge of the Viennese police. As for the provincial police administrations, these were to be run by the various governors, who would report to the *Hofkanzlei*.[25] Kollowrat had finally triumphed.

These measures were evidently meant for the short run only, since Leopold now charged Joseph von Sonnenfels—that old campaigner for reform in Theresian days, who had been almost totally eclipsed in Joseph's reign—with working out a master plan for creating a new police regulation.[26] What Sonnenfels eventually came up with was a massive plan, whose instructions to police district commissioners alone encompassed 134 pages. That it took him only half a year to produce this document was not so much a tribute to the celerity of his methods but rather consequence of the fact that he had only to revive a proposal he had already worked out in Theresian times but had never been asked to submit.[27]

Unfortunately, in at least one important respect, Leopold's reservations about Sonnenfels were only too amply confirmed by this document. The old war horse, while he had lost none of his zeal for anchoring respect for the individual in the law, had also failed to learn anything new in the two decades that had passed since he had originally conceived his plan. Thus he proposed to extend police supervision to such a wide gamut of human affairs that, not only would the expense to the state have been ruinous, but the result would have been the establishment of a police state far more pervasive in its control over the lives of the citizenry than anything that Joseph and Pergen had dreamed of in their boldest flights of ambition. To create the equivalent of a modern social welfare state might just have been possible in one or more of the prosperous German states where the flourishing small town was the dominant social form, where the population was small in relation to the total resources available to the prince, and where the number of individuals requiring state assistance was insignificant. It would have been ruinous in Austria, with its large population of rural indigents and its cities that were beginning to suffer from the problems of overexpansion.

There now ensued a bitter struggle between Sonnenfels, who insisted upon the necessity of adopting his proposals in their entirety, and Count Sauer, whose hand was strengthened by arguments supplied to him by Pergen's ex-assistants, Schilling and Mährenthal, who had been reassigned to the Lower Austrian government—after the dissolution of the ministry of police—but who remained in constant touch with their former chief. Aside from protesting against the infeasibility of Sonnenfels's proposals, they objected that these did not give a place to the secret police, without which a modern state could simply not function. These objections did not go entirely unheeded, as Leopold seems to have acquiesced in Sauer's offer to keep open certain lines of communication running from him to von Beer, and thence to the provincial police commissioners, but in the main the emperor opted in favor of a somewhat reduced version of Sonnenfels' plan, which was enacted into a new police regulation on 1 November 1791.[28] It is difficult to project what the long-term effects of this measure might have been. For the time in which it was in force it applied only to Vienna, where many of the services that the police was now called upon to render already existed in one form or another, so that the expense was kept somewhat in check. In particular, the police doctors who had been employed under the terms of the plan found their services much in demand. A large portion of the population, too poor to afford the services of a private physician, and convinced that to seek treatment at the city's central medical facility—Joseph's *Allgemeines Krankenhaus*—was courting an early death, seems to have used them as a kind of free public health service.[29] What would have happened if the attempt had been made to extend this system to the whole of the monarchy is quite another story, but before this could take place Leopold took ill and died quite unexpectedly, on 1 March 1792. Once again, as had been the case only two years before, there was a general uncertainty about what would now follow.

NOTES

1. Pergen to Kaunitz, 16 January 1790, S.A., Noten von der Polizeihofstelle (hereafter N.v.P.), neu, 21.

2. *Ibid.*

3. For Leopold, see A. Wandruszka, *Leopold II.*, 2 vols. (Vienna, Cologne, Graz, 1963–65). As Wandruszka makes clear, Leopold had very decided opinions about every major issue in the realm he stood to inherit, but took care to entrust these only to his secret diary. Cf. Benna, "Organisierung," 211, who, however, confuses the issue of Leopold's views on the police question by citing A. Fournier, *Die Geheimpolizei auf dem Wiener Kongress* (Vienna & Leipzig, 1913), 4. Benna is arguing that Leopold's Tuscan secret police apparatus was the envy of Vienna, where it was cited in the Staatsrat as an ideal, and that it might well have served as a model and inspiration to Pergen, whereas Fournier maintains precisely the contrary.

4. Benna, "Organisierung," 211; Walter, "Organisierung," 51–52.

5. Walter, Zentral-Verwaltung, II/1/2/1, 93. Officially, it was announced that Pergen, in his capacity of *Landmarschall,* had been placed in "Jubilationsstand," a sort of honorable retirement, but later on he made no bones about his belief that Leopold, from that time on, had intended to put him on the shelf and to dismantle his system (über Haufen zu werfen). Cf. Bibl, Wiener Polizei, 257–58.

6. *Ibid.*

7. Benna, "Organisierung," 211; K.-H. Osterloh, Joseph von Sonnenfels, 149.

8. H. Wagner, *Wien von Maria Theresia bis zur Franzosenzeit: Aus den Tagebüchern des Grafen Karl von Zinzendorf* (Vienna, 1972), 61. As late as the fall of 1790 Pergen was expressing admiration for Leopold's policies in the Austrian Netherlands, where a combination of political moderation and cooperation with the local nobility seemed to have gotten the upper hand over the rebellion. Cf. Pergen to his son, September and October 1790, S.A., F.A.S. 20.

9. Benna, "Organisierung," 211.

10. Pergen to Leopold, 2 March 1790, quoted in Fournier, *Geheimpolizei,* 3–4.

11. Benna, "Organisierung," 211.

12. Bernard, *Limits,* 116–17.

13. Silagi, *Ungarn und der geheime Mitarbeiterkreis Kaisers Leopold II.* (Munich, 1961), 38–39.

14. *Ibid.*

15. Kollowrat to Pergen, 28 July 1790, V.A., P.A. I.

16. Pergen to Leopold, 14 August 1790, V.A., P.A. I. Once Leopold's attention had been drawn to the question of prison diet he soon found this seriously deficient. His late brother had held the opinion that imprisonment ought to be made as harsh and unpleasant as was compatible with the maintenance of life, and the nether limits of human tolerance had been generously estimated. Leopold now decreed that all prisoners, no matter what their offense, were to receive at least a dish of warm soup daily in addition to their bread ration, and were to have a plate of vegetables three times a week. Cf. Wandruszka, *Leopold II.,* II, 337.

17. Pergen to Leopold, 1 July 1790, Niederösterreichisches Landesarchiv (hereafter N.L.A.), Polizeiordnung (hereafter P.O.), 2.

18. *Hofkriegsrat* to Leopold, 17 July 1790, N.L.A., P.O.

19. Lower Austrian Collegium der Stände to Leopold, 26 August 1790, N.L.A., P.O.

20. Wandruszka, *Leopold II.,* II, 337; Bernard, *Limits,* 117.

21. Leopold to Pergen, 15 February 1791, V.A., P.A. VII. Cf. Bernard, *Limits,* 117–18, and *Wandruszka,* Leopold II., II, 337–38.

22. Pergen to Leopold, 3 March 1791, V.A., P.A. VII.

23. Pergen to Leopold, 5 March 1791, V.A., P.A. VII. Cf. Wangermann, *Jacobin Trials,* 94.

24. Walter, "Organisierung," 52. The letter of resignation is dated 3 March

1791, but in view of the fact that Pergen had still been remonstrating with Leopold on 5 March, this seems to have been a case of back-dating, by which Pergen probably meant to convey the impression that, unwilling to put up with Leopold's insulting manner, he had resigned at once. Walter professes to be at a loss to account for Pergen's resignation at this point, but Wangermann, *Jacobin Trials*, 95, is undoubtedly correct in asserting that this dispute was the immediate cause of it.

25. Walter, "Organisierung," 52–53. The instructions accompanying these dispositions alleged that it was essential to bring about a shift in emphasis from Pergen's system, which had emphasized the secret police to the all but fatal neglect of ordinary police business. Cf. Benna, "Organisierung," 212. But what is reflected here is the old Hofkanzlei view of the police as an agency regulating almost all of the internal workings of the state, a concept that Pergen had long before rejected as hopelessly impractical.

26. Sonnenfels, chafing under his isolation from the centers of power as a mere university professor, had been pestering Leopold for employment in some important capacity since shortly after his succession to the throne. Cf. Osterloh, *Sonnenfels*, 150. Curiously, Leopold, who, while willing to concede Sonnenfels considerable abilities, nevertheless thought of him as a vain windbag—who inevitably tended to start more than he could finish, and should therefore not be entrusted with a position of genuine power—yet was willing to entrust this project to him. Cf. Wandruszka, *Leopold II.*, II, 325.

27. Osterloh, *Sonnenfels*, 150–51.

28. *Ibid.*, 152–57; Wangermann, *Jacobin Trials*, 95–99.

29. Wangermann, *Jacobin Trials*, 99; cf. P. P. Bernard, "The Limits of Absolutism: Joseph II and the Algemeines Krankenhaus," *Eighteenth Century Studies*, IX/2 (1975–76), 193–215.

8

Francis II and the Emergence
of the Police State

S HORTLY BEFORE RESIGNING Pergen passed on to Leopold a lengthy
memorandum on secret societies that had been sent him.[1] The
anonymous author of this document contended that these organizations,
while pretending to have no concern aside from improving the lot of
mankind, in fact were dedicated to undermining the power and the
good name of the rulers of the world and to inciting disobedience
among the common people. The revolt of the American Colonies had
been the first in a chain of related conspiracies, of which the overthrow
of the French Monarchy was only the most recent. That the conspirators
were not content to leave it at that could be clearly discerned from the
activities of the emissaries whom they had sent to all neighboring
countries with the undoubted purpose of fomenting rebellions against
their rulers as well. (Here a circular from the Masonic lodge of Bordeaux,
calling for fellow Masons everywhere to support revolutionary activity,
was cited.) One of the most sinister aspects of these conspiracies was the
fact that those most closely involved in them were not crass out-
siders who aroused the immediate suspicion of all right-minded
citizens, rather those who gave every outward reassurance of respect-
ability. A significant proportion of lodge members were former Jesuits
who, while inspiring confidence and sympathy in the populace at
large, were in fact secretly determined to avenge themselves on the
monarchs of Europe for having conspired to dissolve their society.
It would certainly be desirable to ban all secret societies without
exception. Such a step, however, would be counterproductive. Unfortunately, the people who have been drawn into them make up, to
a considerable degree, the most knowledgeable, influential, and

enthusiastic part of society. They should not be turned against the government en masse. That would make them all the more dangerous. Much better to gain their confidence, to subvert their purposes, and to turn them into witting or unwitting supporters of the state. The Prussian government had succeeded in accomplishing just that, and the Berlin lodges now danced to its tune.[2]

On the strength of this Pergen wrote to Leopold, calling the matter to his attention and adding that the allegations in the document seemed to be confirmed as he had recently received a communication from the Vienna lodge *Zur gekrönten Hoffnung,* informing him that some time before they had received the aforementioned appeal from Bordeaux, which, however, the Viennese Masons hastened to assure him, they proposed to ignore.[3] Pergen had advised the emperor that it would indeed be a very useful measure to win these people over to the cause of the government. That they had of their own accord turned over to him the inflammatory letter from their French brothers spoke well for their essential loyalty. They might well serve as a means to convey to the broad public Leopold's own views on social questions. They would have to learn to moderate the tone of their utterances, as biting denunciations, in which they specialized, were never capable of bringing about improvements, but merely fanned the flames of anger in the populace. However, considerable advantages would ensue from having a ready source of information about potential dissidents who would presumably continue to try to enlist the Masons for their ignoble ends, being unaware that these were now working for the state. The Masons would provide the police with a means of gathering information about the activities of such dubious groups as Theosophists, Eclectics, Illuminati, Americans, and *Rosenkreuzer*—to the meetings of which his men had, at present, no access.[4] Pergen closed with some dark mutterings to the effect that a number of the revelations his Masonic contacts had made to him were of such a nature that he could not, in good conscience, commit them to paper. He proposed—as soon as the sciatica that was plaguing him permitted—to make an oral report to the sacred person of the emperor.

Leopold did not trouble to answer this communication, in all probability not so much because he was inclined to dismiss its contents as largely fanciful, but because he was already busily making plans for putting together a secret network of informants and propagandizers outside of Pergen's ken. But it would seem that the heir to the throne, the Archduke Francis, was shown this document, and that it made a profound impact upon him.[5] Indeed, the young crown prince took a close interest in police matters at a very early stage.

In May 1791 he took up the cause of Pergen's old associate, Schilling, who was languishing under the new police administration, and recommended that he be taken into another agency so that his great talents would not go to waste.[6] Leopold agreed and urged Francis to "be solicitous in police matters and see to it that the police show more conscientiousness in watching over papers, brochures, foreigners, and vagrants."[7]

If, in contradiction to what is still often asserted, Francis was merely carrying out his father's wishes in looking upon the police as a central element in the governance of the realm, the two men seemingly did differ on their views about the threat to Austria represented by the events in France. They assuredly took contrasting views on the threat posed by the activities of various Austrian sympathizers with the French radicals. After having been in favor of taking a hard line with France, Leopold, strongly backed by the aged Kaunitz's advice, concluded that it would be foolish to attempt to influence events there by active intervention; only with patience and even stoicism could one hope to weather the storm. Francis, by contrast, argued that the mania for equality between classes—an ideal that could never be realized in practice but was bound to unleash unrestricted fanaticism among the people—would unfailingly cross France's borders, at first into the Austrian Netherlands, later into the rest of the monarchy. Far better to intervene before this came to pass.[8] When the French decided for reasons of their own to push matters to extremes, war between Austria and France came to look more and more like a certainty. Francis, influenced by his one-time tutor, Prince Colloredo, vice-chancellor of the *Reichskanzlei,* and by Kaunitz's second-in-command, Philipp Cobenzl, vice-chancellor of the *Staatskanzlei,* greeted these developments joyously, while Leopold and Kaunitz entertained the gravest doubts about them.[9]

In the midst of these developments, with but a few days left before Austria would have to answer France's latest ultimatum with some positive steps either to demonstrate her peaceful intentions or to face the prospect of war, the emperor Leopold, who had been suffering from a chronic stomach colic, took a sudden turn for the worse. On 1 March 1792, with considerable assistance from his physicians, who bled him incessantly, he died. The twenty-four-year-old Francis now found himself on the throne, ruler over more than 20 million subjects. He did not take up this heavy burden with what one would term supreme confidence in his own abilities, complaining that "I am young and have so little experience."[10]

Modesty becomes a man, all the more if he is in the position of influencing the lives of millions by his decisions. Unfortunately, while

Francis's modesty was anything but feigned, it expressed itself for the most part not in taking care to think through to the end the eventual consequences of his actions, but rather in turning to men whom he trusted for one reason or another, and allowing them a free hand. Immediately after his accession he appointed his old governor, Francis Colloredo—a man of limited ability with no experience in the direction of affairs—as his chief minister. As if that were not enough, he named his one-time tutor, Professor Schloißnigg—whose chief distinction had been to relieve the tedium of trying to teach a willing but inept pupil his lessons with long games of blind man's buff—to be Colloredo's principal assistant. And thus Francis asked the octogenerian Kaunitz, whose policies lay in ruins and whose authority was being openly undermined by his own vice-chancellor, to stay on as chancellor. Given this tendency, it is hardly astonishing that, France having declared war upon Austria in April, and the internal situation of the monarchy beginning to display unmistakable tensions, Francis should have begun to yearn for a trusted hand at the helm of the police too.

Within a matter of days after his accession, Francis was dissuaded, without much difficulty, from implementing a plan prepared for his deceased father to abolish the *robot* in Lower Austria. This was done upon representations from the *Hofkanzlei,* indicating that to give in to the peasants in this no doubt justified desire would only encourage the lower orders to advance further totally inadmissible demands. This hardly constituted a favorable omen for those who, like Sonnenfels, believed that the way to prevent an upheaval like that in France from convulsing Austria was to eliminate at least the most glaring of the social imbalances existing there.[11]

The growing radicalism of the Brissotins in France was responsible for Francis's acquiescence to a tightening of censorship regulations in the monarchy even before the formal outbreak of war between the two powers. Already in March 1792 a Strasbourg newspaper was banned in Austria on Sauer's recommendation, and soon thereafter all local papers were forbidden to print any political discussions whatsoever.[12]

Once the war with France had begun, seizing upon the natural spirit of patriotism that a great conflict inevitably generated to further one's own ends was a considerable temptation for many.[13] Among these oportunists was Count Sauer, who had chafed for some time under the restrictions put on the powers that he exercised as governor of Lower Austria, compared to those that Pergen had enjoyed. In particular, Sauer greatly resented the fact that Sonnenfels's new police ordinance, while in effect making him responsible for providing for the needs of the capital's inhabitants in a whole gamut of areas, prevented him from surveying their activities as effectively as his predecessor had been able to do through the activities of the secret arm of the police. As a first step toward remedying this defect, in June 1792 Sauer created the *Zweigstelle für Anzeigewesen,* a separate registration department within the provincial administration, putting this under the direction of Pergen's old second-in-command von Beer, who was to be assisted by his former aide Märenthal.[14] As Sauer had taken this step on his own authority, he was now obliged to justify it to Francis, and in doing so he let not one but several cats out of the bag. There were present in Vienna, he alleged, several French emissaries, whose task it was to spread the poison of revolution. (If this was known to the police, there was hardly a need for a system of registration to establish the fact.) Worse, some Austrians sympathized with these apostles of revolution, and would have to be kept under close scrutiny. (But as these were presumably residents of Vienna, they would not be affected by the registration procedures.) Finally, in order to keep track of actions and people likely to become dangerous to the state, not only must coffee houses and inns, where strangers were apt to congregate, be kept under close observation, but, above all, secret societies must be watched over. (Would secret organizations whose members duly registered themselves with the police as such still qualify as secret?) Be all that as it may, Francis sanctioned Sauer's innovation, with the observation that, in his opinion, much work needed to be done to bring the police up to its old level of efficiency.[15]

There followed a dispute involving the provincial administration of Galicia, which wanted to reactivate the secret police in that province; Sonnenfels, who was anxious to protect his concept of what the police should and should not do; and Schilling, who saw in this matter an opportunity to convince Francis of the advantages to be gained from a return to Pergen's old system. Although the Galician request was ultimately turned down, largely because Kaunitz saw in it an attempt to undermine the control of his *Staatskanzlei* over that province, Schilling, while presenting his case, had made the point that Sonnenfels's "social" police were costing the state some 150,000 florins annually; even if the secret police were to be reactivated to its old levels, a narrowly defined police force would cost less than a tenth of that. As Francis had declared that he would under no circumstances impose new taxes to finance the war against France, but would, if necessary, pay for it out of his own exchequer, such a prospective saving must have greatly appealed to him.[16]

In September Francis decided that the time had come to consult Pergen. He sent him a note, asking for a detailed description of the secret police as it had functioned under him, and suggested that Pergen, inasmuch as the police had functioned at its best under his direction, should submit a proposal for restoring this crucial and salutary institution to its former state.[17] Pergen, still angered and embittered over the way in which he had been treated by Leopold, would not be mollified quite so easily. He replied that, inasmuch as he had been kept entirely in the dark about the course of events since his resignation, and had indeed never been told why his system had been overturned, he was in no position to give detailed advice in police matters. He had only heard that the new system was both inefficient and hideously expensive.[18]

In these circumstances it was Colloredo whose influence appears to have been decisive. Kaunitz had argued that, in order to prevent the police from acting in a pernicious and arbitrary manner, it was necessary to continue to exercise a strict surveillance over all of its activities in the *Staatsrat* and *Hofkanzlei*. But in October Colloredo submitted a memorandum to Francis in which he not only argued in favor of a secret police responsible only to the emperor, but buttressed this view by sending along a copy of Pergen's "Secret Instruction" of 1786, in which he had developed that very point for Joseph. Moreover, Colloredo offered the opinion that the best course would be to recall the author of that excellent document.[19] Paradoxically, and contrary to Pergen's expectations, these considerations were reinforced by a series of attacks on the inadequacy and high cost of the Sonnenfels system coming from the pen of Kollowrat. Without the least doubt, what the *Hofkanzlei* had in mind was a return to pre-Josephinian days, when internal security was entirely its responsibility, but the effect of these criticisms was merely to convince Francis that it had been a fatal mistake to depart from Pergen's principles.[20]

None of this seems to have been known to Sauer, who was independently pressing for the reestablishment of a ministry of police, and who doubtless saw himself as its chief.[21] Once again, however, the young emperor would opt in favor of putting his trust in experience. Pergen was sounded out on the subject of his willingness to resume his former station. This time he replied that he would gladly serve, on condition that he be given a deputy who could take over his duties during the summer, when he would need to restore his health. This was agreed to, and on 3 January 1793 Sauer was ordered to turn over control of the police to Pergen. An official announcement informed the public that the ministry of police had been reestablished under its former director, and that its authority would again extend over the whole of the monarchy.[22] In a private communication Francis instructed Pergen to restore the police as quickly as possible to the condition that had characterized it in the reign of his late uncle.[23]

Pergen, who now for the second time found himself at the head of Austria's police network, was not quite sixty-eight years old. This was, even then, not an unusually advanced age for a man in robust health. As it happened, Francis was surrounded by a gerontocracy; many of his chief ministers were even older. Still, if much in the way of flexibility and innovation might not be expected from them, they seemed entirely capable of carrying out their duties. What was to afflict Pergen in his second ministry, at least until its later years, was not so much advanced age as ill health—he had partially recovered his sight as the result of a successful cataract operation the year before, but could not put prolonged strain on his eyes—and ill temper.

Whatever attachment to principle he had managed to hang on to after his dismissal from the governorship of Galicia had long ago been sacrificed to expediency in the process of creating a police apparatus capable of pleasing Joseph. The police had been his creation and had become his raison d' être. When Leopold had proceeded to dismantle it, Pergen, who all his life had been an indefatigable accumulator of benefits and emoluments, had not clung to office but had preferred to resign. No doubt the many pensions he had accumulated in Joseph's service enabled him to do so in ample comfort, but the decision had obviously resulted in a financial loss to him. Now that the new ruler had again turned to him and his opinions had been vindicated, he would cling to them with a ferocity and an inflexibility reminiscent more than anything else of Kaunitz's insistence that the French alliance—his cherished creation—must be maintained right up to the point when the legislative assembly was declaring war on Austria.

Much of what would follow can be understood only in terms of a sort of siege mentality that came to dominate Pergen's thinking under the dual impact of his personal humiliation by Leopold and of the objective threat of the spread of French radicalism. It is not easy to see, under these circumstances, what useful and positive steps, if any, might have been taken to strengthen Austria internally so that she might have been relatively immune to the blandishments of French radicalism. Given Pergen's frame of mind, and the great range of powers over the internal affairs of the monarchy that Francis was willing to leave to him, it was clear from the outset that Austria's response to the challenge of the French Revolution would turn out to be repression rather than preventive reform.[24]

Characteristically, Pergen's first official act after accepting Francis's summons was to request that the letter in which the emperor asked him to resume his post of minister be published in the official gazette in the same prominent place in which his letter of resignation had appeared two years before. But he added the request that, in order to spare Sauer's feelings, Francis might see fit to excise from the rationale for taking this step the phrase "in order to correct the present, uncertain state of the police," although, as God knew, this was only too accurate a description of the state of affairs.[25]

Solicitous as he might have been of Sauer's feelings in the matter of the transfer of police authority, Pergen did not hesitate to remind Francis that the *Polizeihaus* as well as the *Zuchthaus,* which had remained with the Lower Austrian provincial administration, consti- tuted a central and necessary element of the police network. If he were to work with any sort of efficiency, these would now have to be trans- ferred to his ministry.[26] Francis at once acceded to this wish.[27] Aside from this matter, which he regarded as crucial, Pergen was careful not to ask for too much too soon. On the contrary, he made a point of insisting that responsibility for various matters that, under the Sonnenfels system, had been the concern of the police now be returned to the political authorities. In doing this he of course merely reasserted his old belief in the narrow interpretation of police duties, but the effect was to give the impression of a most becoming moderation of purpose. Furthermore, in order not to turn the provincial governors against him, since they would now no longer conduct police business independently but rather through a provincial police chief who would be Pergen's subordinate, he assured them that the police in their provinces would be directly under their control. To be sure, there was a hidden signifi- cance in the use of the term *unmittelbar,* (directly), inasmuch as this signified that the whole of whatever local apparatus they had built up would now be absorbed into a centralized agency under the ministry's resident police chief, but the pride of the governors was salvaged.[28]

Pergen also proceeded with a degree of caution in dismantling the various public service elements that had become a hallmark of the police during his absence. He might not be in sympathy with Sonnenfels's ideas about a *Wohlfahrtspolizei,* but there was no doubt in his mind that these had been enthusiastically received by the broad masses in the principal cities of the monarchy. Simply to abolish them would be willfully creating trouble for himself. In consequence, he encouraged the provincial governors to absorb these services into their administra- tions, letting it be known that he was in no way opposed to the creation of a separate body of police officials in the various provinces for this purpose. Underneath this seeming generosity of spirit lay the inescap- able fact that he was shifting the expense of providing social services from his budget to that of the provincial governors. Still, in fairness to him it must be stated that, on von Beer's recommendation, he agreed that the police doctors would continue to provide free medical services to those in need, on the condition that more stringent controls to establish this need would be applied.[29]

Within ten days of Pergen's reappointment to office Francis provided him with a set of guidelines for the conduct of police affairs. The police would, above all, be vigilant. They would behave in a moderate and circumspect manner in carrying out their investigations. They would proceed discreetly and cautiously in the surveillance of suspects. In making arrests they would behave firmly and calmly, and avoid all appearance of arbitrariness. They would be humane in their treatment of prisoners. And, insofar as they might be involved in passing sentence on prisoners (executive sentencing for minor offenses was a common-place under the Austrian judicial system), these pronouncements were to be governed by considerations of justice.[30] Having provided various theoretical safeguards against possible abuses of police power, the emperor got down to actual business. Pergen was immediately to turn his attention to the activities of the many foreigners residing in Vienna. Not only were all of them to be issued police passports, no one would be allowed to stay on without such a document, but the police would keep all foreigners who were given these documents under constant surveillance. Any activities which in any way aroused the suspicion that they might be agents of France were to be reported to him at once.[31]

Fortunately, there was no need to inform Pergen where his duty lay. He was already at work, tracking down whatever evidence of political dissidence he could. The trouble was, there did not seem to be very much. All that Pergen could come up with on the spur of the moment was the case of a certain Joseph Polz, who had been under arrest for some time for having made extremely offensive remarks in public. At the time of the transfer of police authority from Sauer to himself the former had told him that Polz should probably be released, as the evidence against him was shaky at best. However, given the present political climate, the circumstance that Vice-Chancellor Cobenzl had expressed the opinion that people who made speeches approving of the activities of the French revolutionaries belonged in a dungeon, and His Majesty's determination to stamp out all dissident activity, he now requested specific instructions in the matter.[32]

In addition, there was the case of two of Leopold's former secret agents, Stieber and Rühle, who had been arrested, still under Sauer's regime, for having made utterances that could be interpreted as incitements to rebellion. Since the case against them was rather weak, Pergen inquired whether they might be released, but Francis decided to confine them in the fortress of Kufstein for an indeterminate period.[33] Finally, a certain Franz Spaun, a former government servant, while enjoying the hospitality of the governor of Upper Austria, Count Rottenhan, had made some remarks favorable to the French revolutionaries. In spite of attempts of the host to calm the troubled waters, several of the dinner guests had leaped up and accused Spaun of being a "complete Jacobin." Learning of this incident, and encouraged by the disposition of Stieber and Rühle's cases, Pergen thereupon ordered Spaun's arrest and he too was transported to Kufstein without benefit of trial or hearing.[34]

This was a meager harvest, but before long Pergen would be in the position of doing better. At the end of the month he reported that, in the wake of the horrifying news of the execution of the king of France, stricter measures would have to be introduced. To be sure, the immediate reaction of the Viennese populace had been one of outrage and shock, so much so that the police had been forced to intervene in order to prevent demonstrations directed against various resident Frenchmen in the capital from becoming violent; but it was to be feared that soon enough there would be those who would be inspired to imitate this ghastly example.[35] As a preventive countermeasure, he proposed that the clergy be instructed to include in their sermons regular denunciations of this outrage.[36]

Just a few days later Pergen received a letter from Professor J. A. Riegger, informing him that graffiti depicting freedom wreaths with the words *liberté, égalité* woven into them had appeared in two locations in Prague. This could not have happened if the police had been doing their job. If one was to spend good money on them, the least one could expect was that they should prevent outrages of this sort.[37] Whatever his reaction to this rather less than friendly advice may have been, Pergen proceeded to make good use of it. He notified Francis at once that the political climate in Prague had passed the danger point. Secret societies abounded, as well as supporters of the murderous French cabal, or at least of the revolutionary principles infecting that country. While it might at this stage be undesirable to suppress these always noxious organizations by main force, he advised that they should be neutralized by scaring their leaders with massive threats, and by weaning away their cleverest members. Moreover, as it was well known that the universities were the breeding ground for this sort of outrage, their faculties should be thoroughly purged. Sympathizers with radical doctrines should without exception be removed and replaced with men of reliable monarchist opinions. Mere protestations of loyalty should not be taken into consideration; these would come all too easily from a gentry anxious to retain its positions. Anyone not able to demonstrate a record of long-term loyalty should be dismissed. As for the Prague police, it was of course possible that their vigilance had been somewhat lax. He had issued orders to the *Stadthauptmann,* Count Laczanski, to redouble his efforts.[38] It is most instructive to observe what Pergen was capable of making out of a couple of graffiti.

In Vienna, to demonstrate that he at least was not lacking in vigilance, Pergen ordered his police to keep all foreigners under the strictest observation. Inevitably, this soon led to excessive zeal on the part of some of his men. Before long Cobenzl was complaining that the Westphalian legation had protested because one of their nationals, a tailor's apprentice named Kraus, who held a full-time job in the capital, had been arrested by Pergen's police. When they had been unable to make a case of political agitation against him, they had simply declared him a vagabond and turned him over to the army as a recruit. Such arbitrary and iniquitous acts would have to cease; they might well lead to reprisals by other states.[39]

That the Kraus case was not merely the result of muddling on lower police levels is demonstrated by a note of Pergen's to Cobenzl in which he commented on a report circulating in Vienna about Jacobin plans to introduce the revolution into Austria. The origin of this rumor, he informed his ministerial colleague, was an anonymous denunciation whose accuracy could not be established. Nevertheless, the information contained in this document corresponded closely to what was known about the French radicals from other sources, so that there could be no doubt about its substance.[40] In other words, whatever notions were thought suitable by the police in the pursuit of its duties were to be assumed true, without troubling oneself unduly about their actual correspondence to fact.

Francis was seemingly so impressed with Pergen's acumen that he did not confine himself to giving him virtually complete control over the police, but solicited his advice on matters quite unrelated to the business of his ministry. Thus Francis asked Pergen to draw up an evaluation of various highly placed officials in the Galician administration.[41] Pergen was only too glad to comply with this request, as it enabled him, among other things, to settle a number of old scores.

By the middle of March Pergen was back into the thick of routine police administration. He reported that, in accord with His Majesty's express wish, he had increased the bread ration in the prison system to one pound per inmate per day. It had previously been set at 23 *Lott* (230 grams), so that this represented a virtual doubling. It had been possible to take such a step without burdening his already overstretched budget because the price of bread had recently declined and because, as soon as he had returned to office, he had introduced a regulation that all prison inmates who were not bedridden were to be put to work spinning cotton. This had proved to be a relatively profitable operation.[42]

In April Pergen was able to inform the emperor that he had chosen a deputy.[43] This individual would have the right to act in his name in all matters during his absences from the capital.[44] The man he selected to occupy this important position was Count Franz Joseph Saurau, who was then only thirty-three years old. He had gotten his start in the Josephinian *Kreis* administration, having spent five years as *Kreiskommissär* in Traiskirchen. During this period Saurau was a member of the Masonic lodge *Zur wahren Eintracht,* but this circumstance does not testify to a particularly liberal orientation on his part; it was merely fashionable to belong. In 1789 Saurau was summoned to Vienna as *Stadthauptmann,* in which position he functioned as Pergen's deputy.[45] Apparently he had given complete satisfaction in that capacity, as Pergen would hardly have chosen so relatively inexperienced an assistant otherwise.

At any rate, Pergen was now in the position to proceed with the task that the emperor had entrusted to him: the suppression of all manifestations of either sympathy or actual support for the French enemy. After a promising start, the war against France had been going increasingly badly, and various prominent figures within the government had repeatedly expressed the fear that this circumstance was bound to have internal repercussions.[46] Whether or not this was the case, it certainly behooved Pergen to take the threat seriously. Not only would it have constituted a dereliction of duty to neglect it, but, so long as Francis was convinced that it was real, Pergen's own professional interests would obviously be best served by supporting him in that opinion.

In a lengthy memorandum to the provincial governors Pergen insisted that the danger of revolutionary opinions becoming generally accepted in the monarchy was now so great that mere defensive measures would no longer suffice. Positive steps would have to be taken in order to convert those already infected by *Freiheitsschwindel* (the cult of liberty), which was so much in fashion. Three elements were essential in order to gain this end. Men of good will would have to be encouraged to proselytize on behalf of the monarchical principle; pamphlets defending the existing system would have to be composed and circulated, without this being perceived as too obvious an exercise in propaganda; and, above all, teachers on all rungs of the educational ladder would have to be enlisted in the good fight.[47]

It did not take long for the new system, deployed now throughout the monarchy and centrally controlled from Vienna, to register its first major success. In May it was reported that four notorious Jacobins, including, it was claimed, the Deputy Hérault de Séchelles, had appeared in Passau, where, under the cover of assumed names, they were propagandizing on behalf of the revolution.[48] Shortly afterward the police succeeded in arresting these men.[49]

In the wake of this incident Pergen submitted a report that at first glance seems extremely puzzling. He proceeded to inform Francis that, as of the moment, the Bohemian fortresses of Königgrätz, Josephstadt, Spielberg, and Olmütz, traditional places of detention, held no fewer than twenty-four Staatsgefangene between them.[50] Since Leopold had done away with that category of prisoners, the impression given is that, in some surreptitious manner, two dozen unfortunates had been held without the emperor's knowledge. A closer look, however, reveals that, with four exceptions, these prisoners were all French. Four of them were deputies of the legislative assembly who, along with their secretaries and servants, had fallen into Austrian hands. Then there was the luckless Marquis de Lafayette, who had deserted to the Austrians in 1792 but, instead of being welcomed as an emigré, had been arrested as an agent of the revolutionary regime; and the former French minister of war, de Beurnonville, who had been similarly dealt with.[51] The final four were all Poles: the brothers Zazonczeck, one a general, the other a former treasurer of Galicia; General Wieniawsky, the onetime military commandant in Cracow; and the former Abbot Kolonthay—all of whom had been involved in a Polish national conspiracy against Austrian rule. What is not in the least clear is whether Pergen was merely guilty of a careless choice of terms in referring to these men as Staatsgefangene, or if Leopold, indeed, had revived not only the practice of holding certain people without trial (none of the individuals involved was ever convicted in a court of law), but the formal category of Staatsverbrecher as well.[52]

If there had ever been any doubt about the matter, it was now well established that the Jacobins intended to spread their poison within Austria. Less clear, however, was the extent to which they were successful in this effort. But once launched on these waters, Pergen's men could be relied upon to come up with some evidence of an internal conspiracy.

The ominous form that such efforts could take was soon demonstrated by a lengthy memorandum of Saurau's.[53] In this he informed the emperor that one of the newly reactivated Vertraute, a reliable judge of the popular temper, had warned him that one element of the population, namely the Protestants, were thoroughly untrustworthy. Instead of accepting the toleration which His Late Majesty, the emperor

Joseph, had so graciously accorded them, they rejected the very word as anathema and demanded complete equality. To achieve this goal they would not hesitate to support the revolutionaries, whose principles they greatly admired. They had been in the forefront of the Jacobin uprising in Strasbourg and, given half a chance, there was no reason to suppose that they would behave otherwise within the monarchy.

Saurau went on to name specific individuals. The Viennese school superintendent Höck was said to be infected by the Jacobin spirit. So was Professor Hoffmann, a onetime member of Leopold's secret network of agents in Hungary. An officer named Schmied had been overheard making remarks favorable to France. According to the bookseller Grieffer in Pest, a considerable demand arose among his Protestant customers for books dealing with revolutionary subjects. A man named Weinbrenner, a resident of Vienna, had openly called himself a Jacobin. It was well known that this individual regularly took his noon meal in the company of Hofrat Birkenstock, who sent his son to a Protestant university in Germany. If the local university was so bad, why did not Birkenstock, in his capacity as expert adviser on educational questions, make suggestions for its improvement, rather than send his son abroad? Also to be regarded as highly suspicious individuals were the director of the veterinary school, Johann Gottlieb Wollstein; a secretary at the *Magistrat* named Brandstätter; a soap-boiler named Franzl; and Professor F. X. Neupauer, lately of Graz, now practicing law in Vienna. In addition, what amounted to a Jacobin cell had lately developed in the bookshop belonging to Joseph Vinzenz Degen. Degen himself set the tone, and his customers included such notorious Jacobin sympathizers as the court secretary Bartsch, an intimate friend of Sonnenfels's; Professor Lieblein; a certain Arbesser; and the abbé Strattmann, the custodian of the imperial library, who aspired to becoming a second Sièyes.

Saurau commented on his agent's allegations by saying that, in his view, the man's suspicions of the Protestants were fully justified. These people would never be satisfied until they had succeeded in placing their religion on a level with the dominant one. Any concessions would only lead to further demands on their part. Also, the *Vertraute* knew whereof he spoke with respect to the Jacobin sympathizers. It was all too true that a spirit disloyal to monarchical principles was loose among the teachers and scholars of the capital. It was vital to keep these people under close observation, and to keep the censorship in vigilant hands to prevent them from disseminating their dreadful opinions.[54]

One might have supposed that this formless mixture of unsubstantiated allegations, smears, and innuendos would not have had much of an effect on the emperor, who had already demonstrated that he was at heart a fair-minded man, but Francis was sufficiently impressed to order Saurau to keep all these suspicious individuals under intensive surveillance.[55]

Perhaps most interesting in all of this was the reference to Degen, who would within the year play such a prominent role as *agent provocateur* and police spy in Pergen and Saurau's suppression of the "Jacobin conspiracy" in the monarchy. Was Degen in their employ already in 1793, or, as seems more likely, did they apply pressure by threatening to arrest him for allowing his bookshop to be used as a meeting place for dangerous subversives?

In September, back from his holiday, Pergen notified Francis that he had not been wasting his time. During his absence he had been in constant touch with one of his men in Prague about the best means of winning over the Czechs to unquestioned loyalty to the state. The man had submitted a detailed proposal toward accomplishing this end, but it would require the introduction of a large and elaborate secret police apparatus that could no longer be controlled by the provincial governor, which would doubtless lead to a storm of protest from that quarter. For the time being it would be best to confine oneself to distributing appropriate written materials.[56]

Pergen and Saurau were by no means the only source of alarming rumors. By the autumn of 1793 various branches of government had begun to notify the ministry of police of suspicious activities that had, in one way or another, come to their attention. Philipp Cobenzl, in particular, played an active role in making denunciations of this sort. He reported that it had come to his attention that a Baron O'Cahill, residing in Klagenfurt, was a suspicious individual who should be closely watched,[57] and, somewhat later, that Count Rhode was under suspicion of having spread ideas sympathetic to France in Lindau.[58]

In the midst of this atmosphere of suspicion and denunciation, Pergen believed that the moment had come to take a major step in the direction of extending police control into areas that had so far been outside of it. In November he addressed a memorandum to Francis in which he argued that a major part of the damage being done stemmed from the continued circulation of subversive publications, which the existing censorship was apparently either unwilling or unable to suppress. The only practical way to combat this evil would be to require that henceforth all works dealing with political questions, or commenting on current events, be submitted to the ministry of police for precensorship. Moreover, the ministry should be consulted about the possibility of banning already extant works which fell under the suspicion of disseminating revolutionary ideas. At this point, however, the

Hofkanzlei, recently rechristened *Directorium,* which was responsible for administering the censorship, was able to defend its turf successfully. A majority in the *Staatsrat* declared itself opposed to Pergen's proposal, and Francis merely ordered that the ministry of police be kept abreast of all decisions in censorship matters.[59]

Undeterred by this reverse, Pergen soon thereafter attempted to redefine the borders between police and judicial responsibility in questions affecting state security. His argument was that wherever there existed a clear danger to the state the police had to act, with or without the backing of the judicial system.[60] While the emperor apparently failed to endorse this opinion, he also did not reject it outright, so that Pergen could thereafter act upon this proposition without seeming to contravene the imperial will.

NOTES

1. Anon., *Über geheime Gesellschaften im Staate,* (1791), S.A., V.A. 41.

2. The literature on the participation of the secret societies in the European revolutionary movement at the end of the eighteenth century is immense, contentious, and inconclusive. For the Habsburg lands, cf. in particular L. Abafi, *Geschichte der Freimaurerei in Oesterreich-Ungarn,* 5 vols. (Budapest, 1890–97), and more recent and considerably more tendentious, E. Rosenstrauch-Königsberg, *Freimaurerei im Josephinischem Wien* (Vienna & Stuttgart, 1975); *idem,* "Eine Freimaurerische Akademie der Wissenschaften in Wien," J. H. Schoeps & I. Geiss, eds., *Revolution und Demokratie in Geschichte und Literatur* (Duisburg, 1979); *idem,* "Radikal-aufklärerische Geheimbünde in der Habsburger Monarchie zur Zeit der Französischen Revolution (1785–95), O. Büsch & W. Grab, eds., *Die Demokratische Bewegung in Mitteleuropa im ausgehenden 18. und frühen 19. Jahrhundert* (Berlin, 1980). This volume is a collection of papers delivered at an East Berlin congress that is of considerable interest inasmuch as many of the participants, feeling themselves to be *entre eux,* abandoned even the minimal restraints that they normally impose on themselves, and presented an unabashedly doctrinaire Marxist view. For the more radical Illuminati, who, however, do not seem to have made much of an impact on the monarchy, cf. R. Van Dülmen, *Der Geheimbund der Illuminaten* (Bad Cannstatt, 1975).

3. Pergen to Leopold, 4 January 1791, S.A., V.A. 41.

4. It is by no means clear to me what, if anything, could have been meant by "Americans," unless Pergen was using these terms as a catchall for those who sympathized with some of the liberal principles then in the air, without, however, belonging to one of the more formally organized groups. One instance of subversive Masonic activity in Pergen's eyes was certainly the fuss being made about Mozart's *Magic Flute,* which was first performed in Vienna in 1791. The opera went on to establish a record of sixty-two performances in its first run, not least because it was widely rumored that it was to be understood as a

political allegory. Someone even circulated an elucidation of the cast of characters for those too simpleminded to recognize them, in which the Queen of the Night was identified as Maria Theresa and Pamina as Liberty, "always a daughter of despotism." Cf. F. Gräffer, *Josephinische Curiosa,* 3 vols. (Vienna, 1848–50), III, 182–83, and W. C. Langsam, "Emperor Francis II and the Austrian 'Jacobins,' 1792–1796," *American Historical Review,* L (1945).

5. Francis, although only twenty-two at Leopold's accession, was frequently deputized by his father to represent him at various ministerial conferences, and during a prolonged Italian journey of the Emperor's in 1791, he acted as regent. Thus he saw practically all important state papers that crossed Leopold's desk. On Francis, see W. C. Langsam, *Francis the Good* (New York, 1949), and the older but still useful C. Wolfsgruber, *Franz I., Kaiser von Österreich,* 2 vols. (Vienna & Leipzig, 1899). V. Bibl, *Kaiser Franz* (Leipzig & Vienna, 1938), is uneven but uses interesting materials in the Bavarian State Archives.

6. Wolfsgruber, *Franz I.,* II, 177.

7. Quoted in Langsam, *Francis the Good,* 98.

8. Bibl, *Kaiser Franz,* 36–37. While there does not seem to have been much in the way of organized support for the French radicals in Austria at this time—the great majority of Austrians tended to identify with their countrywoman Marie Antoinette and to look upon all threats to the French Monarchy as a direct insult to her—radical revolutionary literature circulated there in spite of Leopold's insistence that the censorship be strictly applied. Thus Count Karl Zinzendorf, a man of broad interests and liberal sympathies, experienced no difficulty in obtaining copies of the *Moniteur,* or even of the most virulently poisonous pamphlets attacking Marie Antoinette. Cf. M. Schubert, "Wie reagierte Wien auf die Französische Revolution?," *Österreich in Geschichte und Literatur,* XIV/10 (December 1970), 509.

9. Bibl, *Kaiser Franz,* 38–39. For an excellent recent treatment of the larger issues involved, see T. C. W. Blanning, *The Origins of the French Revolutionary Wars* (London & New York, 1986).

10. Quoted in Langsam, *Francis the Good,* 142.

11. Cf. V. Bibl, "Das Robot-Provisorium für Nieder-Österreich vom 20. Juni 1796," *Jahrbuch für Landeskunde von Niederösterreich,* N.F. VII (1908), 240, and Reinalter, *Aufgeklärter Absolutismus,* 143.

12. Reinalter, *Aufgeklärter Absolutismus,* 145; cf. E. V. Zenker, *Geschichte der Wiener Journalistik von den Anfängen bis zum Jahre 1848* (Vienna & Leipzig 1892), 89.

13. The outbreak of war, given the fact that the previous, wildly unpopular conflict with the Ottomans had not come to a formal conclusion until the year before, was not precisely greeted with outbursts of joy in the monarchy. Cf. Wangermann, *Jacobin Trials,* 119–21. Nevertheless, once military operations had begun, the great majority of the populace stood behind Francis in what appeared to all but a few a justified intervention on behalf of the king and his Austrian consort. There is no reason to believe, as Wangermann claims, that Francis "decided . . . to reestablish the Josephinian secret police in order to

destroy the political opposition," which, at that point, was far too insignificant to have merited such a response.

14. Wangermann, *Jacobin Trials*, 121–22. The practice of making all strangers who bedded down in the capital register with the police was not new, it had in fact been carried out to everyone's satisfaction under the existing system; there was no great increase in the number of visitors to Vienna, so that Sauer's actions were plainly intended to create an agency that could be used to keep the populace under surveillance. As Schilling, von Beer's other principal assistant, had been attached to Sauer's department at Francis's own request in 1791, Pergen's old inner triumvirate was now reassembled.

15. Wangermann, *Jacobin Trials*, 122.

16. Benna, "Organisierung," 214. Wangermann, *Jacobin Trials*, 123–24.

17. Walter, *Zentral-Verwaltung*, II/1/2/2, 281–82.

18. Wangermann, *Jacobin Trials*, 124–25.

19. *Ibid.*

20. Walter, *Zentral-Verwaltung*, II/1//2/2, 282. Pergen, who undoubtedly was being kept fully abreast of these developments by his various friends in high places, could not forbear from mocking Kollowrat after his recall to office. In a note informing him of his reinstatement he expressed the heartfelt hope that they would soon restore their mutual friendly relations and confidence in one another's judgment.

21. Francis to Sauer, 5 November 1792, V.A., P.A. XVIII/A.

22. Francis to Pergen, 30 December 1792, S.A., H.P. 619; Wangermann, *Jacobin Trials*, 126.

23. Walter, *Zentral-Verwaltung*, II/5, 400–401. Francis wrote that he considered it his holiest duty to watch over the security of his subjects.

24. Wangermann, throughout *Jacobin Trials*, either implies or argues directly that Leopold had been trying to save what was to be saved of the Josephinian reforms in order to carry them over into the new, infinitely more complex, and more dangerous age, and that these efforts failed because the old guard, which had opposed Joseph from the outset, was finally able to regain power under Francis. This is certainly a possible interpretation of these events. The argument here, however, will be that, in the main, it would be disillusioned or embittered Josephinians, Pergen prominent among them, who would preside over the so-called Francisceian Reaction.

25. Pergen to Colloredo, S.A., F.A.S. 76.

26. Pergen to Francis, 11 January 1793, V.A., P.A. I.

27. Francis to Pergen, 12 January 1793, V.A., P.A. I.

28. Walter, *Zentral-Verwaltung*, II/2/1/1, 283–84. Moreover, the governors were assured that they would have direct access to whatever reports the police chiefs would make to him. Cf. Benna, "Organisierung," 216.

29. Osterloh, *Sonnenfels*, 159. Pergen did insist that the police be freed of what he regarded as "senseless scribbling," such as rendering opinions in what were essentially civil disputes. Cf. Oberhummer, *Wiener Polizei*, I, 83–84.

30. Langsam, *Francis the Good*, 155. Langsam cites Pergen's instructions to

the provincial chiefs, issued in April, but these are virtually identical with Francis's orders of January.

31. Francis to Pergen, 14 January 1793, S.A., N.v.P., neu, 21.

32. Pergen to Philipp Cobenzl, 15 January 1793, S.A., N.v.P., neu, 21. Cobenzl, who evidently felt uncomfortable in these waters, hastened to reply that he had only been expressing a general opinion, without knowing the particulars of Polz's case. Decisions of this kind were exclusively in the province of the police. Cobenzl to Pergen, 18 January 1793, S.A., Noten an die Polizeihofstelle (hereafter N.a.P.H.), neu, 1.

33. Reinalter, *Aufgeklärter Absolutismus*, 178.

34. *Ibid.*

35. Schubert, "Wie reagierte Wien?," 508–9. Still, Pergen seems not to have given too much credence to reports that radicalism was rife among French emigrés. When the governor of Carniola, Count O'Donnel, raised the issue his instructions were that letters posted by Frenchmen were to be opened only in cases where there were strong reasons to suspect them of revolutionary activity. Cf. M. Pawlik, "Emigranten der Französischen Revolution in Österreich," *Mitteilungen des Instituts für österreichische Geschichtsforschung*, LXXVII (1969), 114.

36. Pergen to Francis, 31 January 1793, V.A., P.A. X/B1. The emperor approved of this suggestion and informed Pergen that he would personally see to it that the clergy be instructed in this manner.

37. Riegger to Pergen, 7 February 1793, V.A., P.A. X/A2. Riegger, who had been dismissed from a lucrative post as librarian to the Schwarzenbergs in the reign of Joseph, had entertained high hopes of rehabilitation when Leopold came to the throne. He had in fact been encouraged to believe that he would receive an appointment as *Hofrat*, but Leopold had vetoed this, referring to him as "that Jacobin." Doubtless Riegger hoped now to establish his bona fides as a good conservative. Cf. Wurzbach, *Biographisches Lexicon*, XXVI, 35.

38. Pergen to Francis, 14 February 1793, V.A., P.A. X/A2.

39. Cobenzl to Pergen, 24 February 1793, S.A., N.a.P.H., neu, 1. Pergen's excuse for this misadventure was that not the police, but the *Magistrat*, which was under Sauer's authority, was to blame for the fate of Kraus. He had been turned over to it for disposition of his case, and that body had failed to conduct a proper investigation. Pergen to Cobenzl, 28 February 1793, S.A., N.v.P., neu, 21.

40. Pergen to Cobenzl, 24 February 1793, S.A., N.v.P., neu, 21.

41. Pergen to Francis, 1793, S.A., V.A. 40. So as not to interrupt the flow of the narrative unduly, the full text of this document appears in Appendix I.

42. Pergen to Francis, 16 March 1793, V.A., P.A. I. Cf. the *Magistratskundmachung*, January 1793, which required all prison inmates to spin a minimum of twelve bobbins of cotton weekly. Those who fell below that norm were to be punished by reductions in their food allocation, and those who exceeded it were to be rewarded with a bonus of 1 krone for each additional bobbin.

43. Wangermann, *Jacobin Trials*, 126.

44. Pergen to Thugut, 30 April 1793, S.A., N.v.P., neu, 21.

45. On Saurau see *Beiträge Statthalterei*, 349 ff., and Wurzbach, *Biographisches*

Lexicon, XXIII, 192 ff. Cf. also H. Wagner, *Freimaurerei um Joseph II.* (Vienna, 1980), 139. Saurau did not wait long to ingratiate himself with Francis. In May he submitted a lengthy report criticizing the zeal and ability of most of the monarchy's public servants (by implication those of his chief as well) and demanding wholesale dismissals of those incapable of carrying out their duties. Cf. A. Faulhammer, "Politische Meinungen und Stimmungen in Wien in den Jahren 1793 und 1794," *Programm des k.k. Staats-Gymnasiums in Salzburg* (1893), 8–9.

46. As early as December 1792 Sauer rounded up a number of resident Frenchmen whom he suspected of sympathizing with their government in Paris, and several of them were eventually expelled without benefit of trial. Shortly thereafter, the earl marshal, Prince Starhemberg, insisted on the necessity of forestalling the dissemination of revolutionary literature within Austria. Wangermann, *Jacobin Trials,* 128–29. But what Wangermann fails to underline is that these measures seem to have been largely preventive in nature. There were at the time no reports in the police files of any actual manifestations of sympathy for the revolution among Austrians.

47. Benna, "Organisierung," 217.

48. Saurau to Thugut, 23 May 1793, S.A., N.v.P., neu, 21. From this point on, as often as not, communications from the ministry of police to various branches of the government went out over Saurau's name. Since this practice was not the case just in the summer months, it cannot have been the rule only when Pergen was away. It is not really possible to determine whether, during the rest of the year, Saurau signed whenever Pergen was prevented from doing so because of ill health, or because Pergen had turned over to him certain categories of business. Since no very clear pattern emerges, the latter is somewhat unlikely. At any rate, it would seem that Pergen and Saurau were in close agreement on all major issues, so that it makes most sense to think of their direction of the ministry as a cooperative effort, with Pergen at first dominating, and Saurau later on, probably around 1797, beginning to assume a leading role.

49. Saurau to Thugut, 10 June 1793, S.A., N.v.P., neu, 21. Whoever the leader of this French party was, it was not Hérault de Sèchelles, who in June would participate in the arrest of the Girondins in Paris and so could not have been in an Austrian prison. It is not clear at what point the Austrians realized their error. The Austrian prison records list the name of Bancol as a deputy imprisoned in the fortress of Olmütz, but this name does not appear in the authoritative *Dictionnaire parlementaire Français* (Paris, 1891).

50. Pergen to Francis, 1793, S.A., N.v.P., neu, 21.

51. Beurnonville and the deputies were all members of a commission sent out by the convention to the *Armée du Nord* for the purpose of arresting General Dumouriez, who was suspected of collusion with the enemy. Dumouriez turned the tables on them, had them arrested, and turned them over to the Austrians. The two most prominent deputies involved were François Lamarque and Armand-Gaston Camus. The Austrian prison records list the names of the other two as Willmer and Guinette. These names do not appear in the *Dictionnaire.*

52. The natural temptation would be to put these prisoners into the category of those being held in military prisons, outside of civil jurisdiction, were it not for the fact that Pergen later also submitted a list of *Festungsarrestanten*. Cf. *Tabelle über die Festungsarrestanten* (1793), V.A., P.A. V. There were five of these (Ferdinand Rühle, Franz Spaun, Peter Colombat, Franz Großing, and Franz Hanke), all of whom were being held for political crimes, and who would seem, much more so than the Frenchmen and Poles, to qualify as *Staatsverbrecher*. Großing had certainly been one originally. Could the painfully exact Pergen have been guilty of a careless terminological error? It is hardly credible. The details of these five cases will be discussed below.

53. Saurau to Francis, 19 July 1793, V.A., P.A. X/B1.

54. The crudeness and viciousness of the attack on the Protestants, as well as the inclusion of Birkenstock, Pergen's old protégé, leads one to suspect strongly that this document is exclusively the work of Saurau.

55. Marginalium of Francis on the above. Wangermann, *Jacobin Trials*, 149, who fails to quote this document, refers to it as follows: "The police had been aware of the identity and movements of some of the 'Jacobins' since the summer of 1793." This is to dignify Saurau's diatribe with an importance and a trustworthiness that it in no sense deserves.

56. Pergen to Francis, 8 September 1793, V.A., P.A. X/A2.

57. Cobenzl to Saurau, 13 September 1793, S.A., N.a.P.H., neu, 1. In a major reorganization of the chancery following upon the Second Partition of Poland, from which the Austrians had been excluded, Francis split the chancellery into two parts. Cobenzl and Spielmann, who had inherited Kaunitz's mantle, were replaced by Baron Franz Maria Thugut, who, however, was not given the title of chancellor (Kaunitz retained this until his death in the following year), but merely of foreign minister. Cobenzl was shunted off to head a rump, which was intended to deal with Italian domestic affairs. Not surprisingly, he would have been anxious to expand his shrunken dominion. Cf. K. A. Roider, Jr., *Baron Thugut and Austria's Response to the French Revolution* (Princeton, N.J., 1987), 104–9.

58. Cobenzl to Pergen, 16 February 1794, S.A., N.a.P.H., neu, 1. This last denunciation turned out to be superfluous, since Pergen had notified Thugut in November 1793 that his agents were watching Rhode, who was the Prussian ambassador-designate to Portugal, and who had been seen in the company of "the most vocal democrats" of the place. Pergen believed that Rhode intended to arrange for the shipment of wheat from Prussian Neuchâtel to France. Pergen to Thugut, 6 November 1793, S.A., N.a.P.H., neu, 1. Apparently Thugut did not deem it necessary to pass on this manner of intelligence to Cobenzl.

59. Benna, "Organisierung," 221–22; Walter, *Zentral-Verwaltung,* II/2/1/1, 286.

60. Pergen to Francis, 12 December 1793, V.A., P.A. IX/B 18.

Pergen and the "Jacobin" Trials

IN NOVEMBER 1793 Pergen notified Colloredo that he had received a denunciation from a man called Desalleur. The subject of this document was Dr. Franz Anton Mesmer, who had recently returned to Vienna from a long stay in France.[1] Von Beer had launched an immediate investigation of this individual, in the course of which both Princess Gonzaga and Hofrat Stupfel had confirmed that Mesmer not only held extremely dangerous opinions, but took every available occasion to disseminate these in a malicious manner. Pergen's considered opinion was that such an individual represented a clear danger to the state. The very next day he was able to report that Mesmer had been arrested, that his papers had been confiscated, and that in all probability the same fate awaited several other persons who had been in close association with him.[2]

Mesmer had studied medicine in Vienna and, having received his degree, began the practice of that profession in the capital. Soon afterward he undertook the experiments with hypnosis that would ultimately make him famous. At the time, however, they aroused considerable suspicion, and in 1777 he was forced to make a precipitate departure. He traveled to Paris, where he repeated his experiments with success. He was soon very much à la mode in the French capital, and numbered among his patients some of the most prominent members of the aristocracy. Acting upon his conviction that the successful physician treats the whole man, he founded a so-called Society of Harmony. For a time the French police suspected that this was an organization for the dissemination of radical ideas, but the notion was soon dropped due chiefly to the circumstance that the initiation fee into the society was 100 louis d'or, a sum that only the very rich could afford. Mesmer might be bilking the credulous, but he was certainly not disseminating revolutionary ideas. By 1785 he either grew tired of Paris, or equally likely, his experiments in hypnosis were again giving rise to suspicion among his colleagues in the medical profession. At any rate, he left France in that year and spent the next eight traveling in Germany and Switzerland. Shortly before the outbreak of the revolution in France a onetime associate of his, one Guillaume Kornmann, had indeed founded what amounted to a radical branch of the Society of Harmony, but by then Mesmer had been gone from France for some time.[3]

In 1793, his estranged wife having died, Mesmer returned to Vienna to occupy the house they had owned in common on the Landstraße. Part of this mansion was rented to the Princess Gonzaga, and Mesmer now called upon this lady to pay his respects. In the course of their conversation he mentioned that he had spent some years in Paris, whereupon the princess denounced the French regicides as an abomination in the sight of God and man. Mesmer agreed that the Jacobins deserved her condemnation, but added somewhat injudiciously that there were other, more moderate, reformers in France, whose views should not be condemned out of hand. Thereupon the princess had Mesmer thrown out of her apartment and told anyone who would listen that he was a dangerous radical who sympathized with the regicides.[4] This, it would seem, ultimately led to Desalleur's denunciation and Mesmer's arrest.

Mesmer remained imprisoned for some two months, but in spite of the best efforts of the police investigators, nothing could be proven against him, so he finally had to be released. All that Pergen was able to achieve was to have him expelled from Austrian territory.[5] From Pergen's point of view, this was a meager harvest. Once more, as in the cases of Stieber, Rühle, Spaun, and Kraus, the best efforts of the police had been able to produce only unsubstantiated gossip and malicious innuendo. If he were to convince Francis that the danger of internal conspiracy was real and present he would have to do considerably better.

As luck would have it, the solution to Pergen's problem was close at hand, in the person of Ignaz von Martinovics.[6] This individual, a former member of the Franciscan order, had been a prominent member of Leopold's team of secret agents whose task was to influence public opinion in Hungary favorably to the monarchy, as well as to report to the emperor on Hungarian conditions. Although this personal secret service was dissolved after Leopold's death, its director, Franz Gotthardi, the onetime chief of police in Pest and close associate of Pergen's, was retained by Francis in an unspecified capacity with instructions to continue to report on events of interest in Hungary. At first these reports went to Colloredo, but immediately after the reconstitution of the ministry of police, Gotthardi was instructed to work through Pergen.

Gotthardi had retained Martinovics on his payroll throughout this period and considered him to be his most valuable agent, so much so that, being placed once more under Pergen's direction, he even ventured to suggest that the man's activities continue to be known only to himself, to the emperor, and to Colloredo, thus in effect establishing an independent Hungarian branch of the secret police. This request, however, was denied by Francis, and Pergen was soon directing Martinovics's activities himself. In April 1793 he sent him on a tour of Hungary and Transylvania. Upon his return to Vienna Martinovics submitted a series of reports—made up partly of his observations and in part freely invented—the tenor of which was that revolutionary opinions circulated everywhere in the country, various Hungarian regiments were on the point of mutiny, and several of the monarchy's leading officials were openly talking treason. Although Saurau seems to have reacted to these reports with some skepticism, Pergen advised that it would be well to investigate further, as it was known to him through other sources that the general atmosphere in Hungary evidently left much to be desired.[7]

What was not known to Pergen and Gotthardi was that, alongside his activities as a police agent, Martinovics himself was a dabbler in revolutionary politics. As early as the autumn of 1792, he had hit upon the idea of disseminating some notions highly critical of the Austrian regime in the form of a supposed open letter from the Italian count Giuseppe Gorani to Francis. Gorani had in fact published a series of such letters to various sovereigns in the Paris *Moniteur* in the course of 1792. When in September an issue of that paper, for one reason or another, failed to reach Vienna, rumors quickly arose that it had contained a Gorani letter addressed to Francis, and had for that reason been suppressed by the Austrian censorship. It was this supposed letter that Martinovics now composed and circulated. In this document Martinovics accused Francis of having turned his back on the liberal policies of his late uncle, in favor of continuing and enhancing the repressive measures instituted by his father. These circumstances had not gone unnoticed in Hungary, and one day the Hungarian nation would unfailingly rise up to sweep him from his throne.[8] Martinovics apparently put this document away in a drawer where it lay for some months, but by the summer of 1793, after his return from Hungary, and after it had become clear to him that, although he could continue in his present employment, Gotthardi's repeated requests to reward him in some extraordinary manner for his contributions had been turned down, he decided to circulate it among a group of like-minded acquaintances. Prominent among these was the former lottery entrepreneur, Johann Hackl, at whose house Martinovics frequently took his midday meal. Hackl had been barred from further participation in the lottery business for some unnamed transgression, and thus harbored a grudge against the government. But he had accumulated some money and, moreover, had a rich and attractive wife, circumstances that allowed him to set a table for whatever friends cared to drop in. Aside from Martinovics, the regular diners seem to have been the poet Alois Blumauer, the abbé Paul Strattmann, custodian of the imperial library, and the police commissioner of Lemberg, Franz Xaver Troll, another former agent of Gotthardi's.[9] Apparently a frequent topic of conversation among the dinner guests was the latest news from France, which of course was being hotly discussed everywhere in Vienna. According to later but often contradictory testimony, some of those present spoke approvingly about political figures such as Robespierre and even applauded reports of French military victories and occasionally burst into spirited renditions of the *Marseillaise* and of *Ça ira*, with Mrs. Hackl at the piano.[10]

There existed two similar groups in Vienna, both of them also *Tischrunden* in format. One group met at the house of Baron Andreas Riedel, a onetime mathematics tutor of the emperor Francis', and later professor at the military academy in Wiener Neustadt; the other at the home of Dr. Wollstein, the head of the veterinary surgery school. The principal members of Riedel's group seem to have been Lieutenant Franz Hebenstreit, an officer in the garrison regiment in the capital; Count Stanislaus Hohenwart, a student, who appears to have been in love with Riedel's daughter; an employee of the Superior Military Court, Cajetan Gilovsky; and a secretary in the Hungarian chancery, Georg Ruszitska, whom Riedel had employed as music teacher and tutor in his household. Dr. Wollstein's guests included the municipal councillor Martin Joseph Prandstätter; the lawyer and former law professor Franz Xaver Neupauer; and the lawyer Jakob Ignaz Jutz.[11] The Riedel group, in order to economize, shared a subscription to the *Moniteur*, which circulated among its members in a prescribed order. These three groups were aware of one another's existences and occasionally this or that regular dined with one of the others.[12]

Riedel was clearly the best situated and potentially the most influential of the Viennese self-styled Jacobins. As a former tutor of the emperor he could legitimately entertain some hopes of suggesting to him a course of action more favorable to revolutionary France at some critical juncture. It may well be that his inability to gain the ear of any influential figure at the court—he at one time appealed in this sense to Francis's younger brother, Archduke Ferdinand of Tuscany, but was rebuffed—helped him decide to try his luck with more direct methods, but Riedel never seems to have broken away entirely from the notion that somehow, at some time, he would be able to change the course of events by persuading those in power to change their ways.[13]

Of all these dabblers in political theory the most interesting and original was undoubtedly Lieutenant Hebenstreit, who at any rate would have no truck with pallid arguments resting on persuasion. The son of an academic family in Prague, he had received a solid education (he had even attended Sonnenfels's lectures on civil and canon law), but for unknown reasons had chosen in 1768 to enlist in the army instead of pursuing the academic or bureaucratic career for which his background and studies would have qualified him. Five years later he deserted to Prussian Silesia and was subsequently forcibly enlisted in the Prussian army. In 1778, apparently as part of an exchange resulting from the Peace of Teschen, he was returned to the Austrian forces, where he started over as a private in his old regiment. He must have served with considerable diligence, because by 1791 he had risen up through the ranks to *Platz-Oberleutnant* in the Vienna regiment responsible for the protection of the capital as well as the maintenance of public order there.[14] Full of resentment against a society that had failed to recognize his merits, a priest more than a schoolteacher *manqué*, Hebenstreit alternated between violent outbursts in which he insisted that the vague egalitarian notions of his table companions must be translated into action at once and utopian speculations of so abstruse a nature that his companions, mainly men of some education, failed to grasp their meaning. Riedel, however, considered him to be a supernal, never-to-be-equaled genius.[15] Hebenstreit composed a Latin poem entitled *Homo hominibus* in which he developed the idea of the fundamental equality of mankind along lines familiar to the readers of Rousseau. He did make an attempt to fit these notions to the conditions prevailing in Austria by devoting a considerable portion of his epic to rural problems. But his proposed solution to these, namely that the nobility be made to stay on its estates, where it would not be tempted to overspend its income, and where, in the absence of urban cultural stimuli, it would eventually merge into the peasantry, does not strike one as either practical or particularly revolutionary. His associates seem to have shrugged the whole thing off as a hopeless waste of time and effort, incomprehensible to the peasants to whom it was ostensibly addressed, and lacking novelty and cohesion from the point of view of the intellectuals.[16]

Somewhat less esoteric a contribution to the revolutionary cause was the music that Hebenstreit composed to a text written by a Captain Beck, entitled *Eipeldauer Lied,* which rather simplemindedly attributed

Louis XVI's fate to the fact that he had sided with the aristocrats against the people, and by implication suggested that Francis might well come to a similar end if he refused to change his ways.[17] This piece of doggerel was sung occasionally by Riedel's guests, but never in public.

Of a still more practical nature was Hebenstreit's invention of a war engine intended for use against the Austrian cavalry, which on more than one occasion had caused havoc among the loosely deployed French infantry. (The French had learned to fight *en tiralleurs* to good effect in the American Revolution, but there they had not had to face cavalry.) This was an artillery piece mounted on a carriage to which sickle-shaped blades were attached to repel cavalry at close range. Hebenstreit constructed a model of this device—borrowing the wheels from a baby carriage supplied by Gilovsky—and showed it to the Polish count Stanislaus Soltyk, who was in Vienna in an effort to recruit support for the Polish nationalist movement of Tadeusz Kosciuszko. Soltyk was sufficiently impressed by the potential usefulness of this war engine in the uprising that the Poles were planning to pay Hebenstreit 200 florins for a copy of the plans. This money was used by the lieutenant to send two of his friends, a medical student named Denkmann and the Lutheran preacher Held, to Freiburg in order to find a means of getting the drawings to France. After many misadventures Denkmann and Held actually reached the French capital but ran straight into the disorder preceding the overthrow of the Jacobin regime and were lucky to escape with their lives. Hebenstreit's invention, at any rate, did not reach the minister of war, Carnot, in time to be adopted by the armies of the revolution before its overthrow.[18] This incident, inconsequential as it may have been, is of some importance because, along with the one that will presently be described, it brought the activities of the Viennese Jacobins to the attention of Pergen and Saurau, if not to that of the masses.

Hebenstreit, even if his revolutionary efforts failed to arouse much interest or enthusiasm, was, along with Riedel, engaged in another form of literary activity. From roughly the end of 1792, the two friends seem to have produced several—it is not entirely clear how many, but probably a dozen or so—pamphlets extremely critical of the government, expressing admiration for the revolutionary regime in France, and even calling upon Austrians to imitate the common people of France in rising up in rebellion in order to rid themselves of the monarchy. To be sure, the would-be revolutionaries were never able to find a printer for these calls to revolution, so that their effectiveness was considerably reduced, but at least one attempt to distribute them in manuscript was made, in December 1792. On that occasion, however, the still baled packet, deposited on a street corner, was found by a policeman on his rounds, so it evidently failed to reach its intended audience.[19]

The point here is that the police had been aware of the circumstance that someone in Vienna was engaged in writing and attempting to disseminate pro-French pamphlets for some time. Since very probably through Martinovics, and certainly through Degen, Pergen and Saurau were also being kept abreast of the activities of the Riedel, Wollstein, and Blumauer groups, it is necessary to try to determine why they did nothing about any of this until the summer of 1794. Was there insufficient evidence to take action against the presumed Jacobins? Such a lack had not notably deterred Pergen when he had decided, some five years before, that Wucherer represented a clear danger to state security, and there is no reason to think that he deemed it necessary to proceed more scrupulously now.[20] Were they waiting to see how far the strands of the conspiracy stretched, so as to be sure that all the Jacobins in the monarchy would be rounded up once the trap was sprung? Possibly, and in the event it turned out that there had in fact been similar stirrings in Styria, Carinthia, Carniola, Tyrol, and even Vorarlberg.[21] But the police had no inkling of the existence of these provincial societies until just before the arrest of the Viennese conspirators, and moreover, in the event of a genuine and serious plan for a revolutionary uprising, it would have been dangerous to the point of irresponsibility to allow it to ripen in order to make sure that none of the plotters would slip through the meshes of the investigation. The monarchy was denuded of troops and there were French prisoners of war everywhere on its territory, many of them free on parole. If there were in fact contacts between the Austrian Jacobins and their counterparts in Paris, if plans for a genuine revolt existed, the means for putting it down would hardly have been available, once it had begun to spread. The authorities' only hope would have been to nip the conspiracy in the bud, and Pergen was surely the man to insist on such a course if he thought it necessary. Or did he not take the whole affair quite as seriously as its later chroniclers would?[22]

In the absence of any direct evidence one may only surmise about possible answers to these questions. It may be best to try to reconstruct what actually happened from what is definitely known. The more recent accounts of the Austrian "Jacobin" conspiracy all assume that the police had penetrated the secrets of the various groups in the monarchy that looked upon recent events in France with sympathy or even admiration, without, however, explaining what the common link between these various sub-conspiracies might have been. That such a link existed, if in all probability only in the dossiers kept by Pergen and

Saurau, is made clear by the fact that when the police decided to strike, the members of these various widely scattered societies were rounded up within the space of twenty-four hours. How did Pergen and Saurau manage to learn of their existence and to amass incriminating evidence against all of these conspirators, when there is no evidence that their own members were for the most part aware of one another's activities?

There are four possible answers to this question. (1) It may have been that the various Jacobin "cells" in the monarchy arose in various places in spontaneous response to the promise of developments in France and, given the obvious need for secrecy in a nation at war with that country, were, except for the accident of interlocking memberships, largely ignorant of their respective existences. The police, however, with supernal efficiency, managed to ferret out most of them. (2) Although the individual members of the cells knew only about the activities of their immediate associates, there existed a coordinating intelligence at some higher level. In the manner of the "control" who nowadays directs the activities of espionage and subversive groups in hostile territory—while the individual spies and saboteurs know only as much as is necessary for them to carry out their assignments—an agent of the revolutionary government held all the strings of the Austrian conspiracy in his hand. If this person had, in some manner, fallen into the hands of the Austrian police, they would at that point have been in the position of moving simultaneously against all the groups. (3) The link antedated the existence of the cells: that is to say, they were forged not by some master organizer sent out by the legislative assembly, but by an agent provocateur acting on behalf of the police. (4) Finally, it may be that these three elements all played a part in uncovering the Jacobin conspiracy, acting in various combinations.

Let us now examine these hypotheses sequentially. The first may be fairly quickly dismissed as a sufficient explanation. The police continued to be woefully understaffed, just as in Joseph's day; it had been unable to trace the seditious pamphlets found on the street in Vienna to their source, in spite of some fairly obvious clues; to ascribe to it the kind of efficiency and organization that would have been required to discover the activities of a half-dozen or more separate conspiratorial groups would constitute a wild overestimation of its capabilities.

As for the second of these hypotheses, this is the explanation offered by the first detailed account of the Austrian Jacobin conspiracy, published within two years of the events it describes.[23] According to this pamphlet, a complete list of the various Jacobin societies in the monarchy fell into the hands of the Austrian police quite fortuitously in May 1793 with the capture of a senior French emissary, the later Marquis de Sémonville. This liberal *ci-devant* aristocrat, a former member of the national assembly and friend of Mirabeau, was in 1793 ambassador-designate to the Porte. He was on his way to Constantinople, but had also been entrusted by Danton with a highly secret mission, an attempt to trade off the release of Marie Antoinette and her children against some very substantial advantage. While negotiating with Austrian emissaries on neutral ground, in the Grisons, he was, on orders from Vienna, seized and transported to the fortress of Kufstein, where he remained a prisoner for some two years.[24] In his papers, according to an anonymous account, was found a list of all the Austrian Jacobins. It is difficult to decide what to make of this story. While it is hardly inconsistent with the complex machinations that characterized the inner workings of the French government at the time, the circumstance that there is no trace whatsoever of such a document in the (admittedly incomplete) Austrian police archives gives one pause. At this stage no final judgment can be made.

It is, however, possible to account for most of the knowledge of the activities of the Jacobins in the monarchy available to Pergen and Saurau on the basis of the reports supplied to them by their informant alone. All that is necessary to assume is that Martinovics and Degen between them were aware of the existence of all the groups. In that case, since Degen's contacts with even the Viennese groups were of a limited nature, Martinovics, who knew far more about the matter, must have at one point confided in Degen. This too must remain in the realm of conjecture, but as we shall presently see, there can be little doubt that it was on the basis of information supplied by Degen, no matter how obtained, that Pergen finally decided to act against the Jacobins.

As early as January 1794 the police had gotten wind of some highly suspect sermons being preached in the Vienna suburbs of Penzing and Schottenfeld. Since the preachers in question (the vicar of Penzing and two Benedictines) did not stop at expressions of admiration for the French government, but went on to indulge in speculation about the very core of Christian doctrine, it was unnecessary to make a legal case against them; they could be punished under the rubric of police regulations dealing with blasphemy. The culprits were duly sentenced to a year's imprisonment and their congregations, consisting for the most part of artisans (these were working-class suburbs), were given severe warnings.[25] This so-called *Schusterkomplott*, although its roots seem to have been clearly in a populist movement within the Austrian church, directed at the autocratic administration of Cardinal Migazzi, and having very little to do with political issues per se, appears to have convinced Pergen and Saurau that the activities of the Viennese clubs, of which they continued to receive intermittent reports from their man Degen, had produced echos in broader strata of the population, an at least potentially dangerous development.

In June, with the war going relatively well for Austria, Saurau informed Colloredo that, although there were some alarmists and defeatists at work within the monarchy, their number was small and the police was well aware of their activities.[26] But soon enough the tide of battle turned against the Austrians, and French armies poured into Belgium. Saurau now turned to Francis, advising him of the potential danger such ill-disposed people represented at a time when the news from the front was bad enough without being magnified by their efforts. Unfortunately, as he was forced to admit, there was no proof that the Austrian "Jacobins" were doing anything beyond engaging in loose talk, and Francis still insisted on legal proof before proceeding against them.[27]

This impasse was ended with the arrival of a report from Switzerland. The Austrian resident in Bern, Tassara, sent in a detailed account of what he had learned about the activities of Held and Denkmann in that country, along with the information that these gentlemen were presently on their way to Paris, bearing plans of Hebenstreit's war engine which they intended to submit to the Jacobin regime there.[28] Now at last Saurau was in possession of evidence that pointed unmistakably to treason.

As soon as Pergen learned of this development he returned from his summer holiday to take charge of the investigation himself. He now requested from Francis permission to arrest the plotters. He granted the emperor the point that the most undesirable step of all would be to transform his rule into one of ministerial despotism and *lettres de cachet*. Due process must be observed whenever possible. Still, these were perilous times, and the security of the state must not needlessly be exposed to grave dangers. Even the English government had recently found it necessary to suspend habeas corpus. To insist on extending the full measure of legal protections to the conspirators was to invite disaster; by the time a case against them could be made the whole country might well be in open rebellion. It was the responsibility—the sacred duty—of the police to prevent matters from coming to such a pass.[29] Even at that point, however, Francis was unwilling to sanction such extra-legal proceedings on his sole authority. Instead, he sent Pergen's note to the *Staatsrat* for an opinion. The minister of police did not delude himself about his chances of prevailing in that body. Clearly, alternate measures were now called for.

It was Saurau who found the formula that would persuade the reluctant emperor that drastic measures were now required. On 27 June he sent Francis a detailed report about Degen's revelations to him. What his informer had reported, he argued, was clear proof of treasonable activity on the part of the club members; it only remained for the police to follow up these revelations to make a watertight case against the "Jacobins." Francis replied with permission to proceed in this manner.[30]

Pergen and Saurau now prepared the ground for a roundup of the club members. The first step they took was to launch a series of rumors in the capital that the police had uncovered an elaborate Jacobin conspiracy. The plotters had intended to bring about a state of chaos by setting fires, promoting riots, setting off explosions, and assassinating members of the imperial family and prominent nobles. They would then take advantage of the confusion created by these multiple disasters to seize power and establish a Jacobin republic. To give credence to this story, police detachments were posted at the otherwise unguarded gates of Vienna, where all persons going in or out were subjected to strict controls. All this created considerable excitement in the population, and the officially disseminated rumors were soon joined by spontaneous ones about still further Jacobin outrages in the offing. But after a day or two, the basically skeptical Viennese public began to express some doubts about these stories: if such a widespread plot had been hatched, why had not any of one's acquaintances been approached about participating, since such an undertaking would obviously require considerable popular support?[31] The rumors would have to be substantiated in some manner.

At that point Saurau played his trump card and seemingly instructed Degen that he was now to entrap one or more of the conspirators so that a case could finally be made against the lot.[32] As early as 4 June Degen had supplied Saurau with extracts of Hebenstreit's poem *Homo hominibus*, pointing out its dangerous character, qualified, in his opinion, only by the circumstance that it was written in Latin; the poem obviously addressed itself in the main to students, and on this occasion at least, one had reason to be thankful for the deplorable latinity of the monarchy's students. More to the point, Degen also dropped some dark hints about the possibility that the conspirators were in touch with the crown prince of Denmark, a man well known for his liberal sympathies.[33]

Degen himself was not of the opinion that, as he put it, "a mere handful of enthusiasts and intriguers" was capable of arousing much enthusiasm among the mass of the population, which, in his opinion was unshakable in its loyalty to the crown. Still, should the French take the trouble to send a capable emissary to the monarchy, such people might prove to be dangerous.[34] Should this ever come to pass, Degen felt it to be his duty to report that he had learned that there were some other individuals in Vienna who, he had reason to believe, although they were more careful in their utterances, also harbored potentially dangerous opinions. These included an employee of the censorship commission named Eschenreich, the printer Javernez in the *Josefsstadt,* and the director of the Vienna Institute for the Deaf and Dumb, Märzthaler.[35]

Some two weeks after this, Degen reported on two meetings that were to provide Pergen and Saurau with the basis for proceeding against the presumed plotters. The first of these meetings took place on 20 July. Hebenstreit's intimate, the private tutor Jelline, whom Degen had befriended some weeks before, the auditor Billek, and the soap-boiler Franzl came to Degen's apartment. There the host, in his own words, after setting his guests at ease, presented them with a plan meant both to gain their full confidence and to encourage them to reveal the full extent of the Jacobin conspiracy throughout the whole of the monarchy. The recent French victories, he said, presented those of a revolutionary inclination with both an opportunity and a challenge. But before the extent of any action could be decided upon, it was necessary to know precisely what forces one could count on. Once one had a list of all reliable sympathizers, these should be organized into independent cells of five members each, under the direction of a central committee on the French model. His modesty forbade suggesting himself as a member of this body; moreover, it would be wise to select individuals whose position in life was such that the government would think twice about arresting them. Riedel, above all others, seemed to possess the qualities desirable for such a position. Obvious as the bait was, Degen's guests rose to it. They declared themselves in agreement with his notion that the time to act was at hand and qualified his proposal only with remarks to the effect that, while it would—for the tactical reasons he had outlined—be desirable to include a number of well-placed individuals on his proposed steering committee, there should be some little people on it as well. He himself should not be excluded. Jelline then declared that he himself would bring Degen's proposals to Riedel and Hebenstreit. As Degen assured Saurau in a coda to his report, he had set a trap for the conspirators. If as a result they were now to hatch actual plots, the police would be in a position to cut these off whenever they chose to do so.[36]

Jelline was as good as his word, and Hebenstreit, at least, could hardly wait to discuss Degen's proposals with him, arranging to meet him in the Brigittenau on the evening of the same day.[37] These three men, drinking beer at a table in a café in Vienna's *Augarten,* now engaged in a discussion of revolutionary tactics.[38] Hebenstreit did not think highly of Degen's suggestion to organize a central committee and to proselytize in the provinces. People of substance were trustworthy in a revolutionary cause only if their hands were already bloodied; recruiting in the provinces would be fruitless and would merely draw the attention of the police to the movement. What was required was a *coup d'éclat* in Vienna, and possibly also in Prague. Those prepared to carry this out—some thirty-five hundred men would be needed—must be recruited among craft journeymen and day laborers in the capital's various cheap taverns and dives. Such folk, when presented with a dilemma, had only one reaction, smashing in heads, and this must be taken advantage of by the students and theoreticians. As for what needed to be done, he was of the opinion that one must begin by burying sharpened iron bars, spears, scythes and pitchforks in various locations around the capital. Some evening, acting upon an agreed signal, the revolutionary army would unearth these weapons, massacre the night watch, prevent the troops stationed in the city from coming out of their garrisons (the cavalry and artillery units, Hebenstreit added, would in all probability support the uprising in any case), lay their hands on various government treasuries, kill some three hundred aristocrats along with their entire retinues, and physically take hold of the emperor, who would be forced to put his signature on several dozen cartes blanches, to be used in implementing various revolutionary aims, after which he also would be. . . . [39] Only then should one proceed to set up a provisional government and to appeal to the provinces. Such an appeal, however, must be made in the name of the emperor, and the peasantry would have to be deluded into thinking that they were following his orders. Before they could be disabused of this notion, they were to be won over to the cause of the revolution by the abolition of all manorial dues and work obligations. Anyone continuing to demand the performance of the *robot* was to be impaled forthwith. In order to break the habit of automatic obedience to their overlords, any peasant continuing to perform such obligations would be burned at the stake.

While such unrelentingly bloodthirsty expositions are not without their own peculiar charm, one is forced to wonder whether they could have been seriously meant, or if Hebenstreit was not amusing himself at Degen's expense, constructing a madcap caricature of events alluded to in the police-inspired rumors for his interlocutor's benefit. Degen himself had his doubts, pointing out to Saurau that their man was obviously giving way to confused rantings, and that, in the interest of truth and objectivity, he should point out that by this time Hebenstreit had consumed an entire pitcher of beer. Moreover, in a postscript Degen also pointed out that he found inexplicable the readiness of such people to entrust themselves and their secrets to the first comer; how incredibly easy it was to lead them to any desired length once one had decided to make criminals out of them, and it should be no more difficult to secure legal proofs of their guilt.[40]

We may leave unanswered at this point the questions of whether Degen had succeeded in extracting from Hebenstreit a genuine declaration of his intentions, or if he had merely elicited a drunken diatribe on a theme that he himself had introduced. The point is, as Degen admits by implication in the postscript of his communication to Saurau, that Hebenstreit's statements made in the presence of Jelline, who had to be considered a coconspirator, still did not constitute a sufficient legal case against him.[41] If Pergen and Saurau wanted to stay strictly within the law, as the emperor seemed clearly to wish, Degen's denunciations would be insufficient grounds on which to proceed against the "Jacobins."

At this point, however, Saurau seems to have decided that the situation brooked no further delays. Still on 21 July he advised Francis that he had uncovered a vast conspiracy and that the conspirators would have to be arrested.[42] He would certainly not have done so without Pergen's consent.

During the night of 23 July 1794 Riedel, Hebenstreit, Gilovski, Jelline, a Dr. Hanke, Hackl, Jutz, a merchant named Jenni, and Martinovics were all arrested.[43] The evidence of conspiracy contained in Degen's reports seemed sufficiently convincing to the emperor Francis to move him to appoint under Saurau an *Untersuchungshofkommission,* a special commission to conduct the investigation.[44] Thus the police would not have to depend on the courts to build a case against the conspirators. Constant interrogations soon produced various confessions. Riedel admitted the authorship of the subversive tract *Call to the German Nation;* Jelline confirmed the gist of Degen's description of the conversation in the *Augarten,* although he insisted that he and Hebenstreit had been speaking in general terms, not making specific plans; Martinovics, who fainted three times during his initial interrogation, eventually collapsed completely and gave the commission the names of all his Hungarian associates, who were thereupon also arrested; and Hebenstreit, although he denied any intention of carrying out his plans, admitted having spun them, but only as a mere rhetorical exercise, he insisted.[45]

The interrogations were conducted principally by Hofrat Schilling, Saurau's man rather than Pergen's. The minister himself seems to have confined himself largely to coordinating the investigation and to ferreting out any wider aspects that the conspiracy might have had. He was particularly interested in Riedel's revelation, under questioning, that early in July several Styrians, among them Franz Dirnböck, a member of the municipal government of Knittelfeld, had come to Vienna to consult with Riedel. On this occasion they had joined the members of Riedel's group in an outing to a nearby hilltop in the Brühl, where a solemn oath, apparently modeled on that of the Illuminati, had been sworn by all present, who had pledged themselves to root out blind fanaticism wherever they found it and to work tirelessly on behalf of good and virtue. Pergen was apparently very much concerned that Dirnböck's official position might have enabled him to corrupt large numbers of the common people and prevailed upon the provincial governor, Count Welsberg, to arrest him and his associates.[46]

It cannot be our task here to enter into the long and complex arguments about the precise degree of guilt of the various persons implicated in these events. Whether they had confined themselves to making grandiloquent pronouncements and were nothing more than *Schwätzer und Schwärmer*, babblers and enthusiasts, or whether they had been engaging in actual plotting, their behavior in time of war, which included the expression of undisguised enthusiasm for the principles of the enemy, would have led to their indictment under a more tolerant regime than that of the emperor Francis. The real question was, how would they be tried, once Saurau's commission had established an ample presumption of guilt? To allow the ordinary courts to dispose of the matter entailed certain risks from the point of view of the ministry of police. Degen's role in eliciting the one indisputably treasonable utterance made by the accused, Hebenstreit's *Augarten* diatribe, would necessarily emerge, and if Degen were called to testify, he might very well insist on repeating the disclaimers he had included in his communications to Saurau, at which point the entire government case would collapse. It would certainly be preferable to deal with the entire matter in camera. This was not a practical possibility in the case of the Hungarians implicated by Martinovics, since the Magyars would regard any attempt to bypass their judicial system as a further slight, something to be avoided at all costs in those difficult times. The Magyar conspirators would simply have to be tried in Hungary, by the duly constituted courts.

The Austrians, however, were another matter. If the pretrial investigations had been conducted in secret, by an ad hoc commission, why not the trial as well? In October Saurau proposed that a special court, made up in large part of the members of the investigatory commission, and presided over by Count Leopold Clary, the president of the *oberster Gerichtshof*, supreme judiciary, be constituted for the purpose of trying the accused conspirators.[47] This proposal was sanctioned by the emperor, who did not even bother to consult the *Staatsrat*.[48] As has been pointed out, such a step would have gone a long way toward transforming the monarchy into a police state.[49] As it happens, however, Clary, who was favorably disposed toward such a solution, was away on his estates at the time that the emperor's order to establish a special court for trying these cases reached his office. The man in charge was his deputy, Baron Karl Anton von Martini, a distinguished legal philosopher and writer on legal questions. Martini was bound to have a very different view of the matter and, to his eternal credit, did not hesitate to expostulate with Francis. Ignoring due process, he argued at length, would not merely result in a miscarriage of justice: it would lead the general public to lose faith in the emperor, from whom it expected a fatherly concern for the rights of all.[50] These arguments did not fail to have an effect on the emperor, who now, rather belatedly, consulted the *Staatsrat*. When that body agreed with Martini he reversed himself and ordered that the cases be tried by the regular courts.[51]

The result of these trials was in essence predetermined by Count Clary's decision that, of the four sitting justices in these cases, two were to be the same men who had been in charge of the pretrial investigation.[52] Thus the accused were in essence to be tried by their accusers. (Not until the main trials were over was the legality of this procedure successfully challenged by one of the defendants, Dr. Jutz.)

As was to be expected, the harshest sentences were meted out by the military court, which tried the three defendants who were members of the armed forces. Gilovsky and Hebenstreit were sentenced to be hanged and a Captain Billek, who had been involved only at the fringes of the movement if at all, got ten years in irons. Since Gilovsky had committed suicide during the preliminary investigation, the sentence was carried out on his dead body.

Hardly less severe were the sentences in the Hungarian trials. Eighteen death sentences were handed down, and Martinovics and six of his closest associates were in fact executed, the sentences of the others being commuted to indefinite prison terms.

Of the Austrian "Jacobins" tried by the ordinary criminal courts, one, Joseph Wenninger, the mayor of Knittelfeld in Styria, went insane during the proceedings; one, Gotthardi, died in prison; and five were acquitted. While four defendants, against whom there was at best insufficient evidence, were condemned to indeterminate terms of "political imprisonment," fifteen of the principal conspirators were convicted of treason and *lèse-majesté*. The harshest sentence went to Riedel (sixty years); the others received prison terms ranging from thirty-five down to twenty years. The defendants would, in accordance with Saurau's recommendation, serve their imprisonment in the fortress of Munkács, where the conditions were such that they "could expect the end of their lives in a relatively short time."[53]

What should we make of these doubtful convictions; of these draconic verdicts? If Hebenstreit had been technically guilty of offering aid to the enemy in time of war, the device he had offered to the French was of such ludicrous antiquity and inappropriateness for use on eighteenth-century battlefields as to cast serious doubts on his sanity. The others had unquestionably indulged themselves in loose talk as well as copious criticisms of existing institutions, and had no doubt explicitly praised the actions of the enemies of the monarchy. Whether they had in fact conspired together to engage in treasonable actions, or whether all such imputations stemmed exclusively from the ministry of police's agents, can no longer be established.[54] But it is important to judge these events by the standards obtaining at the time. In our own days, especially, but by no means exclusively in time of war, men have been put to death for much less. Eighteenth-century Austria, however, was supposedly a *Rechtsstaat* in which the will of the sovereign was circumscribed by law. True, this admirable precept had, as we have seen, been honored as often in the breach as in the obedience under Joseph. But Leopold had remedied most of these excesses, and Francis had by and large agreed with his father on the necessity of allowing the courts a free hand in deciding questions of guilt or innocence. The verdicts and the sentences in the Jacobin trials constitute a clear aberration from this principle. In all probability we need not look to elaborate conspiracy theories to explain what happened. Threatened by the victorious armies of revolutionary France, in the face of near unanimity among his closest advisers, the emperor Francis would have had to summon up a truly uncommon commitment to the principle of judicial supremacy to resist the pressures for dealing with what he himself probably believed to be a genuine conspiracy. He was hardly the man to do that.

NOTES

1. Pergen to Colloredo, 16 November 1793, S.A., F.A.S. 67.

2. Pergen to Colloredo, 17 November 1793, S.A., F.A.S. 67.

3. R. Darnton, *Mesmerism and the End of the Enlightenment in France* (Cambridge, Mass., 1970), 73–80.

4. V. Buranelli, *The Wizard from Vienna* (London, 1976), 186–87.

5. *Ibid.,* 187. Reinalter, *Aufgeklärter Absolutismus,* 180, garbles the story. He cites Wangermann, *Jacobin Trials,* who in fact does not deal with the Mesmer case at all.

6. For the following cf. D. Silagi, "Aktenstücke zur Geschichte des Ignaz von Martinovics," *Mitteilungen des österreichischen Staatsarchivs*, XV, (1962) 246 ff.; idem, *Jakobiner in der Habsburger-Monarchie* (Vienna & Munich, 1962), 130 ff.; and idem, *Ungarn.*

7. Pergen to Francis, May 1793, S.A., Kaiser Franz Akten (hereafter K.F.A.), 147.

8. Silagi, *Jakobiner*, 148–53.

9. Wangermann, *Jacobin Trials*, 137–39. It does seem to me that Wangermann, 137, rather overstates the case when he calls the activities of this circle "an attempt to organize and coordinate the active opposition to the policies of Francis II's government." Nothing quite that formal ever seems to have taken place. The existence of this group was first established by R. Bartsch, "Die Jakobiner in Wien," *Österreichische Rundschau*, VII (1906), 504–5. For Blumauer see P. P. Bernard, *Jesuits & Jacobins: Enlightenment and Enlightened Despotism in Austria* (Urbana, Ill. 1971), 79–83, and E. Rosenstrauch-Königsberg, "Aloys Blumauer—Jesuit, Freimaurer, Jakobiner," *Jahrbuch des Instituts für Deutsche Geschichte der Universität Tel-Aviv*, II (1973), 145–71. By this time Hackl was more or less subsidizing Blumauer, who was unable to make a living with his pen.

10. Wangermann, *Jacobin Trials*, 139–40; Rosenstrauch-Königsberg, "Blumauer," 163.

11. Wangermann, *Jacobin Trials*, 139. A. Körner, "Andreas Riedel," Ph.D. dissertation (Cologne, 1969), 136–37, gives more details than Wangermann but conflates the two groups. For Hebenstreit see A. Körner, "Franz Hebenstreit (1747–1795)," *Jahrbuch des Vereines für Geschichte der Stadt Wien*, XXX/XXXI (1974–75), 39–61.

12. From the testimony given at the later trial of these men it appears very likely that Martinovics knew all of them and had attended all three *Tischrunden*. This is of course not to say that the information that the police received about their activities came from him, although he had previously, in Hungary, engaged in conspiratorial activities that had gone well beyond what Pergen had instructed him to do, and subsequently informed on his co-conspirators when it suited him better to ingratiate himself in Vienna. Cf. Silagi, *Jakobiner*, 140. Perhaps more to the point is the question of whether, and to what degree, the bookseller and police spy Vinzenz Degen was associated with these groups. L. Stern, "Zum Prozeß gegen die österreichische 'Jakobiner-Verschwörung'," in W. Markov, ed., *Maximilien Robespierre: Beiträge zu seinem 200. Geburtstag* (Berlin, 1958), 482, maintains that Degen frequently attended the meetings of the Riedel group, but Körner, "Riedel," 136, denies this. As we shall presently see, Degen must have been present at some of its dinners, even if he was not a regular guest.

13. Körner, "Riedel," 135.

14. *Ibid.*, 143.

15. Körner, "Hebenstreit," 52–55.

16. A German translation of the poem by Franz-Josef Schuh is reprinted in

A. Körner, *Die Wiener Jakobiner* (Stuttgart, 1972), 53–70.

17. Wangermann, *Jacobin Trials,* 140; Bernard, *Jesuits & Jacobins,* 163.

18. Silagi, *Jakobiner,* 177–78; Körner, "Hebenstreit," 47–48; Bernard, *Jesuits & Jacobins,* 165.

19. Körner, *Wiener Jakobiner,* 13–14. Most of the other pamphlets were undoubtedly circulated in manuscript, but probably got no further than the three *Tischrunden.* Körner's assertion "Die Zahl dieser demokratischen Zeugnisse scheint gering, wenn man sie am überlieferten Schriftgut der herrschenden Klasse mißt; zahlreiche Hinweise beweisen jedoch, daß der Umfang dieser Revolutionsliteratur sehr groß war" seems at best gratuitous.

20. In December 1793 Pergen urged Francis to consider the advisability of giving the police discretionary powers to dismiss from their positions or even to mete out jail sentences to government servants who represented a danger to the state because of their "insolent talk." Francis had temporized, without, however, closing the door on this option. Cf. Wangermann, *Jacobin Trials,* 135–36.

21. The activities of these groups have been minutely reconstructed by Reinalter, *Aufgeklärter Absolutismus,* 272–363.

22. Wangermann, *Jacobin Trials,* 145, admitting that "the evidence concerning the various 'Jacobin' groups in the Habsburg dominions does not trace even the outlines of a powerful 'conspiracy' menacing the foundations of the monarchy," also asks himself why the police should have decided that countermeasures were necessary precisely in the summer of 1794. The answer he arrives at, that this had little to do with the "conspiracy" itself, but rather was the consequence of the overall political situation within the monarchy, is seductive but not entirely convincing. It may well be that the emperor and his minister of police had reached the conclusion that, in view of a deteriorating military situation, internal disaffection represented a genuine danger, but he cites only one bit of hard evidence, a note from Francis to one of his younger brothers in January 1794, mentioning reports of fraternization between soldiers of Wurmser's army and French advanced guards. To conclude from this (146) that "For the French 'enemy' the Austrian soldier tended to feel sympathy rather than hostility" is to go well beyond the evidence.

23. Anon., *Geheime Geschichte der Verschwörung der Jakobiner in den österreichischen Staaten* (London, 1795), reprinted in F. Gräffer, *Franciscéische Curiosa* (Vienna, 1849), 9–18.

24. On Charles-Louis Huguet, created Marquis de Sémonville by Louis XVIII, see *Dictionnaire des Parlementaires Français,* V, 299–300, and *Grand Larousse Universel,* XIV, 527.

25. Wangermann, *Jacobin Trials,* 149–50.

26. Saurau to Colloredo, 1 June 1794, S.A., F.A.S. 162.

27. Wangermann, *Jacobin Trials,* 150–51.

28. Tassara to Thugut, 29 May 1794, S.A., Staatenabteilung, Schweiz, Berichte 193. Cf. Wangermann, *Jacobin Trials,* 151, and F. Schuh, *Franz Hebenstreit* (Trier, 1974), xxiii–xxiv.

29. Pergen to Francis, 23 June 1794, cited in Wangermann, *Jacobin Trials,* 152.

30. Saurau to Francis, 27 June 1794, V.A., P.A. X/B1, and marginalium of Francis. Cf. Wangermann, *Jacobin Trials*, 153, and Schuh, *Hebenstreit*, xxvi.

31. L. Stern, "Prozeß." Stern's account is based on *Österreichische Memoiren aus dem letzten Dezennium des achtzehnten Jahrhunderts* (Leipzig, 1848), 257 ff., an anonymous work by someone with a detailed knowledge of these events.

32. There is no record of instructions to that effect having been given Degen. Wangermann, *Jacobin Trials*, 153, simply assumes this to have been the case, surely not an unreasonable assumption in view of what follows. The alternative is to accept the hypothesis that Degen was acting on his own, which is leaving a great deal of room for the individual initiative of a simple police agent. But, as we shall now see, the matter is an extremely complex one.

33. Degen to Saurau, 4 June 1794, S.A., V.A. 8; cf. F. Schuh, "Die Wiener Jakobiner: Reformer oder Revolutionäre?," *Jahrbuch des Instituts für Deutsche Geschichte*, XII (1983), 81–83.

34. Degen to Saurau, 8 July 1794, S.A., V.A. 8.

35. Degen to Saurau, 10 July 1794, V.A., P.A. X/B1.

36. Wangermann, *Jacobin Trials*, 153–56, translates lengthy excerpts from Degen's reports. The full text in Körner, *Wiener Jakobiner*, 72–76.

37. Wangermann, *Jacobin Trials*, puts the date of this meeting on 21 July, but in a note to Saurau, dated 21 July, Degen writes "Hebenstreit hat mich um eine Zusammenkunft . . . auf gestern ersuchen lassen. . . . " Cf. Körner, *Wiener Jakobiner*, 73.

38. Körner, *Wiener Jakobiner*, 74–76.

39. The monstrousness of this was apparently too much for Degen, who leaves a blank for the obvious imputation that the emperor is to be killed.

40. Körner, *Wiener Jakobiner*, 76.

41. Both Wangermann and Körner miss this point. Under Austrian law an incriminating statement had to be verified by two independent witnesses in order to be accepted as evidence. Degen could be one of these if his position as police agent did not come out during his testimony. But Jelline might very well refuse to testify against his fellow conspirator and therewith the entire police case would be negated. The relevant passage, which Degen appends as a post-script to his letter of 10 July 1794, reads: "Eure Excellenz ersehen aus der unbegreiflichen Unbesonnenheit, mit der diese Leute sich dem Nächsten Besten an den Hals werfen, wie leicht es seyn würde, sie jede Länge zu führen, die man nur will, und daß, wenn man es für ratsam findet Verbrecher zu machen, auch die rechtsbeständigen Beweise nicht schwer fallen dürften, welche Bemerkung ich E. E. zum weiteren Nachdenken hiermit unterlege. Wenn mit Hebenstreit eine andere als nach politischen Rücksichten zu bestimmende Untersuchung vorgenommen werden sollte, und folglich vor moralischer Imputation die Rede wäre, so müßte ich noch zur Treue der Wahrheit anmerken, daß er vorher einen ganzen Krug Bier zu sich genommen hatte."

42. Wangermann, *Jacobin Trials*, 156, quoting V. Franknòi, *Martinovics élete* (Budapest, 1921), who cites Saurau's note, which can no longer be traced.

43. Silagi, *Jakobiner*, 182. For Hanke see H. Wagner, "Der Plan zur Organisation

einer geheimen Gesellschaft des Arztes Dr. Franz Stephan Hanke 1794," in I. Ackerl, W. Hummelberger, & H. Mommsen, eds., *Politik und Gesellschaft im alten und neuen Österreich: Festschrift Rudolf Neck*, 2 vols. (Munich, 1981), I, 45–61.

44. Wangermann, *Jacobin Trials*, 157. Whatever differences one may have with Wangermann on other questions, his treatment of the following investigation and trials is exemplary, both for its mastery of complex detail and for its judiciousness, and my account is based largely on his.

45. Schuh, "Wiener Jakobiner," 100–101; Wangermann, *Jacobin Trials*, 157–58.

46. Wangermann, *Jacobin Trials*, 142, 158–59; cf. K. Hafner, "Franz Josef Graf von Saurau," *Zeitschrift des Historischen Vereines für Steiermark*, VII (1909), 26–27.

47. Kabinettsbefehl, 1 October 1794, S.A., V.A., 33.

48. *Ibid.*

49. Wangermann, *Jacobin Trials*, 161.

50. *Ibid.*, 162–64.

51. *Ibid.*, 164–65.

52. For the trials and their verdicts see Wangermann, *Jacobin Trials*, 168–71.

53. S.A., V.A. 24.

54. To no one's astonishment, the various interpretations of these events offered by historians accord closely with their own predilections. Silagi, *Jakobiner*, 197, while granting that the Austrian regime was partly motivated by a war psychosis, maintains that the conspirators were indeed guilty of treasonable actions, and had thus brought the verdicts down on their own heads. Stern, "Jakobinerverschwörung," 490–93, speaks of a *Staatsintrige* (a government plot). Schuh, "Wiener Jakobiner," 125–26, while denying the established guilt of the "Jacobins," wants nothing to do with a "government plot": this would undermine belief in the existence of a real "democratic" movement in the Austria of the time. Curiously, Wangermann never really pronounces a definitive judgment on the guilt or innocence of the defendants whose trials he chronicles so minutely.

10

The Consolidation of
State Control

O N 23 JUNE 1794, while Saurau was devoting all his attention to uncovering the details of the various Francophile conspiracies that had come to the attention of the police, Pergen sent a long letter to Francis that went well beyond these particulars.[1] It was, he contended, a cardinal duty of the police, not just to discover and to neutralize individuals who, by their actions, represented a threat to the security of the state, but to assist the government in discovering and identifying conditions that were apt, sooner or later, to lead to trouble. The French example had shown that violent actions against the state (*Staatserschütterungen*) invariably began in large cities in which agitators had found a fertile ground for their poisonous opinions among the free-floating population that had flocked there. Now as everyone knew, the population of Vienna had risen alarmingly since the late emperor Joseph's accession. It had been that monarch's laudable intention to attract numerous foreign industrialists to the capital and to encourage them to establish plants there by promising them partial immunity from taxation and the like. This intention, unfortunately, had been only very imperfectly realized by the time of Joseph's death. The result had been that tens of thousands of propertyless individuals, attracted by rumors of gainful employment, had settled in Vienna, but had for the most part failed to find employment. Hence the population of the capital now consisted not of well-to-do, upright members of the middle classes, but of people reduced to living off their wits. This class of people harbored no loyalty for the monarch, frequently parroted some foolish slogan, and forever ran after change because it had, in any case, nothing to lose.

While these had been common characteristics of the *Pöbel* (lower classes) throughout the course of history, conditions now made them infinitely more dangerous because of the dense concentration of such people in the large cities, and because of the active propaganda of the French Jacobins directed toward them. Things had come to such a pass that most of the primary and secondary school teachers in the towns of the monarchy had become infected with such opinions and were doing their utmost to spread them among that portion of the urban populace as yet unaffected by them. Although these allegations could not be supported by *legally valid proofs,*[2] it was the unshakable opinion of the state police that it was in a better position to judge the truth of the matter than the judicial authorities, whose procedural limitations would always prevent them from coming up with convincing proofs in these murky areas. His Majesty would do well to take his warnings seriously. As a first step it would be necessary to *reduce the population of the capital*[3] by whatever means were thought appropriate. The *Staatsrat* should receive immediate instructions to that effect. No further construction should be allowed in the capital, particularly no permits for the building of new factories should be issued (here Pergen appears to be arguing in a sense contrary to the position he has previously expounded); journeymen not admitted to become masters in their trades should be prevented from marrying; and all persons unable to prove regular employment should immediately be expelled. While heretofore under existing legislation, *every foreigner who had not been convicted of a crime had enjoyed the right of residing in the capital, it would be far more in keeping with present conditions if all such foreigners who were unable to prove to the satisfaction of the police that they pursued legal and regularized occupations be expelled.*[4] If Francis were to see his way clear to authorizing these measures, Pergen would guarantee that they would be carried out humanely and without imposing undue hardship on those affected.

Finally, Pergen thought it essential to point out that there was a further major obstacle in the path of a really efficient administration of police business. The courts insisted on treating cases brought to them by the police as part of their normal *Gerichtsordnung* (docket) and to circumscribe them with all of the formalities attendant upon judicial procedure. Now it was his devoutest wish that His Majesty's subjects should for all time be preserved from ministerial despotism and *lettres de cachet.* Nevertheless, there was a via media between such excesses and the ponderous procedures insisted upon by the courts, and it would be essential to follow this middle way if irremediable catastrophe were not to ensue. Unfortunately, in the situation in which the monarchy presently found itself, there were numerous cases in which crimes against the state were committed, but no legal proofs could be produced against their perpetrators. This was in part because the witnesses necessary to obtain convictions would be reluctant to testify in public because of possible retribution from those of a mind with the accused; and partly because it would not be in the interest of the state itself to reveal certain crucial sources of information. At all times, even under the mildest of governments, police cases having to do with the security of the state itself have been exempted from judicial formalities. It is the sacred duty of the police not just to uncover crimes that have already been committed, *but also to prevent dangerous crimes against the state from being committed at all.*[5] It is essential to give the police the *political dispositions*[6] that will enable them to perform this essential duty. There is no reason to fear that such a system would be subject to abuse, since under the current practice all arrests of persons dangerous to the state, along with reports of their interrogations, are routinely made known to the emperor.

This document represented far more than a request for emergency powers. If Francis were to accede to Pergen's demands, not only would this mean that the extraordinary powers of the secret police would at the very least be restored to the level at which they had been under Joseph in the 1780s, but with considerably greater resources at Pergen's disposal; the principle that the ministry of police could dictate policy in questions with a bearing upon state security would be firmly established. Francis, at any rate, seems to have understood the seriousness of the matter and, rather than deciding it on his own authority, submitted it to the *Staatsrat.* This body, in effect, ruled against Pergen by refusing to sanction the extraordinary powers he had requested, although eventually the economic restrictions on Vienna's growth that he had proclaimed essential were enacted into law.[7] Nevertheless, if Pergen had failed in his attempt to make his police formally independent of judicial review, the fact that he had so openly and strongly developed this argument, and that the emperor, knowing where his minister stood, kept him in office, could not have failed to have a part in the subsequent development of the Franciscan police.

Pergen was well aware of the paradox that attended the activities of the secret police: so long as these remained wholly hidden from view, the general public would remain in ignorance of the great dangers that the police were protecting them from. Consequently the arguments of men like Zinzendorf, who continued to criticize the extra-legal elements of Pergen's conduct in the *Staatsrat* would continue to convince. In his eagerness to strengthen his position Pergen finally went so far as to abandon his all but paranoid insistence on absolute secrecy. It might not be a bad idea, he concluded, if the public were to be informed about police investigations of crimes against the state, once these had been concluded, and so long as the information released was kept in general terms.[8] Was he also putting subtle pressure on Francis?

Looking back upon the successfully concluded action against the Austrian and Hungarian Jacobins, Pergen, after urging Francis to reward Saurau, Schilling, and Mährenthal with substantial raises in salary for their parts in uncovering the conspiracy, went on to warn the emperor that, in his view, the danger was by no means past. The fatal combination of lack of true faith, mockery of the established religious order, democratically inspired freedom-swindles, and antimonarchical sentiment had, in spite of the best efforts of the police, not disappeared from the scene. Just recently a captured French emissary named Probst had confessed that his government continued to support clandestine activities in the monarchy. In combination with the ongoing Prussian efforts in support of Hungarian dissident movements, this could at any time bring about a situation every bit as critical as that which had existed in the spring of 1794. Only unremitting vigilance on the part of the police could preserve the monarchy in these circumstances.[9]

The rewards requested by Pergen were duly granted. He asked Colloredo to express his thanks to Francis for this largesse and added that, when the emperor had asked him to come out of retirement to restore the Josephinian police system that had been wholly dismantled through lack of comprehension, he had not hesitated a moment to heed this call. Nor would he hold back an ounce of whatever strength he still possessed in order to protect the sacred person of His Majesty.[10]

Inevitably, in the pursuit of so important a goal, excesses of zeal occurred. Thus, a man named Franz Pauer was arrested on suspicion of complicity in the Jacobin plot. Under questioning he admitted his guilt and gave the police a list of his co-conspirators. His case was turned over to the judiciary for trial, but by this time, the initial "Jacobin" hysteria having subsided, not to the special court created by Francis for the purpose of dealing with the "conspiracy," but to the ordinary superior court in Vienna. That body not only found Pauer innocent, but determined that his confession had been extracted from him against his will. Thereupon Pauer asked to be indemnified for the harm that had been done him. Pergen was indignant. Such calumnies could not be permitted to circulate. Pauer was to be told that any further vilifications of the police would inevitably result in his punishment: he had only himself to blame for making up fanciful stories and confessing to crimes he did not commit. He was a *Schwärmer,* nothing more.[11]

This misadventure failed to inculcate any caution in Pergen. Later in 1795, after conferring with the chief officials of his ministry, he addressed a lengthy memorandum to the chief justice of the superior appellate court, Count Clary.[12] The recently concluded proceedings against the "Jacobins," he wrote, revealed that the conspiracy went deeper than the police had originally suspected. Sympathizers with the detestable French ideas were to be found in all social classes, and most alarmingly even among His Majesty's public servants. Specifically, the most suspicious individuals were Paul Strattmann, the custodian of the Imperial Library; Joseph Ratschky, a secretary employed by the *Hofkanzlei;* the poet and publicist Alois Blumauer;[13] Hackl's wife, Katherine; and one Lörmann.

Clary followed up these allegations, deciding that those implicated were to be interrogated, but without being put under arrest, since there seemed to be no clear-cut evidence that they had committed any illegal acts. Not much came of this, as might have been expected under the circumstances. The interrogations elicited only an admission on the part of Strattmann that, during a journey to France in 1770, he had been deeply shocked by the degree of rural poverty that he had observed. Nevertheless, Clary was in favor of dismissing Strattmann and Ratschky from their posts: to have fallen under suspicion was in itself a sign that one did not deserve the imperial confidence. However, the majority of Clary's colleagues on the superior court refused to go along with him and were upheld in this opinion by the *Staatsrat* and eventually by Francis.[14]

A rather more sinister offshoot of the conspiracy mentality is represented by the case of the manufacturer Franz Jenne. His name had come up occasionally during the interrogations of those arrested as being that of someone who was not unsympathetic to their ideas. As luck would have it, just at that point the Vienna police received a letter from their colleagues in Basel, informing them that Jenne was apparently implicated in Denkmann and Held's mission to Paris on behalf of Hebenstreit's war engine. Thereupon Saurau did not hesitate to order Jenne's arrest. Soon enough, however, it turned out that Jenne was the victim of mistaken identity. The man in question was named Jenni. Unfortunately for Jenne, however, it had emerged during his preliminary interrogation that he was acquainted with a Captain Laszkovícs, who was under arrest as one of Martinovic's principal collaborators. In consequence, Jenne was not released as soon as the police learned that they had taken the wrong individual into custody, but rather held in jail for some four months. By the time he was finally let go, his reputation had suffered to such an extent that his business soon failed.[15]

In the wake of these events Jenne applied to the superior court for restitution. He had after all been ruined as the consequence of a judicial error. When queried about the case Pergen developed a truly remarkable argument: the responsibility for the mistaken identity could not be laid at his door, anyway such errors could not be prevented in the course of police work. Moreover, if the state was to be protected from hostile elements, both internal and external, the police must have the right and the means to oversee both the political and the moral conduct of the citizens, without the latter feeling that they were in some manner being offended by this surveillance. Any infringement of this necessary police function would, in the last analysis, compromise the security of all. As for Jenne, his actions had hardly been above suspicion; had he not corresponded with a notorious conspirator, a man since executed for treason? He had no claim to restitution; it would be more than generous to allow him 100 florins toward his expenses in leaving the monarchy.[16] Francis concurred and thus Jenne was the poorer for his experience. But insofar as Pergen's views on the proper functions of the police would now prevail, so was the monarchy.

If Pergen could be utterly indifferent to the fate of an individual who had been implicated as the result of pure error, connections still counted for something with him. Young Count Hohenwart, the nephew of the bishop of St. Pölten, a member of Riedel's circle, had been arrested with the others in July 1794 and had eventually been sentenced to thirty years in the fortress of Kufstein, along with deprivation of nobility. The sentence had been unusually harsh, since all that could be proven against Hohenwart was that he had been aware of the sentiments that had regularly been expressed at Riedel's table, without having objected to them; and that at one time he had expressed a desire to have a democratic constitution in the monarchy at some point in the future. Now in 1796, expressing the opinion that young Hohenwart really represented no danger to anyone, Pergen recommended that he be released into the custody of his uncle, which was presently done.[17]

In the years that followed, Pergen increasingly left the routine business of police administration to Saurau. Occasionally he would take an interest in a case, whether it was to pursue some will-o'-the-wisp in the form of yet another supposed "Jacobin" conspiracy in 1797, which turned out to be entirely imaginary,[18] or to appear in an avuncular guise, as when he pointed out that a recent innovation in the capital, the erection of wooden railings to enable pedestrians to ascend steep streets in the outskirts more easily, was basically a good idea, but it had to be taken into consideration that little children might come too close to the edge and fall over; this could be corrected by putting up a second crossbar at a lower level.[19] But by and large, Pergen seems to have been content to enjoy the prerogatives of the position that he had at last achieved.

Early in 1798, when the war had at long last ended, and the Jacobin threat had comfortably receded, Francis asked Pergen to report on the status of the *Staatsgefangene:* was it necessary, in the circumstances, to continue that institution? There were only four persons held as such, Pergen replied.[20] (The Jacobin conspirators, who had been given public trials, did not of course fall into that class.) These were Friedrich Rühle and Franz von Spaun, both held since early 1793 for having expressed *staatsgefährliche Gesinnung,* ideas dangerous to the state; the French subject Peter Franz Colombat, majordomo in the household of Prince Colloredo, condemned to be imprisoned until the end of the war for having been overheard making "democratic" statements and being known to entertain close relationships with several of his countrymen; and the physician Franz Stephan Hanke, accused of high treason in the wake of the Jacobin affair in 1795 but not convicted, and subsequently, in view of his dubious principles, being held for an indefinite period as a necessary measure, dictated by caution.

Pergen was of the opinion that Hanke, who was sick in body and mind, could be released without much danger. Not so, however, the others. As for Colombat, it was true the fighting had ended, but no peace treaty had as yet been signed, so that he could not properly claim that the war was over. In addition, he had throughout his imprisonment complained about conditions in the *Polizeihaus,* yet when Pergen himself had asked him for particulars, had answered that he would go into the details of his mistreatment only after his release. Thus, it was to be expected that, if released, he would shamelessly importune His Majesty. As for Rühle and Spaun, they had both demonstrated an active aversion to the monarchical form of government, and should continue to be held in prison.

One should be careful not to exaggerate. Four individuals being held without benefit of trial, largely for having been overheard to make remarks critical of the government (which of itself was not a crime), do not, by themselves, constitute a concentration camp state. Refusing to free a prisoner because he might after his release make embarassing revelations about his treatment does not yet mean a police out of control. But none of this accords with the principle of a *Rechtsstaat,* a society run on precepts of legality. Nor does it accord very well with the tenets of the Enlightenment, to which Pergen, in his younger days had subscribed. In all probability he had not even set out to become the implaccable pursuer of the otherwise-minded, the inflexible upholder of the monarchical system that he finally was. Rather, after a long period of embarassing failures, he had experienced some success with defending the established order. Ultimately, he identified with his own creation to the extent that he was no longer capable of perceiving the elementary proposition that it ran counter to pretty much everything he had previously stood for. Most likely he saw himself as a conscientious public servant, performing a necessary if unpleasant task for the good of all.

The elements for totalitarian control over the state were all present in Austria by the end of the eighteenth century. So far as at least Pergen and his associates were concerned, so also was the will to impose it. What was still missing were the means: a mechanical and technical infrastructure making it possible to impose this sort of control systematically over large populations. That would come later. But it may surely be asserted that Pergen had created the mechanisms that, in a very direct fashion, made possible the police state of the Metternich era. How may this be reconciled with his undoubtedly genuine admiration for the Enlightenment that was so dominant a characteristic of his younger years? Doubtless his opinions, like those of many both before and after him, became more conservative as he grew older. Presumably there were occasions on which he simply opted for advancement over principle. We may grant him the benefit of a reasonable doubt and assume that, with the collapse of the old regime in France staring him in the face, he became genuinely convinced that the liberal views with which he had once sympathized led inevitably to the ruination of the state, and thus of all organized life. Finally, there is some reason to believe that his view of the Enlightenment was narrowly circumscribed; he seems to have understood it as nothing more substantial than the consistent taking of anticlerical positions.

In 1804[21] Pergen, covered with honors and rewards, asked to be retired, citing his deteriorating health as the reason; he was, after all, almost eighty years old. He would still, on occasion, submit lengthy reports on various matters of state, banking law among them, but there is no evidence that anyone paid much attention to them. He died on 12 May 1814, some nine months short of his ninetieth birthday.

NOTES

1. Pergen to Francis, 23 June 1794, S.A., F.A.S. 76.
2. Italics Pergen's.
3. Italics Pergen's.

4. Italics Pergen's

5. Italics Pergen's

6. Italics Pergen's

7. Wangermann, *Jacobin Trials*, 152, 176–77.

8. Pergen to Clary, 10 February 1795, S.A., V.A. 107.

9. Pergen to Colloredo, 10 August 1795, S.A., F.A.S. 76.

10. Pergen to Colloredo, 15 August 1795, S.A., F.A.S. 76.

11. Pergen to Löhr, 21 January and 15 May 1795, S.A., V.A. 19.

12. Pergen to Clary, 26 September 1795, S.A., V.A. 13.

13. Blumauer, who was involved in these events to a more considerable extent than a number of the individuals who had actually been arrested, managed to extricate himself by admitting to a series of minor indiscretions vis-à-vis Degen, as he evidently knew that the latter had reported these to the police anyway, but denying any knowledge of any genuinely seditious pronouncements. Cf. protocol of Blumauer's interrogation, 25 April 1795, S.A., V.A. 12.

14. Wangermann, *Jacobin Trials*, 184–85.

15. Pergen to Clary, 9 April 1796, S.A., V.A. 13.

16. Pergen's response quoted in Clary's report, 22 April 1796, S.A., V.A.

17. Reports of Pergen, 15 May 1795 and 1 November 1796, S.A., V.A. 8.

18. A man named Nikolits, who was being held in an investigation of some fraudulent business, had accused two Jewish merchants in Miscolz of involvement in a plot to establish a revolutionary regime in Hungary. Eventually, it turned out that he had merely been attempting to curry favor with his accusers. Cf. Pergen to Clary, 17 March and 1 October 1797, S.A., V.A. 21.

19. Pergen to Francis, 1797, S.A., F.A.S. 76.

20. Pergen to Francis, 2 February 1798, S.A., F.A.S. 76.

21. Not in 1802, as Wangermann, *Jacobin Trials*, 191, suggests.

Appendix

Pergen is evidently trying to curry favor with Joseph here by (1) demonstrating his comprehensive knowledge of the qualities of persons in
several branches of government service at different levels, and by (2)
showing him that he is aware of the various subtleties that those who
actually direct the course of affairs, as distinguished from those who
merely carry out orders, must operate with. What is of particular
interest is Pergen's explicit assumption that the top ranks of the administration should be occupied by members of the aristocracy, a point that
under Joseph could not always be taken for granted; and his repeated
insistence that an overview, to be sure one based on accurate information,
is superior to mere mastery of the facts, which constitutes an implied
criticism of Joseph's well-known opinion that his administrators should
push papers around until they dropped in their tracks. It is not altogether clear if Pergen's criticisms were of an unconscious nature, or if he
was sufficiently naive to believe that Joseph would be pleased to act
upon the plain truth once he heard it. The full text of his memorandum
follows:

Wenn es dem Kaiser darum zu thun ist, die Direkzion der vornehmsten
Zweige der Staatsverwaltung nach und nach in die Hände solcher
Individuen auszutheilen die würklich bloß für die gute Sache, und frei
von allen personal Kollisionen arbeiten, die die Geschäfte nicht einseitig
sondern in dem wechselseitigem Zusammenhange treiben in welchem
sie behandelt werden sollen; um da sich die verschiedenen Zweige
nicht statt gehörig in einander zu greifen, und mit vereinten Kräften
zum gemeinschaftlichen Zwecke aller öffentlichen Anstalten zu arbeiten,
vielmehr beständig kreutzen, und ihre Wirksamkeit selbst unter einander
addiren, so fehlt es ihm keineswegs im Lande an brauchbaren, als

Augendiener, sondern mit dem wahren Eifer für die gute Sache wirkenden Männern.

Er hat ferner unter den schon itzt dienenden Kavalieren (und für Präsidenten sind doch Edelleute aus weiten politischen Rücksichten immer am besten geeignet) so ausgezeichnete Individuen daß sie in jedem Lande unter die erste Klaße gezählt werden würden.

Er hat ferners unter den subalterneren Stellen Leute von gründlichsten Kenntnißen und der hoffnungsvollsten Anlage bei denen es nur darauf ankömmt, daß die oberste Geschäftsleitung sich angelegen sein laßen sei hervor zu suchen, in jene Wirkungskreise zu versezen zu denen sie sich nach ihrem Disposizionen gerade am beßten schicken.

Unter die erstere können ohne nur die wirklich im Ministerio als Gouverneure angestellte Individuen zu rechnen, und unter denen sich insbesonders Gr. Rottenhann eine so allgemeine einstimmige Hochachtung erworben hat wie sich vielleicht noch wenige Minister rühmen können unter dem dermal noch als untergeordnete dienende Kavaliers zu zählen.

Gallenberg der seit beinahe einem Jahre das Gubernium in Galizien und vormals die in diesem Lande so wichtige Direktion, welche nicht mit dem Dienst eines bloßen Regißeurs zu vermengen ist, führte; der jeder Landesstelle mit dem beßten Erfolg vorzustehen im Stande sein würde, der aber noch weit nützlicher im Cameral Fache, und besonders in der Leitung der Gefälle und der Accisen anverwendet werden könnte, weil er einerseits die Manipulazion, und den inneren Gang der Gefälls Administrazion praktisch kennt, den Scharfen Blick und den Kombinazions Geist besitzt der hinzu nötig ist, und andererseits dabei auch die politischen Verhltniße der verschiedenen Klaßen der Kontribuenten kennt und daher den wesentlichsten Gesichtspunkt zu faßen im Stande ist, den leider die meißten Kammeralisten verfehlen, nämlich die Leitung der Gefälle und Accisen mit dem Wohl des inneren Handels und Wandels zu kombinieren, und nicht durch unüberlegte Plusmacherreien die Accise für den Kontribuenten ut 10. lästig zu machen, während daß die wirkliche Staatseinnahmen doch unter ut 1. dabei gewinnet.

Philip Herberstein der dermal bei der Rechenkammer arbeitet, ein tief denkender Mann, der nachdem er einige Jahre wirlich bei der ehemaligen Regierung gearbeitet, nacher seine ganze Zeit dem Studio und der Lektüre gewidmet, und insbesondere das Finanzfach mit unermüdeten Fleiße studiert hat, der den ganzen Umfang der Staatswirtschaft und den sistematischen Gang der Staatsrechnung kennt, und mit einem Worte die vollkommenste Anlage zu einem wahren

Financier besitzt, wie sich ihn der Kaiser zur Leitung der Staats Controlle nicht geigneter wünschen könnte.

Herberstein Mattheus hat sich ebenfalls während der Zeit, die er im Privatleben zugebracht die gründlichsten Kenntnisse in allen Fächern der Staatsverwaltung gesammelt, hat auch schon wirklich bei dem Referate, worinn er den dermaligen Referenten Sumerau supplirt, actenmäßige Beweise seiner richtigen Theorie in allen Theilen der Gesezgebung gegeben hat, aber noch im besonderen sich vorzüglich auf das Kommerzienfach verlegt, und darinn gerade jene praktische Kenntniße gesammelt die zur Leitung des Commerz Departments unumgänglich nötig sind, und ohne welche das Gouvernement nie ein gründliches Commerzial System faßen kann, und die Hofkammer immer die Dupe ihrer Mäkler sein muß.

Saurau der dermal bei der Hofkanzlei das böhmische Landesreferat führt, würde in jedem Lande der Welt unter die ausgezeichnetesten Subject gerechnet werden, und könnte bei der gründlichsten und gelehrten Theorie die er besizt der praktischen Kenntniße die er erworben das beschwerlichste Gouvernement mit Zuversicht übernehmen. Er hat aber nebst diesen noch eine ausgezeichnete Fähigkeit zur oberen Geschäftsführung die ihn fähig macht gerade bei der politischen Hofstelle im Centro der Geschäfte mit vorzüglichem Nuzen gebraucht zu werden. Es ist bei der Direkzion der politischen Hofstelle nicht genug, daß sie das materielle der Geschäfte kenne, sie muß vorzüglich auch die Verhältniße, die Stärke und Schwäche, die Rechte und Vorurtheile der verschiedenen Claßen und Individuen kennen, die in den verschiedenen Staatsgeschäften konkurieren, und durch die das Gouvernement wirken muß. Zur Leitung der politischen Hoffstelle die zugleich der unmittelbaren Ratgeber, und der erste Werkzeug des Souverains ist, zugleich die Entschlüße vorschlagen, und allen Anordnungen den ersten schwung geben muß, ist die bloße Dicasterialische Genauigkeit nicht hinlänglich; sie erfordert viel Menschenkenntniß, einen weit aussehenden Blick und den in allen Geschäften so wesentlichen vorurtheilfreien Kombinazionsgeist, der durch eine geschickte Einleitung Dinge mit Leichtigkeit in Erfüllung zu bringen weiß, die mit dem mechanischem Dicasterial Gang, niemals zu Stande kommen können. Der Staats Körper ist, er mag auf was immer für ein Art organisirt sein, immer eine aus vielen Treibrädern zusammengesezte Maschine, und keine Kraft in der Welt ist im Stande, sie im gehörigen Gange zu erhalten, wenn sie nicht zugleich auf die natürliche Leitung dieser Treibräder rechnet, und dem dadurch erwachten den Wiederstand abzufelschen weiß; dies ist das wesentlichste Geschäft der Hofstelle, und deswegen sind gerade da solche tiefdenkende, und vorurtheilsfreie Ratgeber wie Saurau ist am nützlichsten.

Eben so ist der Galizische Landes Referent *O'Donel* ein Mann von ausgezeichneten Genie, Gelehrsamkeit, und besonderer Lebhaftigkeit des Geistes.

Bei der Hofkammer führt schon dermal *Wrbna* Bergwerksreferat, der aber nicht allein in diesem für unsere Monarchie so wichtigem Reiche, man darf sagen exzellirt, sondernüberhaupt ganz die reine Beurtheilungskraft, die gründlichen Kenntnisse, und den tähtigen unbefangenen Eifer besizt, um in allen Geschäften mit Ruhm zu arbeiten.

Dies sind nun die vorzüglichsten unter den Mir bekannten ausgezeichneten Subjekten, die der Kaiser gleich zu der wirklichen Leitung der verschiedenen Zweigen der Staatsverwaltung und Gesezgebung verwenden kann, und mit denen, wenn sie zweckmäßig ausgetheilt sind er mehr als mit einer Legion bloßer Dikasterialisten auszurichten vermögen wird.

Nebst diesen sind unter der Subalternen:

Wratislaw dermal als Kreishauptmann nach Böhmen bestimmt, ein sehr fähiger und brauchbarer junger Mann der mehrere Jahre im Kreis- und Gubernialdienste sich gebildet, und anbei einen besonders lebhaften Geist hat.

Wallis dermaliger Rath bei den Landrechten, der des allgemeinen Rufes eines äußerst thätigem Arbeiters genießet.

Ein sicherer *Schilling* der als Hofsekretär bei dem ehemaligen Polizei Departement angestellt war, der aber nicht alleine in diesem sondern auch in anderen Fächern, und vorzüglich im geistlichen und Studien Departement außerordentlich brauchbar ist, als welche er a fond studiert hat, un worinnen er die geläutertesten Grundsäze besizt, folglich als Rath wesentliche Dienste leisten könnte.

Ein gewißer *Zahlhaf* dermaliger Regierungs-Sekretaire der während der 6 Jahre als er bei Regierung dient immer mehr zu außerordentlichen Arbeiten als zu den gewöhnlichen Expeditionen verwendet worden, der nun zwei Jahre das Stiftungsreferat wiwohl nur als Sekretär führt, und jede Rathstelle mit wesentlichem Nuzen zu versehen im Stande wäre; der aber insbesondere das so weitwendige, Stiftungs-Departement, die Ordnung der hinzu gehörigen detaillierten Administrazion, den Gang der Buchhaltereien und den Zusammenhang der verschiedenen Stiftungs und Verpflegs Anstalten, und dazu gehörenden abgesonderten Fonds so gründlich kennt, und dabei cine so unermüdete Genauigkeit besizt, da man ihm ganz blindlings die Direkzion der ausgedehntesten Administrazion oder des verwickeltesten Buchhalterei Geschäfte anvertrauen könnte, und als Mitglied der Stiftungschofkommißion, oder Bucchalterei wesentliche Dienste zu leisten im Stande sein würde.

Graf Degenfeld dermal als Supernumerär Rath in Vorderösterreich angestellt, der die gründlichste Studien und die vortreflichste Grundsätze mit einem außerordentlichen Arbeitseifer verbindet.

Der Appelations Rath Hienmayer der dermal bloß im Justizfach arbeitet, der aber auch zu politischen Geschäften viele Fähigkeit besitzt.

Ein sicherer *Welser*, Regierungs-Sekretär der nunmehr schon 20 Jahre bei Regierung mit Auszeichnung dient, und schon lange als Rath oder als Hof-Sekretär mit so wesentlichem Nuzen hätte verwendet werden können, als es hauptsächlich notwendig ist, daß bei den Hofstellen solche Individuen vorhanden seien, die die Data und den Gang der unteren Stellen praktisch kennen.

Der geheime Staats-Offizial *Collenbach* der außerordentlich gründliche Kenntniße, scharfe Beurtheilungskraft, ausgezeichnete Gelehrsamkeit, und unermüdete Arbeitsamkeit besitzt.

Es ist dermal in Warschau beinahe ganz vergraben ein sicherer De Caché als Resident angestellt, der nun seit 16 Jahren die Geschäfte dieses so häcklichen Posten in der allerunangenehmsten Lage nämlich ohne Ansehen, und mit äußerst geringem Gehalt gerade in einem Lande wo das äußerliche so wesentlichen Einfluß auf die Geschäfte hat mit bewunderungswürdigem Erfolge und Klugheit führt, und einmal im Bureau der Staatskanzlei mit vielem Nuzen gebraucht werden könnte.

Dies sind nur einige der mir gerade am genauesten bekannten vorzüglichsten Subjekten, und dient diese Erinnerung auch nur zum Beweis, daß wenn ich dem niemand Ursache haben kann seine Talente zu zeigen, so vorzüglich, und in so vielen und verschiedenen Fächern anwendbare Subjekte anzuzeigen im Stande bin, sich wohl mit Evidenz darauß schließen ließe, daß es unter der großen Anzahl der mir teils weniger genau, teils ganz unbekannten Individuen, die dermalen in den verschiedenen Stellen und Gubernien zerstreut sind, in dem Verhältnis unmöglich an brauchbaren Köpfen mangeln könne, wenn sich das Ministerium, der Staatsrath, oder wem diese Sorge übertragen sein mag, die Subjekten aufzusuchen und in der Vertheilung darauf bedacht zu sein sich einen Nachwachs für die verschiedenen Zweige der Geschäfte zu bilden.

Diese Vorkehrung sich einen Vorrath von geschickten Leuten zu sammeln, verschiedene Anlagen der vorgeladenen Individuen genau auszurechnen und das Studium jeden in den Wirkungskreis zu sezen, zu dem er gerade am beßten geeignet ist, ist eines der wichtigsten Geschäfte der obersten Leitung, und gerade dies ist vielleicht bisher am meißten vernachläßigt worden. Mancher Geist ist für den methodischen Gang der Dikasterial Geschäfte zu lebhaft, und eben darum zur Direkzion geschaffen, mancher würde als Rathgeber da wo es auf Ausarbeitung der Grundsätze ankämme die besten Dienste liefern, und ist zur Expedition nicht so gut geignet; Mancher hat die vollständigsten Kenntniße und größte Findigkeit zu Finanz und Kammer Geschäft in dem die Genauigkeit fehlt die zu Gouvernement und Justiz Geschäften erforderlich ist et vice versa.

Wenn die oberste Leitung diese Nuancen nicht beobachtet, die Subjekten die zur Direkzion geignet wären nicht von jenen die sich beßer zur detaillierten Expedizion schicken, unterscheidet, und mit einem Worte nicht ein eigenes Studium aus der Beurtheilung und Bildung ihrer vorhandenen Individuen macht, so wird sie auch bei dem größtem Reichthum an ausgezeichneten brauchbaren Köpfen, doch immer bei jedem vorkommenden Fall in stätter Verlegenheit bleiben, und die verschiedenen Stellen werden immer so unzusammenhängend fortarbeiten, als es vielleicht dermal leider der Fall ist.

Bibliography

Archival Sources

Haus-, Hof- und Staatsarchiv, Vienna
  Staatskanzlei:
    Grosse Correspondenz
    Interiora, Personalia
    Interiora
    Vorträge
  Reichskanzlei:
    Ministerial Korrespondenz
  Hofreisen
  Familien Archiv:
    Sammelbände
  Handbillets-Protokolle
  Noten von der Polizeihofstelle
  Noten an die Polizeihofstelle
  Kaiser Franz Akten
  Staatenabteilung:
    Schweiz, Berichte
Hessisches Staatsarchiv, Marburg
  Politische Akten nach Philipp dem Grossen
    Kaiser-, Reichs- und Kreisakten
Verwaltungsarchiv, Vienna
  Adelsinkolate
  Nachlass Pergen
  Hofkanzlei
    Galizien
  Pergen Akten
    Personalien
  Präsidialakten

Archiv der Stadt Wien
  Annalen des Wiener Kriminal Gericht
Niederösterreichisches Landesarchiv, Vienna
  Polizeiordnung

Printed Sources

Anon. *Geheime Geschichte der Verschwörung der Jakobiner in den österreichi-schen Staaten.* London, 1795; reprinted by F. Gräffer as *Francisceische Curiosa.* Vienna, 1849.
Anon. *Österreichische Memoiren aus dem letzten Dezennium des achtzehnten Jahrhunderts.* Leipzig, 1848.
Anon. *Über geheime Gesellschaften im Staate.* 1791.
Arneth, A. v. *Briefe der Kaiserin Maria Theresia an ihre Kinder und Freunde.* 4 vols. Vienna, 1881.
Beer, A. *Joseph II., Leopold II., und Kaunitz: Ihr Briefwechsel.* Vienna, 1873.
Beiträge zur Geschichte der Niederösterreichischen Stadthalterei. Vienna, 1897.
Bittner, L. *Gesammtinventar des Wiener Haus, Hof- und Staatsarchivs.* 5 vols. Vienna, 1936.
Dictionnaire parlementaire Français. Paris, 1891.
Friedel, J. *Freye Bemerkungen und Zweifel über das Armeninstitut in Wien.* Vienna, 1785.
Gräffer, F. *Francisceische Curiosa.* Vienna, 1849.
———. *Josephinische Curiosa.* 3 vols. Vienna, 1848–50.
Grand Larousse Universel.
Journal de Francfort. July 1753.
Justi, J. H. G. *Grundriß der Polizeywissenschaft.* 1759.
Keith, Sir R. M. *Memoirs and Correspondence.* 2 vols. London, 1849.
Magistratskundmachung. January 1793.
Schlitter, H., et al., eds. *Aus der Zeit Maria Theresias: Tagebuch des Fürsten Johann Josef Khevenhüller-Metsch.* 10 vols. Vienna, 1907–72.
Wraxall, N. W. *Memoirs of the Courts of Berlin, Dresden, Warsaw, and Vienna.* 2 vols. 3rd ed. London, 1806.
Wurzbach, C. v. *Biographisches Lexicon des Kaiserthums Oesterreich.* 60 vols. Vienna, 1856–91.

Secondary Sources

Abafi, L. *Geschichte der Freimaurerei in Oesterreich-Ungarn.* 5 vols. Budapest, 1890–97.
Aretin, Karl Otmar v. *Heiliges Römisches Reich, 1776–1806.* 2 vols. Wiesbaden, 1967.
Arneth, A. v. *Geschichte Maria Theresias.* 10 vols. Vienna, 1863–79.
Bartsch, R. "Die Jakobiner in Wien." *Österreichische Rundschau,* VII (1906).

Bauer, Roger. "Kaiser Joseph und die literarischen-Folgen." *Wien und Europa zwischen den Revolutionen (1789–1848). Wiener Europagespräch 1977. Wiener Schriften* 39. Vienna and Munich, 1978.

Bauer, Werner M. *Fiktion und Polemik: Studien zum Roman der österreichischen Aufklärung.* Vienna, 1978.

Beer, A. *Die erste Theilung Polens.* 3 vols. Vienna, 1873.

Beidtel, Ignaz. *Geschichte der österreichischen Staatsverwaltung: 1740–1848.* 2 vols. Innsbruck, 1896–98.

Benda, Kalman. "Probleme des Josephinismus und des Jakobinertums in der Habsburgischen Monarchie." *Südost-Forschungen,* XXV (1966).

Benna, Anna Hedwig. "Die Polizeihofstelle." Ph.D. dissertation. Vienna, 1941.

——. "Organisierung der staatlichen Polizei unter Kaiser Joseph II." *Mitteilungen des österreichischen Staatsarchivs,* VI (1953).

——. "Organisierung und Personalstand der Polizeihofstelle (1793–1848)." *Mitteilungen des österreichischen Staatsarchivs,* VI (1953).

Bernard, P. P. *Jesuits and Jacobins: Enlightenment and Enlightened Despotism in Austria.* Urbana, Ill. 1971.

——. *Joseph II and Bavaria.* The Hague, 1965.

——. "Joseph II's Last Turkish War Reconsidered." *Austrian History Yearbook,* XVII/1 (1988).

——. "Kaunitz and the Cost of Diplomacy." *East European Quarterly,* XXVII/1 (March 1983).

——. "The Limits of Absolutism: Joseph II and the Algemeines Krankenhaus." *Eighteenth Century Studies,* IX/2 (1975–76)

——. *The Limits of Enlightenment.* Urbana, Ill., 1979.

——. "The Philosophe as Public Servant: Tobias Philip Gebler." *East European Quarterly,* VII/1 (1973).

Besterman, T. *Voltaire.* New York, 1969.

Bibl, Viktor. "Das Robot-Provisorium für Nieder-österreich vom 20. Juni 1796." *Jahrbuch für Landeskunde von Niederösterreich, N.F.,* VII (1908).

——. *Die Wiener Polizei: Eine kulturhistorische Studie.* Leipzig, 1927.

——. *Kaiser Franz.* Leipzig and Vienna, 1938.

Blanning, T. C. W. *The Origins of the French Revolutionary Wars.* London and New York, 1986.

——. *Reform and Revolution in Mainz 1743–1803.* Cambridge, 1979.

Bodi, Leslie. "Enlightened Despostism and Literature of Enlightenment." *German Life and Letters,* XXII (1968–69).

——. "System und Bewegung: Funktion und Folgen des Josephinischen Tauwetters." *Wien und Europa zwischen den Revolutionen (1789–1848). Wiener Europagespräch 1977. Wiener Schriften* 39. Vienna and Munich, 1978.

——. *Tauwetter in Wien: Zur Prosa der österreichischen Aufklärung: 1781–1795.* Frankfurt a. M., 1977.

Böhm, Wilhem. "Die Konservativen in Österreich." In *Rekonstruktion des Konservatismus,* edited by Gerd-Klaus Kaltenbrunner. Freiburg, 1972.

Buranelli, V. *The Wizard from Vienna.* London, 1976.

Cloeter, Hermine. *Johann Thomas Trattner: Ein Grossunternehmer imTheresianischen Wien.* Vienna, 1952.

Conrad, H. *Deutsche Rechtsgeschichte* 2 vols. Wiesbaden, 1954.

——. *Rechtsstaatliche Bestrebungen im Absolutismus Preussens und Österreichs am Ende des 18. Jahrhunderts.* Cologne and Opladen, 1961.

——. "Zu den geistigen Grundlagen der Strafrechtsreform Joseph II. (1780–88)." *Festschrift H. v. Weber.* Bonn, 1963.

——. *Recht und Verfassung des Reiches in der Zeit Maria Theresias.* Cologne and Opladen, 1964.

Darnton, R. *Mesmerism and the End of the Enlightenment in France.* Cambridge, Mass., 1970.

Dickson, P. G. M. *Finance and Government under Maria Theresia, 1740–1780.* 2 vols. Oxford, 1987.

Dreyfus, F. G. *Socités et mentalités a Mayence dans la seconde moitié du xviiiéme siècle.* Paris, 1968.

Ehalt, H. *Ausdrucksformen absolutistischer Herrschaft.* Munich, 1980.

Ellemunter, A. *Antonio Eugenio Visconti und die Anfänge des Josephinismus.* Graz and Cologne, 1953.

Emerson, D. E. *Metternich and the Political Police.* The Hague, 1968.

Ernst, W. "Die Preissenkungsaktion Kaiser Josephs II." *Österreichische Volksstimme,* CCCI (1951).

Faulhammer, A. "Politische Meinungen und Stimmungen in Wien in den Jahren 1793 und 1794." *Programm des k.k. Staats-Gymnasiums in Salzburg* (1893).

Finger, August. *Das Strafrecht.* 3 vols. 3rd ed. Berlin, 1912–14.

Franknoi, V. *Martinovics élete.* Budapest, 1921.

Franz, E. G., et al. *Darmstadts Geschichte.* Darmstadt, 1980.

Fournier, August. *Die Geheimpolizei auf dem Wiener Kongress.* Vienna and Leipzig, 1913.

——. "Joseph II. und der geheime Dienst." *Historische Studien und Skizzen,* III. Vienna and Leipzig, 1912.

Glassl, Horst. *Das österreichische Einrichtungswerk in Galizien, 1772–1790.* Wiesbaden, 1975.

Gnau, Hermann. *Die Zensur unter Joseph II.* Strassburg and Leipzig, 1911.

Goldinger, Walter. "Kant und die österreichischen Jakobiner." In *Beiträge zur neuere Geschichte Österreichs,* edited by Heinrich Fichtenau and Erich Zöllner. Vienna, Cologne, Graz, 1974.

Grab, Walter. "Demokratische Freiheitskämpfer Österreichs im Zeitalter der Französischen Revolution." *Wien und Europa zwischen den Revolutionen (1789–1848). Wiener Europagespräch 1977. Wiener Schriften 39.* Vienna and Munich, 1978.

Gragger, R. *Preußen, Weimar und die ungarische Königskrone.* Berlin, 1923.

Grodziski, S. *W Králestwie Galicyi i Lodomerii.* Kraków, 1976.

Groß-Hoffinger, A. J. *Joseph II. als Regent und Mensch.* Stuttgart, n.d.

Grüll, Georg. *Bauer, Herr und Landesfürst. Sozialrevolutionäre Bestrebungen der oberösterreichischen Bauern von 1650 bis 1848.* Graz and Cologne, 1963.

Guglia, E. *Maria Theresia.* 2 vols. Munich and Berlin, 1917.

Gutkas, K. "Der Kaiser und seine Mitarbeiter." In *Österreich zur Zeit Kaiser Josephs II,* edited by Karl Gutkas et al. Melk, 1980.

———. "Österreich unter dem geistigen Einfluss von Aufklärung und Josephinismus." *Österreichische Bildungs-und Schulgeschichte von der Aufklärung bis zum Liberalismus.* Eisenstadt, 1974.

Hafner, K. "Franz Josef Graf von Saurau." *Zeitschrift des Historischen Vereines für Steiermark,* VII (1909).

Hartl, Friedrich. *Das Wiener Kriminalgericht.* Vienna, Graz, Cologne, 1973.

Haselsteiner, H. *Joseph II. und die Komitate Ungarns.* Vienna, Graz, Cologne, 1983.

Hatschek, O. "Studien zum österreichischen Polizeistrafrecht." *Archiv für Strafrecht und Strafprozess,* (1910).

Häusler, Wolfgang. *Das galizische Judentum in der Habsburger-Monarchie.* Vienna, 1979.

Heinisch, Reinhard Rudolf. "Der Josephinische Staat." In *Österreich zur Zeit Kaiser Josephs II.,* edited by Karl Gutkas et al. Melk, 1980.

Helfert, A. v. *Das System der österreichischen Volksschule.* Prague, 1861.

Hock, Carl v., and Hermann Bidermann. *Der österreichische Staatsrath (1760–1848).* Vienna, 1879.

Hoegel, H. *Geschichte des österreichischen Strafrechts.* Vienna, 1904.

Hollerweger, Hans. "Tendenzen der liturgischen Reformen unter Maria Theresia und Joseph II." In *Katholische Aufklärung und Josephinismus,* edited by Elisabeth Kovacs. Munich, 1979.

Hubatschke, Harold. "Die amtliche Organisation der geheimen Briefüberwachung und des diplomatischen Chiffrendienstes in Österreich." *Mitteilungen des Instituts für österreichische Geschichtsforschung,* LXXXIII (1975).

Hundert, G. "The Implications of Jewish Economic Activities for Christian-Jewish Relations in the Polish Commonwealth." In *The Jews in Poland,* edited by C. Abramsky et al. Oxford, 1986.

Ingrao, Charles W. *The Hessian Mercenary State.* Cambridge, 1987.

Just, Leo. "Zur Kirchenpolitischen Lage in Österreich beim Regierungsantritt Franz II. (März bis Dezember 1792)." *Quellen und Forschungen aus Italienischen Archiven und Bibliotheken,* XXVII (1931–32).

Kallbrunner, J. "Die Wiener Polizei im Zeitalter Maria Theresias." *Monatsblatt des Altertumsverein zu Wien,* XI (1911).

Kaplan, H. *The First Partition of Poland.* New York, 1962.

Karniel, Josef. "Das Toleranzpatent Kaiser Josephs II. für die Juden Galiziens und Lodomeriens." *Jahrbuch des Instituts für Deutsche Geschichte der Universität Tel-Aviv,* XI (1982).

Klingenstein, Grete. "Akademikerüberschuss als soziales Problem." In *Bildung, Politik und Gesellschaft,* edited by G. Klingenstein, Heinrich Lutz, and Gerald Stourzh. Munich, 1978.

——. "Bildungskrise: Gymnasien und Universitäten im Spannungsfeld theresianischer Aufklärung." In *Maria Theresia und Ihre Zeit.* Vienna, 1979.

Koplenig, Hilda. "Conrad Dominik Bartsch (1759–1817): Freimaurer und Journalist." *Wiener Geschichtsblätter,* XXXII/3 (1977).

Körner, A. "Andreas Riedel." Ph.D. dissertation. Cologne, 1969.

——. "Andreas Riedel (1748–1837): Zur Lebensgeschichte eines Wiener Demokraten." *Jahrbuch des Vereines für Geschichte der Stadt Wien,* XXVII (1971).

——. *Die Wiener Jakobiner.* Stuttgart, 1972.

——. "Der österreichische Jakobiner Franz Hebenstreit von Streitenfeld." *Jahrbuch des Istituts für Deutsche Geschichte der Universität Tel-Aviv,* III (1974).

——. "Franz Hebenstreit (1747–1795): Biographie und Versuch einer Deutung." *Jahrbuch des Vereines für Geschichte der Stadt Wien,* XXX/XXXI (1974–75).

Kretschmayr, Heinrich, ed. *Die österreichische Zentralverwaltung.* Vienna, 1938.

Langsam, Walter Consuelo. "Emperor Francis II and the Austrian 'Jacobins', 1792–1796." *American Historical Review,* L (1945).

——. *Francis the Good: The Education of an Emperor.* New York, 1949.

Lorenz, Reinhold. *Volksbewaffnung und Staatsidee in Österreich (1792–1797).* Vienna and Leipzig, 1926.

Löw, Alois. "Zur geschichte des Wiener Jakobiner Prozesses." *Monatsblatt des Altertum-Vereines zu Wien,* VII (1905).

Lunzer, Marianne. "Josephinisches und antijosephinisches Schriftum." In *öffentliche Meinung in der Geschichte Österreichs,* edited by Erich Zöllner. Vienna, 1979.

Lutz, H., and H. Rumpler, eds. *Österreich und die deutsche Frage im 19. und 20. Jahrhundert.* Munich, 1982.

Maasburg, M. Friedrich v. *Die Strafe des Schiffziehens in Österreich (1788–1790).* Vienna, 1890.

Markov, Walter. *Aufgeklärter Absolutismus und Revolution: Zur Geschichte des Jakobinertums und der frühdemokratischen Bestrebungen in der Habsburgermonarchie. Veröffentlichung der Kommission für neuere Geschichte Österreichs 68.* Vienna, 1980.

——. "Jakobiner in der Habsburger-Monarchie." In *Jakobiner in Mitteleuropa,* edited by Helmut Reinalter. Innsbruck, 1977.

Mathy, Helmut. "Uber das Mainzer Erzkanzleramt in der Neuzeit." *Geschichtliche Landeskunde,* II. Wiesbaden, 1965.

Mayer, F. M., R.F. Kaindl, and H. Pirchegger. *Geschichte und Kulturleben Österreichs.* 3 vols. Vienna and Stuttgart, 1965.

Moos, Reinhard. *Der Verbrechensbegriff in Österreich im 18. und 19. Jahrhundert.* Bonn, 1968.

Müller, M. G. *Die Theilungen Polens.* Munich, 1984.

Oberhummer, Hermann. *Die Wiener Polizei*. 2 vols. Vienna, 1937.

Ogris, Werner. "Joseph II.: Staats- und Rechtsreformen." In *Im Zeichen der Toleranz,* edited by Peter F. Barton. Vienna, 1981.

Orieux, J. *Voltaire*. New York, 1979.

Osterloh, Karl-Heinz. *Joseph von Sonnenfels und die österreichische Reformbewegung im Zeitalter des aufgeklärten Absolutismus*. Lübeck and Hamburg, 1970.

Pawlik, M. "Emigranten der Französischen Revolution in österreich (1789–1814)." *Mitteilungen des Instituts für österreichische Geschichtsforschung,* LXXVII (1969).

Raeff, M. *The Well-Ordered Police State*. New Haven, 1983.

Reinalter, Helmut. *Aufgeklärter Absolutismus und Revolution: Zur Geschichte des Jakobinertums und der frühdemokratischen Bestrebungen in der Habsburgermonarchie*. Vienna, Cologne, Graz, 1980.

——. *Aufklärung, Absolutismus, Reaktion: Die Geschichte Tirols in der 2. Hälfte des 18. Jahrhunderts*. Vienna, 1974.

——. "Aufklärung, Freimaurerei und Jakobinertum in der Habsburger-Monarchie." *Jakobiner in Mitteleuropa,* edited by Helmut Reinalter. Innsbruck, 1977.

——. "Der Jakobinerpriester Joseph Rendler. Versuch einer Biographie." *Mitteilungen des Instituts für österreichische Geschichtsforschung,* LXXXII (1974).

——. *Der Jakobinismus in Mitteleuropa*. Stuttgart, 1981.

——. "Die Gesellschaftspolitischen Vorstellungen der österreichischen Jakobiner." *Jahrbuch des Instituts für Deutsche Geschichte der Universität Tel-Aviv,* VI (1977).

——. "Die Jakobiner in der Habsburgermonarchie." In *Revolutionäre Bewegungen in Österreich,* edited by Erich Zöllner. Vienna, 1981.

——. "Einwirkungen der Französischen Revolution auf die Innen- und Aussenpolitik des Kaiserhofes in Wien." In *Deutschland und die Französische Revolution,* edited by Jorgen Voss. Munich, 1983.

——. "Gesellschafts-politische Konzeptionen österreichischer Jakobiner." In *Die Demokratische Bewegung in Mitteleuropa im ausgehenden 18. und frühen 19. Jahrhundert,* edited by O. Busch and W. Grab. Berlin, 1980.

——, ed. *Jakobiner in Mitteleuropa*. Innsbruck, 1977.

Roider, Jr., K. A. *Baron Thugut and Austria's Response to the French Revolution*. Princeton, N.J., 1987.

——. "The Oriental Academy in the Theresienzeit." *Topic,* XXXIV (1980).

Rosenstrauch-Königsberg, Edith. "Aloys Blumauer—Jesuit, Freimaurer, Jakobiner." *Jahrbuch des Instituts für Deutsche Geschichte der Universität Tel-Aviv,* II (1973).

——. "Eine Freimaurerische Akademie der Wissenschaften in Wien." In *Revolution und Demokratie in Geschichte und Literatur (Festschrift "Walter Grab"),* edited by J. H. Schoeps and I. Geiss. Duisburg, 1979.

——. *Freimaurerei im Josephinischen Wien: Aloys Blumauers Weg vom*

Jesuiten zum Jakobiner. Vienna and Stuttgart, 1975.

——. "Radikal-aufklärerische Geheimbünde in der Habsburger Monarchie zur Zeit der Französischen Revolution (1785–1795)." In *Die Demokratische Bewegung in Mitteleuropa im ausgehenden 18. und frühen 19. Jahrhundert,* edited by O. Busch and W. Grab. Berlin, 1980.

Sashegyi, Oskar. *Zensur und Geistesfreiheit unter Joseph II.* Budapest, 1958.

Schenk, E. *Mozart and His Times.* New York, 1959.

Schenk, H. G. "Austria." In *The European Nobility in the Eighteenth Century,* edited by Albert Goodwin. New York and Evanston, Ill. 1967.

Schimetschek, Bruno. *Der Österreichische Beamte.* Vienna, 1984.

Schlitter, Hans. *Die Regierung Josephs II. in den österreichischen Niederlanden.* Vienna, 1900.

Schlitter, Hans, et al., eds. *Aus der Zeit Maria Theresias: Tagebuch des Fürsten Johann Josef Khevenhüller-Metsch.* 8 vols. Vienna, 1907–1972.

Schmidt, J. *Entwicklung der katholischen Schule in Österreich.* Vienna, 1958.

Schnür-Peplowski, S. *Z Preslosci Galúczi 1772–1862.* Lwów, 1895.

Schonemann, K. *Österreichs Bevölkerungspolitik unter Maria Theresia.* Berlin, n.d.

Schubert, M. "Wie reagierte Wien auf die Französische Revolution?" *Österreich in Geschichte und Literatur,* XIV/10 (December 1970).

Schuh, Franzjosef. "Analyse von Verhörsprotokollen und Prozessakten der Wiener Jakobinerprozesse 1794–1798." In *Die Demokratische Bewegung in Mitteleuropa im ausgehenden 18. und frühen 19. Jahrhundert,* edited by O. Busch and W. Grab. Berlin, 1980.

——. "Die Wiener Jakobiner: Reformer oder Revolutionäre"? *Jahrbuch des Instituts für Deutsche Geschichte der Universität Tel-Aviv,* XII (1983).

——. "Einige Beobachtungen über Rechtsstaat und aufgeklärten Absolutismus im Österreich der Jakobiner-Prozesse." In *Revolution und Demokratie in Geschichte und Literatur (Festschrift "Walter Grab"),* edited by J. H. Schoeps and I. Geiss. Duisburg, 1979.

——. *Franz Hebenstreit.* Trier, 1974.

Silagi, Denis. "Aktenstücke zur Geschichte des Ignaz von Martinovics."- *Mitteilungen des Österreichischen Staatsarchivs,* XV (1962).

——. *Jakobiner in der Habsburger-Monarchie.* Vienna & Munich, 1962.

——. *Ungarn und der geheime Mitarbeiterkreis Kaisers Leopolds II.* Munich, 1961.

Sommer, Friedrich. *Die Wiener Zeitschrift (1792–1793): Die Geschichte eines antirevolutionären Journals.* Zeulenroda and Leipzig, 1932.

Stern, L. "Zum Prozeß gegen die österreichische 'Jakobiner-Verschwörung.' " In *Maximilien Robespierre: Beiträge zu seinem 200. Geburtstag,* edited by W. Markov. Berlin, 1958.

Strakosch, Heinrich. "Das Problem der ideologischen Ausrichtung des österreichischen aufgeklärten Absolutismus." In *Forschungsband Franz von Zeiller (1751–1828),* edited by Walter Selb and Herbert Hofmeister. Vienna, Graz, Cologne, 1980.

——. "Zu wenig: Die Tragik des Rechtsstaates in österreichischer Sicht." *Zeitschrift für neuere Rechtsgeschichte,* I (1979–80).

Strakosch-Grassmann, G. *Geschichte des österreichischen Unterrichtswesens.* Vienna, 1905.

Strasser, Kurt. *Die Wiener Presse in der Josephischen Zeit.* Vienna, 1962.

Strauss, B. *La culture française à Francort au xviiiéme siécle.* Paris, 1964.

Valentinitsch, Helfried. "Das Grazer Zucht- und Arbeitshaus 1734–1783: Zur Geschichte des Strafvollzugs in der Steiermark." In *Festschrift Hermann Bath,* edited by Kurt Ebert. Innsbruck, 1978.

Valjavec, Fritz. "Die Anfänge des österreichischen Konservatismus. Leopold Alois Hoffmann." In *Festschrift Karl Eder,* edited by Helmut J. Mezler-Andelberg. Innsbruck, 1959.

——. "Die Josephinischen Wurzeln des österreichischen Konservatismus." *Südost-Forschungen,* XIV (1955).

Van Dulmen, Richard. *Der Geheimbund der Illuminaten.* Bad Cannstatt, 1975.

Voltelini, Hans V. "Der Codex Theresianus im Österreichischen Staatsrat." In *Festschrift zur Jahrhundert-Feier des Allgemeinen Bürgerlichen Gesetzbuches.* 2 vols. Vienna, 1911.

——. "Eine Denkschrift des Grafen Johann Anton Pergen über die Bedeutung der römischen Kaiserkrone für das Haus Österreich." *Gesamtdeutsche Vergangenheit.* Munich, 1938.

Volz, Gustav Berthold, and Georg Kuntzel, eds. *Preussiche und Österreichische Akten zur Vorgeschichte des Siebenjährigen Krieges.* Leipzig, 1899.

Wagner, Hans. "Der Höhepunkt des Französischen Kultureinflusses in Österreich in der zweiten Hälfte des 18. Jahrhunderts." *Österreich in Geschichte un Literatur,* X (1961).

——. "Der Plan zur Organisation einer geheimen Gesellschaft des Arztes Dr. Franz Stephan Hanke 1794." In *Politik und Gesellschaft im alten und neuen Österreich: Festschrift Rudolf Neck,* edited by I. Ackerl, W. Hummelberger, and H. Mommsen. 2 vols. Munich, 1981.

——. "Die Organisierung der Staatlichen Polizei unter Kaiser Joseph II." *Mitteilungen des Vereins für Geschichte der Stadt Wien,* VII (1927).

——. "Die Zensur in der Habsburger Monarchie (1750–1810)." In *Festschrift für Hans Wagner,* edited by Hans Wagner. Salzburg, 1982.

——. *Freimaurerei um Joseph II.* Vienna, 1980.

——. "Joseph II., Persönlichkeit und Werk." In *Festschrift für Hans Wagner,* edited by Hans Wagner Salzburg, 1982.

——. *Wien von Maria Theresia bis zur Franzosenzeit: Aus den Tagebüchern des Grafen Karl Zinzendorf.* Vienna, 1972.

Walter, Friedrich. "Die Organisierung der staatlichen Polizei unter Kaiser Joseph II." *Mitteilungen des Vereins für Geschichte der Stadt Wien,* VII (1927).

——. *Die Österreichische Zentral-Verwaltung in der Zeit Maria Theresias.* Vienna, 1938.

——. "Kaunitz' Eintritt in die innere Politik." *Mitteilungen des Instituts für Österreichische Geschischtforschung,* XLVI (1932).

——. *Österreichische Verfassungs- und Verwaltungsgeschichte von 1500–1955.* Vienna, Cologne, Graz, 1972.

Wandruszka, A. *Leopold II.* 2 vols. Vienna, Cologne, Graz, 1963–65.

Wangermann, Ernst. *The Austrian Achievement in the Age of Enlightenment.* London, 1972.

——. *Aufklärung und Staatsbürgerliche Erziehung: Gottfried van Swieten als Reformator des österreichischen Unterrichtswesens 1781–1791.* Munich, 1978.

——. "Deutscher Patriotismus und österreichischer Reformabsolutismus im Zeitalter Josephs II." In *Österreich und die deutsche Frage im 19. und 20. Jahrhundert,* edited by Heinrich Lutz and Helmut Rumpler. Munich, 1982.

——. *From Joseph II to the Jacobin Trials.* 2nd ed. Oxford, 1969.

——. "Josephiner, Leopoldiner und Jakobiner." In *Die Demokratische Bewegung in Mitteleuropa im ausgehenden 18. und frühen 19. Jahrhundert: Ein Tagungsbericht,* edited by Otto Busch and Walter Grab. Berlin, 1980.

——. "Reform Catholicism and Political Radicalism in the Austrian Enlightenment." In *The Enlightenment in National Context,* edited by Roy Porter and Mikulas Teich. Cambridge, 1981.

Weckebecker, W. *Von Maria Theresia zu Franz Joseph.* Berlin, 1929.

Wertheimer, E. "Baron Hompesch und Joseph II." *Mitteilungen des Instituts für sterreichische Geschichtforschung,* VI. Ergünzungsband, 1901.

Wolfsgrubber, Cölestin. *Franz I., Kaiser von Österreich.* 2 vols. Vienna and Leipzig, 1899.

Wotke, Karl. *Das österreichische Gymnasium im Zeitalter Maria Theresias. Monumenta Germaniae Paedagogica* 30. Berlin, 1905.

Yurenko, M. *Galicia-Halychyna from Separation to Unity.* New York, 1967.

Zenker, Ernst Viktor. *Geschichte der Wiener Journalistik von dem Anfängen bis zum Jahre 1848.* Vienna and Leipzig, 1892.

Zwitter-Tehovnik, Dana. *Wirkungen der Französischen Revolution in Krain.* Vienna and Salzburg, 1975.

Index